Reuben Peiss July 2, 1912 - Feb. 23, 1952

Alfred Hessel

A HISTORY OF LIBRARIES

translated, with supplementary material,
by
REUBEN PEISS

REUBEN PEISS MEMORIAL EDITION

The Scarecrow Press
New Brunswick, N.J.   1955

Copyright, 1950, by Reuben Peiss

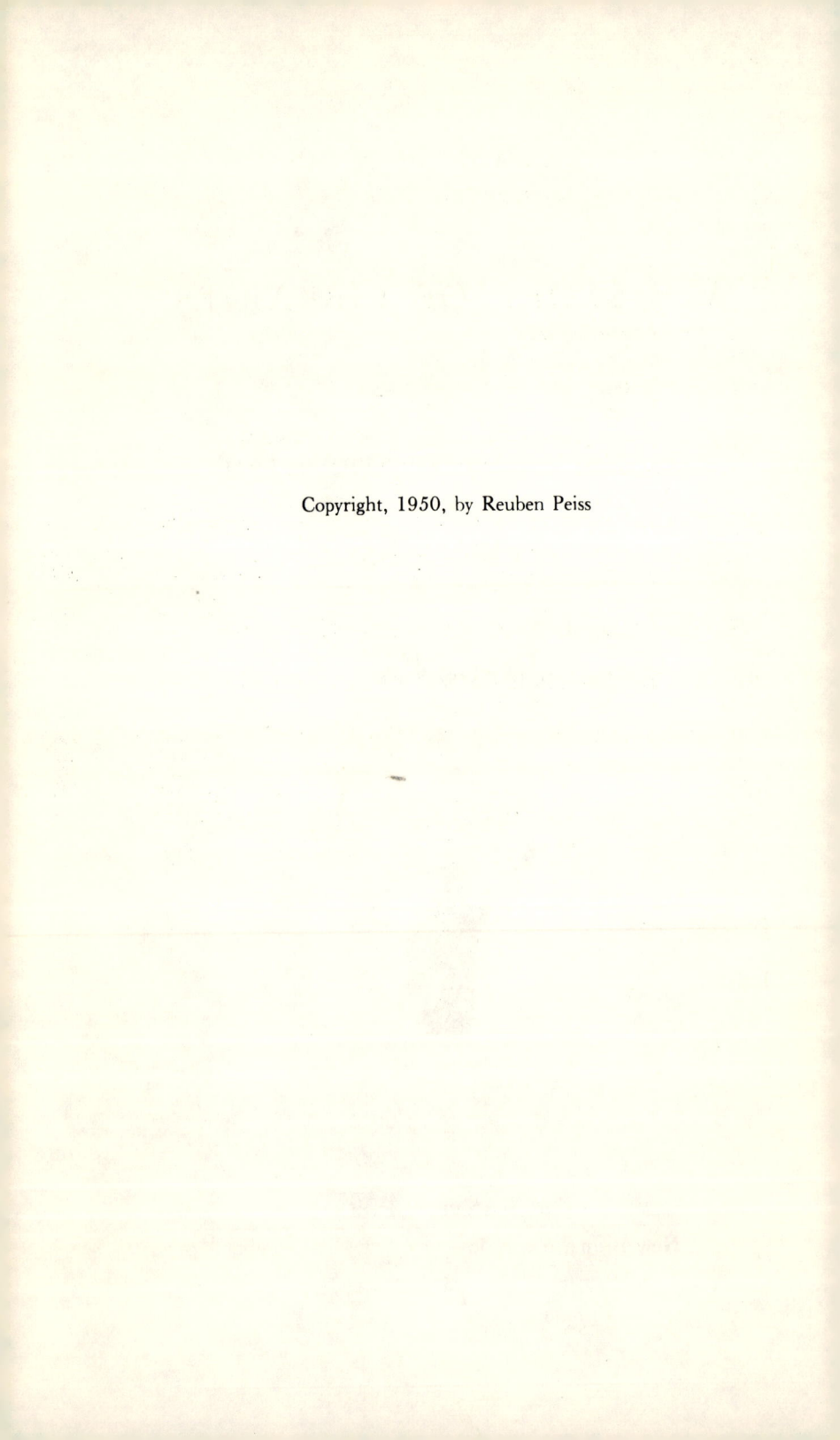

CONTENTS

Preface	III — V
I. The Ancient World	1
II. The Middle Ages to Charlemagne	9
III. The Post-Carolingian Age: Ninth to Twelfth Centuries	19
IV. The Late Middle Ages	28
V. The Renaissance	39
VI. The Reformation and the Seventeenth Century	51
VII. The Enlightenment	62
VIII. The French Revolution and the Nineteenth Century	76
IX. From the Nineteenth to the Twentieth Century	90
Footnotes	129
Bibliography	142
Index	181

REUBEN PEISS, A MEMORIAL

A good general, up-to-date history of libraries, written in English, was lacking in 1937 when Reuben Peiss began his library-school studies at the University of Michigan. German librarians, however, had made fairly notable contributions to library history. Hessel, for instance, at the University of Göttingen, had provided a small work which gave both historical facts and philosophical reflections on the development of libraries from antiquity to the twentieth century. It was natural, therefore, for one of Reuben's professors, in reviewing library history as an introduction to the course in library administration, to mention Hessel's book as worth reading for those students who could manage German. And it was characteristic of Peiss's inquiring mind that he followed up the suggestion: read Hessel through, bought a copy for himself, and quietly set to work to make an English translation.

His fine qualities of mind were evident all through his life. The eldest child of Alexander and Rose Pasternack Peiss, he was born in Hartford, Connecticut, on July the second, 1912. He attended the Northeast Elementary School and the Weaver High School in Hartford, graduating from the latter as salutatorian of his class.

In 1929 he entered Trinity College, Hartford, as the Hartford Scholar, holding the local alumni-association scholarship. He continued on scholarships throughout his entire stay at Trinity. He was Holland Scholar in 1930/31 and 1932/33 (the Holland Scholarships valued at $600 a year being awarded to the highest ranking student in the freshman, sophomore, and junior year). He was elected to Phi Beta Kappa in his junior year. He received the first Alumni prize of $60 for English composition in 1932, the following year the third Alumni prize of $25, and in 1932 he was also awarded the Van Zile poetry prize. While philosophy was his major subject, he graduated in 1933 with honors in both philosophy and English, and as valedictorian of his class.

Upon graduation, when Trinity College awarded him its best scholarship, the Mary A. Terry Fellowship which carried a stipend of $1,000, Peiss went to Harvard University for a year's study in philosophy. There he received his Master's degree in 1934. His desire was to stay on at Harvard to study for the Ph. D. in philosophy, but failure to procure a fellowship at Harvard made him give up that idea. Thereupon he returned to Hartford where he taught English and philosophy for three years at the Hartford Federal College (a Federal Emergency Relief School which ran from 1934 to 1939). In this way he was able to help his mother support the younger children, his father having died some years before.

In his Harvard days Peiss came to realize the affinity that exists between philosophy, as the love of knowledge, and libraries which are repositories of knowledge. Hence in 1937 he decided to give up teaching and go into the library field. He entered the Department of Library Science at the University of Michigan, where he took work among others with Dr. Bishop, Margaret Mann, and Eunice Wead (who regarded him as one of the finest reference students she had ever had).

His first library position was at Harvard where he was put in charge of preparing the data to be reported for inclusion in the second edition of the Union List of Serials. This was no easy assignment. Harvard University has one of the most decentralized library systems in the world, so Peiss had his troubles gathering, coordinating, and checking information. The Harvard entries in the first edition of the Union List of Serials were very inadequate, even to the extent of creating ghosts. The library's serial records were not always reliable; frequently it was a case of checking the pieces on the shelves; recataloging was often necessary before holdings could be reported accurately; and in Widener matters were complicated still further because the Official Catalog contained few added entries for variant titles. At times Peiss resorted to the device of tracing items in numbered monograph series through the aid of entries in national bibliographies. But he surmounted all difficulties. In fact, his bibliographical contribution was so excellent that Winifred Gregory, editor of the Union List of Serials, soon realized Peiss's ability and thereupon made Harvard her first source of outside help.

It was typical of Peiss that, starting with slight knowledge of the field, he quickly made himself master of the intricacies of serials. So it came as a particularly well deserved tribute when Miss Gregory sent him a special letter of thanks after she had completed the editorial work on the second edition of the Union List of Serials.

His next assignment was subject cataloging in the Harvard College Library, but that task was soon interrupted by a call from the Office of Strategic Services in Washington. Its Interdepartmental Committee for the Acquisition of Foreign Publications needed a field representative in Portugal to acquire publications issued in the Axis countries. Since these publications were largely serial in character, a man with good serial experience was sought. Peiss filled the bill excellently.

So in 1943 he went to Lisbon where for fourteen months he was Chief of the Interdepartmental Committee's outpost. Because of his great abilities, Peiss often participated in clandestine intelligence activities in addition to his major assignment of acquiring publications from enemy and enemy-occupied areas. An incident which occurred in the spring of 1944 demonstrates his great physical courage. An ambiguous message from Washington asking him to lay plans for a transfer to Switzerland (but which for security reasons did not state that the Seventh Army would be interrupting his communications by invasion during the coming summer) misled him into interpreting the instruction as ordering him to Switzerland immediately. He replied saying that he was arranging for a fake passport and visas, and would fly to Stuttgart in a German airplane; at Stuttgart he would transfer to an airplane bound for Switzerland; but he made no mention of the great danger awaiting an American citizen traveling through Germany.

His thought was only to do everything he could. Needless to say, orders were immediately telegraphed to Lisbon instructing him to stay there.

In the fall of 1944 he did leave Lisbon to set up an outpost for the Interdepartmental Committee in Bern, Switzerland, where he remained for nearly a year. During the period 1943 to 1945 he also spent short periods of time in England, France, and Spain.

In May 1945 he left Switzerland with an Interdepartmental Committee team to set up a post in Wiesbaden. Almost immediately after that Peiss borrowed a photography truck from the Seventh Army and with two enlisted men made a special journey to Leipzig which had fallen shortly before. He brought back with him two microfilm records of great bibliographical value: the one a copy of the cards which listed accessions in the Deutsche Bücherei from 1937 to 1945; the other the Deutsche Bücherei's current checking record of serials.

In mid-July the Interdepartmental Committee began to release its overseas agents. At the same time the Library of Congress Mission in Germany was established by an agreement between the Library (representing American libraries), the Department of State, and the War Department. The Library immediately authorized the transfer of Peiss to its staff to organize the Mission and recruit assistants. Although he did not actually go on the Library of Congress rolls until September 16, 1945, he was busy with the affairs of the Mission from the first week in August when he arrived in Frankfurt to set up headquarters.

The Mission's history is a matter of record. From Frankfurt Peiss supervised collection posts in Berlin, Munich, Stuttgart, Baden-Baden, Hamburg, and Vienna. He also supervised purchasing operations in Belgium, Holland, and Switzerland. One of his colleagues on the Library of Congress Mission, Harry Miller Lydenberg, remembers him as follows.—

When the six of us—one woman and five men—on the Library of Congress Mission sailed in January 1946, none, so far as I know, had worked with Peiss, nor seen him. I had heard that a man was in government service on the Continent who had worked in the Harvard Library and was in touch with it on matters of common interest; had the impression he was alert and competent; knew nothing of his personality. We all knew he would head our work, all agreed that it was both duty and pleasure to hail and heed him as such. Not even the shivering in that railroad station at Frankfurt a. M. that biting January morning as we tried to get in touch with the Mission headquarters, not even that, lessened our pleasure at the thought of being soon at work with him for so worthy a cause.

At last—mighty long last it seemed—the "touch and go" telephone connections did get through and we six did meet the other two members of the Mission in a less shivery room, there to learn that Peiss was in the hospital but work was moving along as well as possible under the circumstances. We got our billet assignments, our blanket rolls, and then early in the afternoon Clift and Lydenberg went to the hospital. Peiss by that time was "ambulatory," but greeted us curled up in bed. First glance showed he never would make the crew or the football team. I noted too how when he greeted us he put down The Education of Henry Adams, armed-services edition, he had been reading, soon saw how much that told of his tastes. It took no time at all to let us see he was quite in command of the situation, knew what was to be done first off and how to do it as the lead to other progress, knew surprisingly well what each of us seemed best fitted for. His mind was as clear, his personality as forceful, as his body was frail and slight, not one bit of weakness in either mind or body. And as I look back at it all I see clearly how the general plan as first sketched came from a man who knew the conditions and had the general plan of campaign clearly in mind. Changes did come, now and then, of course, but they were incidental and with no harmful effect on the outcome.

As I came to work and travel with him later I heard much of his life at Lisbon, Bern, Geneva, Paris, but always with fitting and characteristic acceptance and silence as to the confidential sides. His life in those and other places on the Continent had brought him into touch with many men of

high and low degree, and as I saw some of those earlier
acquaintances renewed, I came to see what an unusual joy
he had in knowing people, how gladly people accepted him
at his worth, how outstanding was his judgment as to importance and significance of each man or woman, what an
enviable memory he had for names and faces, these on
both sides of the fighting lines. This all helped much for
such results as the Mission was able to show. Of course
his command of foreign languages was a real advantage,
but that alone would have been of little help had it not
been backed up and bolstered by such a personality, such
a character.

    The work of the Mission suffered nothing by his
hospitalization nor his leave of absence to let him get back
on his feet again, so wise had been his planning. One more
instance of the laying down of aims and principles with
sensible freedom as to working out details. As I think back
to those days I feel sure each of us was happy to see how
work went on in spite of such handicaps, but quite plainly
as the result of long distance and constant contact with it.

    After he got in the saddle again and after Clift and I
came home in June I was privileged to keep in touch with
him as the Mission came to close up, as he came to take up
new tasks at home, little chance to talk face to face, much
by letter right up to the last. Impressions of mental alert-
ness, mental integrity, clear and dispassionate judgment of
men and of causes were strengthened and deepened the
longer I knew him. I felt honored beyond merit by letter-
chats with him as work on Hessel went on. I was grateful
for what he said about library work over here as he saw it
in east and west, on the people he worked with, about the
books he read as part of his work and as part of his independent mental life.

    I believe he took no active part in land or water
sports, recall no word about the fun of walking or hiking,
about joy in the woods or farm pastures or on mountain
trails. I know he had plenty of experience in driving a car
in Germany, Switzerland, even in Paris. No faltering of
nerves or coordination. I've no right to say that sport or
quiet enjoyment of nature around him was out of his world,

merely that I recall little to show that side of the man. I know full well how strong was his support of a cause he felt was right. No doubt was there as to where he stood or what he would do if need arose. Nor any suspicion of forcing his own judgments or opinions on the other fellow. By no means a resident of the ivory tower, by no means aloof from or superior to the daily life bustling around him, by no means an unpractical visionary, his chief interests were in the things of the mind and the intellect.

Few equals have come into my ken.

One incident—out of many—from the crowded events of the Mission's brief but effective life may be recalled to attest the quality of Reuben's instincts and reactions. On May 20, 1946, the famous Allied Control Authority Order No. 4 was promulgated ordering the surrender by all German institutions of the Nazi books in their possession, together with the cards from their catalogs representing such books. This was interpreted in the United States as a book-burning order, and the American Library Association, of which Ralph Ulveling was then President, promptly protested to the White House. Reuben, though he did not believe that the order was primarily one for suppression, but rather for converting the enormous stocks of propagandistic literature to a more practical use in the German economy—wood pulp—immediately went into action. In conferences with Brigadier General Eyster, Chief of the Public Relations Division of General Clay's command, and with General Lucius Clay himself, he rapidly worked out a method for systematically assuring that copies of all confiscated propagandistic literature would be conserved for purposes of administration, education, and research. So prompt and effective were his efforts that by June 30, 1946, the Office of Military Government (US) had issued a preliminary directive, implementing Order No. 4 in the American Zone, and providing such assurance. A later order of September 10, 1946, specifically provided for the stockpiling of 150 reference copies of confiscated Nazi literature and for the role of the Mission in this stockpiling. And on September 13, 1946, the Allied Control

Authority amended Order No. 4 carrying the principle advocated by Reuben to the whole of occupied Germany.

In carrying out its part in the stockpiling, the Mission secured the use of the Siemens villa in Lankwitz in south-west Berlin. Thither copies of confiscated materials were brought and sorted out into sets by displaced civilians under the Mission's direction. On October 23, 1946, Reuben, who was then preparing to return to the United States, reported to General Clay that 10,000 titles had been cataloged.

Amid the organizational confusion of an occupation army impatient at its task of civilian rehabilitation, "operators"—that group of the military and para-military who specialized in finding or contriving channels for action unimpeded by red-tape—thrived. Peiss knew the tricks, and appreciated the wit behind them, but his personal ethics barred his indulgence. His experience and persuasiveness helped him to get the action he needed through proper channels.

Careful advance preparation was necessary to produce a convoy of U. S. Army trucks complete with a liaison officer from the Russian Army to penetrate the Eastern Zone as far as Leipzig. As an expedition it was completely successful; the books and journals stored by Otto Harrassowitz and others for American research libraries were collected, loaded, and shipped. And Reuben capped this professional triumph by beating his Russian escort at chess.

Two strong motives dominated much of Reuben's work in Germany, one professional and the other cultural. At times they merged, and his instinct for librarianship and his strong sense of identification with Western culture became one.

He was professionally concerned with the completeness of the bibliographical record. Whether the aspect was toward research collections and bibliographies of wartime imprints, the outpourings of a revived German printing industry, or microfilm of the periodical checking records of the Deutsche Bücherei at Leipzig, his insistence on total cognizance and comprehensive acquisition was constant. This philosophy, as Reuben carried it out, made its mark on American library practice, demonstrating in practical terms many of the virtues and some of the hazards of comprehensive acquisition programs such as the Farmington Plan.

Closely associated with this motive was a keen awareness of the cultural heritage of which German books and journals were the tangible evidence. Reuben was a scholar before he was a librarian, and the whole world of Western thought was his homeland. Salvage of the works of scholarship from the rubble of Leipzig bookshops satisfied only part of his scholarly instinct; in addition to preservation there must come rebuilding. Thus it was that Reuben was vitally concerned with the cultural effects of the split between Eastern and Western Germany, as evidenced by the independent paths taken by the Deutsche Bücherei and the Bücherei des Westens. Finding emergency channels for the post-war resumption of international exchange of publications was a constant challenge; German cultural institutions were to be rehabilitated not because this was the policy of military government, but because they preserved the world of Leibnitz, Spinoza, Luther, Bach, and Mozart; and Reuben was imbued with a sense of urgency for the continuity of Western culture.

Many of the Mission's staff envied Reuben his enthusiasm for fresh experience. A few examples of his appetite come to mind: Reuben rerouting his Leipzig-bound Mercedes so he could show his Russian escort the Schlosskirche in Wittenberg where Luther nailed his theses, visiting the Kurhaus in Wiesbaden to see the head of Nefertiti, critically evaluating the performance of a Stalin prize quartet in Berlin, or enthusing over a Staatsoper performance of Die Entführung aus dem Serail. Characteristically, Reuben was one of the first to build, on his return to the United States, a high-fidelity set to indulge his insatiable hunger for good music.

There is no doubt that the tremendous pressure of his activities as head of the Library of Congress Mission contributed to his decline in health. It was in July 1946 that Peiss suffered the first of the serious attacks which brought him back to the United States the following December almost a wraith. He remained on the Library of Congress staff until December 17, 1946, when he went home to Hartford for a visit with his family and for further medical treatment.

On his European assignments Peiss had demonstrated his outstanding ability as an acquisition librarian. As soon as his health permitted, then, it was natural for him to accept an offer from the Department of State (which in the meantime had absorbed that area of the Office of Strategic Services with which Peiss had formerly been connected) to be chief of the Acquisition Section of its Intelligence Acquisition and Distribution Division. He remained at the Department of State from March 26, 1947, until three years later when he went to teach at the University of California.

During this term at the Department of State Peiss put the finishing touches on his translation of Hessel. He spent endless hours running down references, polishing the translation, completing the bibliography, and writing a supplementary chapter to bring the work up to date.

Peiss had a happy knack as a translator. His work is distinguished by the fact that time and time again he hits on just the right expression in English, an expression which most translators would have missed in their literal-mindedness. The ability to write which won him acclaim at Trinity College was clearly in evidence throughout the translation.

Never robust, for he was the living embodiment of a wonderful mind in a frail body, Peiss wisely decided to give up the stresses of government service in favor of a teaching life in California when in 1950 an offer came to be an associate professor in the School of Librarianship at the University of California.

David H. Clift, who had been with Peiss on the Library of Congress Mission, remembers the enthusiasm with which he set out to teach in California and recalls him in the following terms.

He was a delightful companion and none better for traveling. His many personal qualities encouraged conversation; his intellectual characteristics sparked it. My last trip with Reuben, from Connecticut to ALA in Cleveland, reminded me of all the other trips we made together here and abroad. He was forever interested in opinions and in man's behavior. His mind was questing and philosophical; his critical judgments always tempered by charity and understanding.

Along with talking about anything, he could also become very quiet but you could be sure that his mind was busy, gathering scenery and props for introduction into the conversation of some subject that had come to mind by memory of a book, a news story, some passing scene, or the mention of a friend. He could also, it seemed, fall asleep on a moment's notice; for he had learned, wisely and necessarily, to sustain his strength by little cat-naps that he could apparently take anywhere and under any circumstances.

On the way to Cleveland he was full, as always, of the job ahead. He seemed glad of the teaching prospects in front of him and he showed enthusiasm at this return to academic life. I suspect he felt something of regret, too, at parting with the hectic life he had known since the early war days, for it is probably true that the man of action within him never quite left the man of intellect completely free. I doubt that either ever completely won. In the meantime, he faced life with deep interest, critical speculation, and unwavering confidence. There was pain but there was always tomorrow. If his tomorrows had been as many as his friends, he would write words about all of us.

One of his colleagues at Berkeley, William B. Ready, speaks thus of his term in the library school.

California welcomed him. It is wonderfully surprising how in the brief time that was remaining to him he became so much at home at Berkeley; in classroom, conferences, and meetings he became a prime mover in California library affairs until his death not two years later on the twenty-third of February, 1952.

He was in pain or in its shadow nearly all that time. Clawed by pain he would fight it down and do a man's work or more in his classroom and office before participating to the full in the administrative affairs of the Library School. He was a beloved and respected member of the Faculty Club, and his grinning wit and humor in the teeth of his malignant danger is remembered by his friends there still; they speak of him with pride and affection.

Reuben's subtle fertile mind, his power of analysis, and his critical perception were wedded to his generous and humane nature, making him a dear member of any group or society. He was the best of chairmen and of rapporteurs, a grand raconteur.

It is not easy to assess exactly those qualities in Reuben Peiss that inspired the deep and enduring affection of his friends. Possibly, most of all it was his love of life and of the living; to him there was a place for Spinoza and Whitehead, for Groucho Marx and for Lou Holtz's Yankee Doodle Boy. He loved bridge and fine music, Sherlock Holmes and the speculation of Santayana. He was interested in every manifestation of the creative powers of men and he condemned nothing but the bogus, the shoddy, the dishonest, and the hypocritical. Whatever were the qualities that awoke the love that his friends bore him, his death is an irrevocable loss; his memory will be green among us for aye. His untimely passing has deprived the library world of the full fruition of his mind, of the important bibliographical work that he had planned—"cut is the branch that might have grown full straight."

Published Writings of Reuben Peiss

"Acquisition of Foreign Scientific Publications," Chemical and Engineering News 28:1364-6, 1950.

"European Wartime Acquisitions and the Library of Congress Mission," Library Journal 71:863-76, 1946.

Hessel, Alfred. A History of Libraries. Translated, with supplementary material, by Reuben Peiss. Washington, D. C., Scarecrow Press [1950]. v, 198 p.

"New England Meeting," Library Journal 68:468, 1943.

"Order No. 4," Library Journal 72:372-4, 1947.

"Report on Europe," College and Research Libraries 8:113-9, 1947.

Review: Bibliographic Organization: Papers Presented before the Fifteenth Annual Conference of the Graduate Library School, July 24-29, 1950. Edited by Jesse H. Shera and Margaret E. Egan. Chicago, University of Chicago Press, 1950. In: Library Quarterly 21:229-30, 1951.

Verner W. Clapp, Library of Congress
David H. Clift, American Library Association
Frederick G. Kilgour, Yale University Medical
  School
Harry Miller Lydenberg, Formerly of the New
  York Public Library
Keyes D. Metcalf, Harvard University
Andrew D. Osborn, Harvard University
William B. Ready, Stanford University

PREFACE

The history of libraries is represented by a truly vast literature, which has been augmented in recent years by a number of useful books. Aside from more specialized works there have been Popular Libraries of the World, edited by Bostwick, The World's Great Libraries, by Esdaile and Burton, and the Survey of Libraries, edited by McColvin, as well as the most comprehensive work on library history yet published, the third volume of the monumental Handbuch der Bibliothekswissenschaft, of which the section on English and American libraries has been translated by Lawrence S. Thompson. Nevertheless, there is no adequate short history of libraries in English. The present translation has been made to fill the gap.

I first came across Hessel's work in 1937, when I was studying at the University of Michigan School of Library Science, and quickly found it to be the best single volume for the student. It combines soundness on technical matters with historical insight. Perhaps its finest quality is constant emphasis upon the development of the library as an institution within the framework of general cultural trends.

The present volume consists of a straightforward translation of the first eight chapters of Dr. Hessel's Geschichte der Bibliotheken, with a new ninth chapter by the translator. The original ninth chapter ended with the first World War, and in the intervening years there have been new developments, not the least of which has been another devastating war. I have therefore tried to bring library history more nearly up-to-date. The manuscript was completed in 1943, when I went abroad, and it has now been difficult to decide upon a terminus ad quem. There is still insufficient reliable data concerning the effects of the late war upon libraries to make profitable any attempt to bring the story up to the moment. Although there have been some developments worth noting in America during the past five years, they have not seriously affected the general trends which were apparent in 1943. I have therefore proceeded by the principle of expediency. When a statement made in 1943 would be an obvious anachronism in 1948 (as, for example, many statements about German libraries would be), it has been changed to embody the latest available information. Moreover, whenever there has been a significant change in one of the main subjects originally selected for treatment in the final chapter--or a significant publication bearing upon these subjects--I have made the necessary modifications. Aside from these ad hoc revisions, there has been no systematic attempt to bring the history up-to-date or to cover the literature of the last five years thoroughly.

In the ninth chapter I have used Hessel's materials-- and occasionally sentences or longer passages--but the great bulk of the text is my own. I have tried hard to keep its length in proportion to the rest of the history and to conform to Hessel's general method of focusing upon significant trends; nevertheless the vigorous development of libraries in recent years has required extended treatment. Not quite so much emphasis upon German libraries will be found in the last chapter as in those that precede, for reasons which should be obvious. Limitations of space have required the omission of a number of countries and reduced others to passing mention. The library history of Canada is closely linked with that of the United States, but substantial space might have been devoted to several countries in Europe as well as in the Orient, Australasia, and Latin America. Literature on some of these countries is available in the publications by Bostwick, Esdaile and Burton, and McColvin mentioned above and, of course, in the Handbuch der Bibliothekswissenschaft. The Actes du Comité International des Bibliothèques contain summaries of yearly activities in many countries. Several national library surveys have been made with the financial support of the Carnegie Corporation; these are listed in The Diffusion of Knowledge, by Gourley and Lester.

In making this translation I have kept constantly in mind American librarians and library students. Insofar as possible I have anglicized names and titles, usually giving the original in parentheses the first time it occurs. All passages in languages other than English have been translated, and the original quoted. I have also added explanatory notes where allusions or references might not be clear to the American reader, whose general background differs to some extent from that of the average German. In footnoting I have tried to avoid preciosity but to supply brief information on points that might be obscure.

A number of bibliographical footnotes have also been inserted. The original text had no footnotes, and I have been somewhat reluctant to add them, but those books and articles which have been cited are important sources of information of particular interest to American students who wish to look a bit further into library history. The original bibliography itself has been expanded and rearranged. Exact details are given in the note preceding the formal bibliography.

This manuscript was completed in 1948. However, Dr. Shera's Foundations of the Public Library, published in 1949, is of such great importance that it has been added to the materials cited.

There remains the pleasant task of acknowledging many obligations. The first and greatest of these is to Andrew D. Osborn, who first called my attention to Hessel's work, encouraged me to translate it, and has since given unsparingly of his time and counsel. He has carefully gone over the entire manuscript, which owes much to his scrupulous scholarship. H. M. Lydenberg's scholarly criticism has improved my work at many points. Fritz T. Epstein has read the manuscript and made many helpful suggestions. He has also performed the onerous task of checking some of the bibliography. Keyes D. Metcalf has been responsible for a number of improvements in the last chapter. Walter Sollmitz has provided expert advice on the translation of Latin passages. It is not possible to name all those, particularly friends and former colleagues at the Harvard College Library, who have given me aid at various times, but I do wish here to record my lasting gratitude.

Washington, D. C.   March 15, 1950

CHAPTER I. THE ANCIENT WORLD

The founding of the Library of Alexandria may be called the greatest accomplishment in the library history of ancient times.(1) The planning of this library is ascribed to Ptolemy Soter (d. ca. 283 B.C.), the first of the Diadochian dynasty in Egypt, and the execution of the plan to his son, Ptolemy Philadelphus. Since they proposed nothing less than collecting the whole of Greek literature, these rulers must have had to make available very large funds. Furthermore, they did not balk at various unscrupulous methods: for example, they confiscated the book cargoes of ships anchoring in the harbor of Alexandria, and (the story goes) having borrowed from Athens the works of the three great tragedians, they returned not the official text which had been borrowed but only a copy of it. The number of papyrus rolls finally assembled was reckoned to be several hundred thousand--a prodigious total, even when one considers that in it were included many duplicates and that, moreover, a single literary work as a rule covered several rolls. The library was in two divisions, the large one within the royal palace in the Brucheum section of the city, and the small one in the Temple of Serapis. After the former was destroyed in 47 B.C. during Caesar's campaign in Alexandria, the Serapeum became the real book center of the city.

Historians have done much hard research in the attempt to discover what institutions could possibly have served the Ptolemies as library models. In this attempt earlier, and even modern, scholars have gone as far back as the "antediluvian" period. We have misgivings about following their example: we had rather confine our investigation to the centuries just preceding the founding of the Alexandrian Library.

The logical step would be first to seek its prototypes in ancient Egypt. Here was the home of the ancient writing material, papyrus; in science and belles-lettres the Egyptians produced a very extensive literature--indeed probably nowhere at the time was writing so widely and actively carried on as in the land of the Nile. There was also an excellent system of archives and public records with a sizeable staff, but of large libraries comparable to that of Alexandria we hear nothing. Only the temples had libraries in conjunction with the archives, and these were primarily for liturgical and educational purposes.

We come across similar collections of administrative records, and even of literary remains, in the temples of the

Assyro-Babylonian civilization. Surpassing them all in volume and significance is the library of Assurbanipal, whose clay tablets were brought to light during excavation of the royal palace at Nineveh about the middle of the last century. Assurbanipal (668-626 B.C.) belonged to the last great dynasty of Assyrian kings, the Sargonids. Even more than his predecessors he devoted himself to promoting cultural activities. He was himself very carefully educated, so much so that he could boast of "being able to read stone inscriptions which date from the time before the deluge." Once upon the throne, he undertook the systematic collection of Assyro-Babylonian literature, in the course of which he issued careful instructions for provision of the necessary texts, kept busy a host of copyists, and insisted on careful work. The library had its own staff; the books were well arranged by subject and bore stamps indicating their position in the collection;(2) moreover, catalogues facilitated its use. From its collected holdings--there were deeds, documents, and letters; religious texts; historical accounts; and works in the most diverse fields of knowledge--there shines forth the purpose for which it was designed: it was to serve state as well as church, to promote the lasting fame of its founder as well as scientific knowledge.

There were undeniably remarkable resemblances between the libraries of Nineveh and Alexandria. Both were institutions of a universal character brought into being by reigning princes. It is also proper to point out that in more than one respect the inner organization of the Hellenistic library calls to mind the Assyrian library, and that there are even many similarities in the treatment of the individual literary work in both places despite the difference in writing material (clay tablets at Nineveh, papyrus rolls at Alexandria). Nevertheless it seems to me at present still too risky to insist upon establishing a direct connection of Alexandria with Nineveh. Between them lie four centuries; between them lies the reign of the Medo-Persian kings, who, so far as is known, paid no attention to library matters. It must be left to the future to disclose lines of connection which at present are obscure.

An investigation into library conditions in Greece gives promise of better results: indeed the word for the institution points to Greece as its native land. (3) Libraries were still unknown to Greece in classical times. The tradition that in early days Pisistratus of Athens and Polycrates of Samos had erected libraries does not deserve belief. There was, to be sure, a well-developed book trade in the time of Pericles, but it does not appear to have been customary for collections of manuscripts to be set up by the community, nor was a private library in those days a necessary constituent of an aristocratic home. At the onset of the fourth century B.C. it became more frequent for scholars or literary men to collect libraries of their own. For example, a remark in one of Aristophanes' comedies makes it probable that Euripides did so. (4) The true development of the Greek library began, then, in the very decades which embraced the activity of those two intellectual giants, Plato and Aristotle.

The Academy and the Peripatetic school can claim the glory of having created "not only the learning of Greece but of classical antiquity as a whole." Here there developed for the first time "a large-scale organization of cooperative work" under the leadership of a single individual. Plato undertook a methodical investigation into the fields of mathematics and natural science. Aristotle strove, insofar as possible, to collect completely and establish on a sound footing the facts in all the branches of knowledge, and he became the father of the disciplines of philological criticism and literary history. The work of both these men unquestionably presupposes the existence of a considerable library. With regard to Plato we have no definite report of such a library; of Aristotle, on the contrary, we hear that he collected manuscripts systematically, and we know also of the vicissitudes suffered by the library which he left behind.

Aristotle's pupil, Alexander the Great, opened a new period of ancient history through his campaigns. Greek culture broadened its scope, becoming a world civilization. An international class of educated men came into being. In Hellenistic culture scholarship and erudition became important factors of intellectual life. The seed sown by Aristotle now bore rich fruit, yet there was at the same time a change in the direction of scholarly endeavor. The unifying bond with which the master had connected the special fields of knowledge became more and more relaxed. These individual fields of knowledge became independent; investigations were confined to limited subject matter; and not infrequently the accumulation of knowledge handed down by preceding generations took the place of creative work. Furthermore, the outer form of intellectual cooperation also changed. The free school of philosophers turned into a monarchical organization. For Hellenism adopted as its own form of state the kingdom of the Diadochi, and these princes considered it their task to foster and to propagate Greek culture.

Alexander himself died too early to raise the large-scale organization of scientific studies in the spirit of the Stagirite to the status of a governmental program. This was accomplished by the first Ptolemy, who found a spiritual adviser in the Peripatetic, Demetrius of Phalerum. The Museum was founded on the Athenian model, and the most outstanding scholars of the time were called to the Egyptian court, so that Alexandria swiftly developed into the center of Hellenistic learning. The library constituted the most important working unit of the Museum. A systematic study of Greek literature was undertaken, authoritative texts put together by means of philological and historical criticism, problems of authorship and authenticity investigated, and the extent and division of literary works determined. At the same time the Alexandrian school had an epoch-making effect upon the whole field of the book arts, in that it produced standard copies of individual authors and of the different forms of literature. These were reproduced by a large number of copyists, and copies were then placed on sale. Thus it was to the Museum and its library that Alexandria owed its monopoly on the book trade, which it maintained up to the time of Caesar.

From what we have already said it is easy to understand that administration of the Alexandrian collections was entrusted only to coryphaei of learning, especially since they had, at the same time, to occupy the exalted position of royal tutor. The first of these was the great grammarian, Zenodotus of Ephesus (d. ca. 260 B.C.). He began the arrangement of the book stock and started the editing of Greek literature with his edition of Homer. Of his successors we must mention Eratosthenes, a universal mind encompassing the arts and sciences, known above all as the founder of chronology and of mathematical geography, and Aristophanes of Byzantium, whose most important contribution is to be found in the field of lexicography. Callimachus of Cyrene occupied a special place in this list. Some do not consider him a member of the library staff at all; others consider him some kind of subordinate official. The scholarly reputation of Callimachus rests upon his Pinakes, which he produced about the middle of the third century B.C., probably by availing himself of previous foreign work and the help of disciples. These comprised catalogues of the manuscripts in the library, separated prose writers from poets, and broke up both divisions into subject groups. Within each of these groups the authors were arranged alphabetically and each one provided with a biographical notice and a list of his writings. Finally, the individual work was described as to title, first words, and number of lines. These Pinakes for a long time enjoyed a canonical reputation and formed the basis of all later bibliographies of antiquity.

Concerning the spatial arrangement of the Library of Alexandria we know nothing definite. This makes even more valuable, therefore, the results obtained by the German excavations at Pergamum at the end of the last century. The library there was the work of the Attali: Eumenes II (197-158 B.C.) is considered its founder. Near the temple of Athena Polias an open court with a two-storied portico with four adjoining rooms was uncovered. In the largest was found the great statue of Athena and also pedestal inscriptions referring to well-known writers of Asia Minor, among them one in verse on Homer. Here we have the typical layout of the ancient library: the stoa serving as a study, the entrance hall adorned with statues, and the remaining chambers given over to book storage--the whole closely adjoining a temple.(5)

Only very slight information has come down to us concerning the founding of libraries by others of the Diadochi, for example the libraries of the Seleucids, which were certainly very important. On the whole, the sources for that period are so meager that the very important process of development which the Hellenistic library had then to undergo has remained almost totally unobserved. From all appearances the manuscript collection at Alexandria represented originally only a research tool for a limited group of scholars. Gradually the number of users must have become larger and larger. Thus the library at the Athenian academy located within the Ptolemeum may already have taken on more the appearance of a modern university library. It represented another important step forward when to those interested in scholarship was added the broad circle of educated men in general. Thereby the library for the first time acquired a truly public character and no longer confined itself to serving as a place for work, but existed now, to use Vitruvius's phrase, "for the enjoyment of all" (ad communem delectationem). This type, too, we may assume, the Hellenistic period had already worked out; for this it was which the civilization of the eastern Mediterranean handed over to the western Mediterranean at the end of the first century B.C.

"Conquered Greece subdued her savage conqueror,"(6) says the ancient poet. Modern scholarship sees in the culture of the Roman Empire only a continuation and further development of Hellenistic culture.

From the middle of the second century B.C. Roman generals began to bring home Greek libraries along with other booty. The first to do this was Aemilius Paulus, and in the next century Sulla and Lucullus followed his example. Toward the end of the first century B.C. love of books spread among the Roman aristocracy. Cicero valued his collection very highly and saw in it the heart of his home. His friend Atticus was Rome's first large publisher and dared even to compete with the Alexandrian book trade. He was himself well-educated and he employed a staff of collaborators thoroughly trained in philology, among them Varro, who even wrote a treatise entitled De Bibliothecis.(7)

Caesar was eager to avail himself of Varro's help so that by founding a state library he might, as Mommsen says, "bind together world domination and world literature." Culturally Caesar's endeavors show themselves clearly patterned after Hellenistic models. There is a good deal of evidence that he harbored the intention of transplanting the Alexandrian Library to the Tiber. But not until after his death was the first public library established in Rome in the Atrium Libertatis. It was one of Caesar's intimate friends, Asinius Pollio, who in this way "was the first to make men's talents public property."(8) Augustus followed suit by establishing two collections--one on the Palatine at the temple of Apollo, the other in the Porticus Octaviae. At the opening of the fourth century A.D. the public libraries in the capital city numbered twenty-eight. Only a few of them can be identified. Still, we are justified in assuming that collections were hardly wanting at the great forums and baths. The most important was the Bibliotheca Ulpia near the Column of Trajan.(9) Like the others, it was divided into a Greek and a Latin division, and it served also as the archive for important state documents. Heading these libraries at first were distinguished scholars with the rank of procurator. Later there developed a distinction between the administrative officials proper and the scholarly directors. Under them served slaves or freedmen so numerous as to require their own physician.

The cities of Italy and the provinces endeavoured to follow the example of Rome. Neither the casual references in literary remains nor the results of excavations undertaken

in various places permit even an approximate estimate of
the number of public libraries in the expanse of the Empire.
One gets the impression that probably the majority of the
larger provincial cities with intellectual interests had their
libraries.(10) Occasionally they were indebted for their
erection to the munificence of an emperor--thus the Greek-
loving Hadrian presented to Athens a magnificent library,
the ruins of which one can still marvel at today--but mostly
they were due to the liberality of private citizens. These
people looked after their own needs no less earnestly, for
bibliophilic inclinations were in fashion in the time of the
Roman Empire. No aristocratic city palace, no grand villa
found it seemly to fail to have its book collection. Hence
Seneca's jibe: "Nowadays a library is considered a necessary ornament with which to adorn a house along with hot
and cold baths";(11) and, in another place: "What is the use
of innumerable books and libraries if in a lifetime the master hardly reads the titles??(12) There were private libraries with 30,000 and even 60,000 rolls. The master of the
house either kept educated slaves for their production or he
met his needs with the help of the very highly developed
book trade. Among the educated, Greek authors were much
preferred. Our most reliable information concerning the
contents of such a library comes from the famous discovery
of book rolls at Herculaneum, which is today one of the
treasures of the museum at Naples.

    In general the physical arrangement of Roman libra-
ries followed the principles already familiar to us from
Pergamum, though naturally this did not preclude individual
differences. Thus the latest excavations at Ephesus have
brought to light a book-room without a portico but having
instead a facade with ornamental columns and an outside
staircase.(13) Vitruvius urged that the rooms face the East
to take advantage of the morning light, but in practice his
requirements were not always fulfilled. In order specially
to protect the papyrus rolls from dampness an outer wall
was frequently built around the inner wall, so that a narrow
passage ran between the two. For the rest, so far as stone-
work, architectural style, and artistic decoration are concerned, libraries resembled the other monumental structures of the age. Very likely there was always a statue of
some deity which was placed usually in a recess of the great
hall. Accompanying it were busts and medallions of scholars and writers "whose immortal souls speak in these very
places" (immortales animae in locis iisdem loquuntur). A

good deal of ornamentation was in evidence, but in order to spare the eyes, gold was avoided and a greenish marble selected for the floors. The book rolls, with tickets bearing their titles outward, lay in the pigeon-holes of the wooden presses. These were often symmetrically arranged and sunk into niches in the walls. When necessary there were several such rows, one above the other. The top rows were then reached by means of galleries, which rested on columns. We can say nothing exact about leading practices in the arrangement of the book stock, since only quite scanty fragments of catalogues have been preserved. Some of the public libraries circulated their books. Their administration was frequently in the hands of priests when, as very commonly occurred, they were connected with a temple.

  The history of Graeco-Roman libraries covers a period of about 600 years. It could point to achievements which the Christian West was able to match only after a period of development three times as long. This superiority of the ancient libraries was indeed well known to succeeding generations. Our exposition will show in how many ways the creations of antiquity hovered before the eyes of much later library reformers as ideals.

CHAPTER II. THE MIDDLE AGES TO CHARLEMAGNE

Historians nowadays avoid drawing a sharp line of demarcation between the ancient world and the Middle Ages; instead they suggest a period of transition lasting a good five hundred years. Accordingly no exact span of years can be specified in which the ancient library ceased to exist and the medieval library had its inception. Scholars must content themselves with identifying each of the main factors which determined the character of this new type of library and with following the course of its development.(14)

A signal characteristic of the ancient library is the papyrus roll, of the medieval library, the parchment codex. In the preceding chapter we became acquainted with papyrus as the writing material of ancient times. Even then, as a matter of fact, parchment was used for less important purposes, but artistic and literary evidence indicates that it first came into more general use in the third century A.D., and by the fifth century it had almost entirely supplanted papyrus. In this period, therefore, took place the transcription of most of the extant literature from the one writing material to the other, a process whose importance for the textual criticism carried on in modern philology is well known. And now, corresponding to the substitution of parchment for papyrus, in these centuries the parchment codex with a stiff cover replaced the papyrus roll as the physical form of books. It is to be expected that the infiltration of the parchment codex brought with it certain changes in the internal structure of the library. Still, these could not have been of a revolutionary nature; at least a mosaic of the fifth century (Plate II) and a miniature of the sixth century show that the codices were kept in chests, just as the rolls had been formerly (Plate I). If accommodating the new form of book demanded considerably more space than before, this disadvantage was in a measure compensated for by the fact that a single codex could contain the texts of a whole series of papyrus rolls.

Its real advantages--greater durability and ease of handling, the possibility of writing on both sides, and other features--decided the victory of the parchment codex over the papyrus roll. But we should also consider the simultaneous operation of non-material factors. Thus it seems to have been a time in which the new form of book was propagated by the religious power then coming to the fore, Christianity, while pagan culture, placed on the defensive, was clinging to the form which was on the way out. It was probably about the same time that the Christian library entered into competition with the pagan.

The fate of the pagan library was closely tied up with that of ancient culture. With that culture falling into decay, one school of rhetoricians after another shutting down, and the number of unlettered people rapidly increasing, desolation settled upon the places where formerly those interested in pagan science and literature used to foregather. In the fourth century Ammianus Marcellinus is already lamenting the "libraries closed forever like tombs" (bybliothecae sepulchrorum ritu in perpetuum claustrae).(15) Upon the heels of desolation came destruction. We have practically no trustworthy accounts of the dispersal of manuscripts and the tearing down of buildings. The Alexandrian Library appears to have fallen prey to Christian fanaticism at the end of the fourth century; and it is said that the same Gregory the Great who preached the famous "funeral sermons" to a Rome oppressed by the Lombards caused the imperial book collections to be burned. This comes down, to be sure, as a much later tradition of the Middle Ages, yet it contains the kernel of truth latent in every legend.

In structure Christian libraries copied the pagan ones. As so many of the latter were located within temples, it was natural to bring the former within houses of worship and therewith to assure them of the protection of the Church. The books of the Bible (hence also designated biblia sacra or divina) everywhere formed the basis of the collection. To these were then added liturgical and exegetical writings, and from the time when Christian apologetics began to expand, the works of the theologians and their heathen opponents could no longer be missing. Finally, for studying and gaining proficiency in the language of the Church, be it Greek or Latin, the remaining profane literature was needed.

We have information about many a church library, especially in Africa, even before the reign of Diocletian. Many fell victim to his great persecution. But, from the time the Church was raised by Constantine to the rank of a state institution, the disciplinary, organizational, and dogmatic duties of each bishop forced him at least to maintain a library of moderate compass. At the opening of the fifth century Paulinus of Nola even built at his episcopal seat a Christian reading room and provided it with the inscription: "Here he whose thoughts are on the laws of God may sit and ponder over holy books." (16)

Tertullian (ca. 200) was one of the first of the Church Fathers whose library we can picture today. Then we also have details of the widely renowned library of Caesarea in Palestine. The oldest part of its collection consisted of the manuscripts of Origen, which his pupil Pamphilus (d. 309) copied and industriously augmented. Approximately one hundred years later Jerome made use of them and was able to report that two bishops of Caesarea had transferred to parchment the papyrus rolls of Pamphilus. Jerome was himself an ardent book-collector. His contemporary, the great Augustine, also left valuable manuscripts to the Church at Hippo. These scholars' libraries divided naturally into three parts: two profane, divided by language, and one Christian. The Church Fathers no longer used profane literature in the classical way, for because of their faith they could never overcome a deep-rooted aversion to pagan literature. It served them much more simply as an expedient, a base upon which to build Christian knowledge.

The fifth and sixth centuries brought the political collapse of the Roman Empire and the founding of the German states in the western provinces. Most recent studies have been right in trying to delimit the effect of these events upon the general development of culture, and, above all, in denying the theory of a general catastrophe. In contrast to former centuries there was a strongly increasing influx of Germanic peoples who found themselves up against a strange culture and language. As a consequence, the kind of education provided in ancient times became even less widespread among the laity and, correspondingly, the Church securely established its position as the dominant spiritual power of the times.

In contrast to the Western Empire, the Eastern Empire maintained its independence for a while. Consequently tradition could preserve itself there for a longer time. The succeeding centuries nevertheless brought about such considerable losses of power externally and such radical upheavals internally that even Byzantine culture took on more and more of a medieval character.

The Emperor Constantine built a library along with the academy at Byzantium, and was particularly solicitous for Christian texts. His successors took pains to enlarge the library, so that before the great fire of 476/7 it contained a very large number of books. After the fire it was soon restored. Thereafter, however, ensued a dark period, in which intellectual life fell into decline and did not revive

until after the iconoclastic controversy. During this period
many ancient literary monuments were lost. Those remain-
ing--still a considerable number--were collected by the
distinguished scholar Photius (d. 897/8), who in his bibliography, the Myrobiblion, also analyzed 280 works critically
and supplied biographical notices for the authors. After him
came the age of the great Byzantine encyclopedists. We do
not know whether the imperial library was entirely destroyed
or in what fashion it was later reconstructed, but we can assume that from this time on it continued to exist, right
through the catastrophe of the Latin Crusade, up to the sack
of Constantinople by the Turks.

Besides the imperial library there were ecclesiastical
libraries, like those of the patriarch, and, most important of
all, the collections of the monasteries. During the early
Christian period hermits as well as monks were already
busy in the East studying and copying manuscripts, and the
monasteries, following the rule of Pachomius, acquired
their own book-collections. The fashion for the Middle
Ages proper was set by that great reformer of Byzantine
monastic life, Abbot Theodore of Studium (d. 826), whose
regulations treated of the scriptorium, the library, and the
duties of the librarian. In his abbey at Studium there developed a model school of calligraphy. Even today one can
note the influence of Theodore in the monasteries of Mt.
Athos, though they retain but a small remainder of their
former manuscript treasures.

We have had to stop for a moment to examine the state
of Byzantine culture because in what follows we shall take
the opportunity in several places of referring back to it.
Our main attention, however, focuses on the West, for from
the book-collections which originated there in the early
Middle Ages a continuous line of development can be traced
right down to the libraries of the immediate present.

The papacy considered the cultivation of the Christian
tradition in the West one of its most important missions.
Hence the papal library can look back upon a history of almost two thousand years. Its origins remain veiled in ob-
scurity. We have a report dating from the beginning of the
third century concerning the solicitude of one of the popes
for the preservation of the acts of the martyrs. From the
time when the library comes clearly into view it appears
always to be closely connected with the archives. Damasus
(d. 384) housed both in the Basilica of San Lorenzo. In the
seventh century at the latest came its removal to the Lateran.

At that time the library was often used in connection with Roman synods, and the works of the Church Fathers, as well as heretical writings, were borrowed from it. In the eighth century we first encounter the important office of bibliothecarius, which was filled at the end of the next century by Anastasius, who deserved high praise for his translations of Greek authors. Up to this time Rome was still the great book-mart whence the whole West secured its manuscripts.

We can take it for granted that the other Italian bishops, at least from the time of Constantine, provided for libraries, large or small. Just as in the East, these were now joined by monastery libraries. St. Benedict, the founder of the Benedictine order, can hardly be counted the father of Western monastic libraries, but his rule does mention "library codices" (codices de bibliotheca) and enjoins the brothers "to occupy themselves with reading the sacred books" (occupari in lectione divina).(17) Nevertheless it was far from Benedict's mind to make scholars of the monks, and so his establishment at Monte Cassino hardly possessed an important manuscript collection at the beginning. Such a collection first came into being at Monte Cassino in the second half of the eighth century, when the monastery had become a widely influential center of learned studies and sheltered within its walls Paul the Deacon, to whom we shall refer later in another connection.

Chief credit for having made a home for Western culture in the monastery belongs to Cassiodorus. A Roman nobleman, he was a statesman in the service of Theodoric, the great King of the Goths; then, about the middle of the sixth century, he withdrew into the monastery of Vivarium, founded by himself, in southern Italy. There, following Eastern models, he organized a kind of Christian academy and wrote for it his Institutiones divinarum et saecularium litterarum, which have rightly been characterized as the scholarly rules of the monastery. They contain methodical guides to the study of Church writers as well as classical authors. At the same time special reference is constantly made to the library of the monastery, and the brothers are admonished to copy texts industriously. "Satan receives as many wounds," one passage reads, "as the monk copies words of the Lord." Just a short time before, Bishop Caesarius of Arles had directed the nuns of the convent founded by him "to make beautiful copies of the sacred books" (libros divinos pulchre scriptitare). But Cassiodorus was truly the first man in the West thus to aspire to a systematic collection of necessary religious and profane literary works. Even Greek texts were procured from the East and translated at Vivarium. Cassiodorus took care that the manuscripts should have a good appearance, but he laid the stress upon correctness of the texts. Such endeavors connect him with the scholars of Alexandria before him, and with Charlemagne and his learned advisers who were to come. To Cassiodorus we are indebted above all for the transmission of many literary monuments from antiquity to the Middle Ages.

At the side of Cassiodorus we must place the Spaniard, Isidore of Seville (d. 636). Probably no German tribe became so swiftly Romanized as the West Goths. The church of the Iberian Peninsula distinguished itself by a most active spiritual life up to the Arab conquest, and among the high clergy there were many ardent book-collectors. In this, however, Isidore of Seville surpassed all others. He was the greatest scholar of his time, a typical polyhistor who brought together in his Etymologiae the cumulative result of contemporary knowledge and so produced the first Christian encyclopedia. His own rich library furnished the material. We can get a tolerably clear picture of it thanks to the fact that lines have come down which once adorned the bookcases or the walls, upon which also, after the ancient fashion, portrait medallions apparently were hung. There was very probably over the door an inscription reading: "Here is much that is sacred as well as much that is wordly." (Sunt hic plura sacra, sunt mundalia plura).(18) The inscriptions on case or wall made reference to the Bible, the Fathers, Christian poets, historians of the church, and the ancient jurists. A couplet was also devoted to the scriptorium.

Things developed much less propitiously in Gaul than in Spain, although this particular Roman province experienced a resurgence of late classic rhetoric and poetry during the fourth and fifth centuries, when some impressive libraries came into being (for example, that of the prefect Tonantius Ferreolus), and it enjoyed a most lively literary intercourse, as the quick spread of the Vita S. Martini indicates. But with the beginning of Frankish rule culture in general sank back to a lower level. A long time passed before a new rise got under way, and this even required aid from abroad, which the Irish were the first to supply.

On the Emerald Isle, which had remained untouched by the storm of tribal migrations, there had emerged a monastic life of a very special kind in which ascetic piety combined with the most diligent cultivation of art and scholarship. Here in the far Northwest there was a genuine knowledge of things Greek. Here the book was especially treasured and adorned with script and miniature which testify alike to an original sense of beauty. The designation "scribe" (<u>scriba</u>) was a title of honor, with its functions often attached to the abbotship. An astonishing missionary zeal animated the Irish, and wherever their urge to "wander about in the service of Christ" (<u>peregrinari pro Christo</u>) led them, they brought along their manuscripts.

About 590 the most important of the Irish missionaries, St. Columban, set foot on the continent and founded upon Gallic soil the abbey of Luxeuil. From here a number of other monasteries were established, among them <u>Corbie</u> and <u>St. Gall</u>. In all these establishments the arts of script and book unfolded anew. In upper Italy the monastery of <u>Bobbio</u> owed its origin to the Irish missionary. He himself seems to have laid the foundation of the library there, and it soon became one of the most important in Italy. It has been shown that most probably a large part of the manuscript treasures of Vivarium was transferred to Bobbio and thus preserved for posterity. The fact that most of the palimpsests known today come from Bobbio bespeaks the eagerness of Columban's disciples to enlarge their collection by copying. We have no further direct knowledge of the early period of the library. In the statutes of the abbey in the year 835 appears the decree: "The librarian shall have charge of all books, of reading, and of the scribes." (19) The oldest catalogue of the books, dating from the tenth or eleventh century, shows a collection, astonishing for its time, of over 650 volumes.

England was converted by missionaries from Ireland and, at the same time, from Rome. Under this double influence the highly gifted Anglo-Saxons appropriated and assimilated with comparative speed the material introduced by their teachers. The very first emissaries of the Pope carried manuscripts with them. Somewhat later Anglo-Saxon pilgrims travelled to Rome and returned with further treasures. Benedict Biscop, abbot of the double monastery of Wearmouth and Jarrow, made his way over the Alps five times, and on his deathbed could commend to his brothers "the most noble and copious library which he had brought from Rome" (bibliothecam quam de Roma nobilissimam copiosissimamque advexerat). In this abode lived and labored until 735 the Venerable Bede, who surpassed all his contemporaries as scholar and teacher.(20) He based his works upon Isidore, yet differed markedly from him. Isidore, a Roman by birth, wished to transmit the culture he had inherited to his new compatriots of alien blood. The Anglo-Saxon Bede was filled with the awe of the youthful Germans for the superior old culture. The way in which he tried to assimilate it shows already a character wholly medieval.

The Anglo-Saxons shared the missionary zeal of the Irish, and they followed the trail of their teachers, which led to the continent. St. Boniface chose as the field of his missionary endeavors a still unconverted Germany and carried thence across the sea, along with the new faith, the culture developed in England, as is shown by the insular script and insular miniature decoration of the oldest manuscripts originating east of the Rhine and north of the Main. From the beginning Boniface had at his disposal a collection of books and, as his correspondence reveals, added to it by having books sent from his native country. These he had with him up to the time of his martyrdom. The favorite establishment of this apostle to the Germans, the monastery of Fulda, possessed under its very first abbot, Sturm (d. 779), a productive scriptorium.

Nothing characterized the age we are describing better than this wandering and spread of manuscripts from monastery to monastery, first from South to North, then back again in the opposite direction. Then, as the eighth century faded into the ninth, the great Emperor of the Franks brought about a collection of the materials hitherto scattered throughout the West.(21)

Charlemagne's efforts were consciously directed toward raising the general standards of religion and education by combining them with the Christian heritage of late antiquity and, above all, toward bringing the clergy to be teachers of the people and giving to all the clergy a definite amount of knowledge to carry with them through life. To this end he brought to his court helpers from neighboring lands at that time culturally more advanced. Thus there came from Italy Paul the Deacon and from England Alcuin, who brought with him across the Channel the learning of a Bede.(22) Alcuin took over direction of the palace school, which thereupon became a model for the organization of schools in all churches and monasteries. Objectives which leaders like Cassiodorus, Bede, and Boniface had pursued now became regulatory for the whole Frankish Empire. The central government saw to the setting up of scriptoria in religious establishments and required work correct in form and substance. A reform of writing issued from the court, and book decoration adjusted itself to the new ideals of beauty. There ensued a carefully planned collecting and sifting of liturgical and scholarly literature, in which sound philological criticism according to the principle that "the source offers purer water than the stream" was applied. The best texts existed mostly in Italian manuscripts; authentic copies of these were made, and care taken to distribute them. In this way the scholars of Charlemagne's time made secure a good part of our tradition.

The seed sown by this great emperor yielded its finest fruits under his grandson, Charles the Bald, who is rightly called the first princely bibliophile of the Middle Ages. The splendid codices produced at his behest are among the finest of the age. To his palace school he called the great philosopher, John Scotus, and had him translate important works from the Greek. At that time, moreover, Abbot Lupus of Ferrières, the learned philologist, was indefatigably tracking down manuscripts of classical authors and seeking such mastery of his subject as only modern scholars, strictly speaking, have again aspired to.

The points already made concerning the tendencies and results of the so-called Carolingian Renaissance enable us to conclude that it paid particular attention also to library affairs. Charlemagne bade foreign scholars bring manuscripts with them from their native countries. To Paul the Deacon we are indebted for many classics, to Alcuin--using the words of the sources--for "the flowers of Britain" (flores Britanniae). The latter built the library in his abbey of St. Martin of Tours entirely on English lines, and the collection at Tours then served as a model for other ecclesiastical institutions, for now each institution felt obliged to have a library as well as a school. The palace library, however, was the center of traffic in manuscripts. Here standard texts were deposited and made available for use to anyone interested. Charlemagne was anxious to make this collection as complete and comprehensive as possible. Hence we may take it that the lines addressed to the emperor refer to the library: "Who can even enumerate the series of books which are gathered at your direction from many lands?"(23)

Besides the palace library there was yet another separate personal library of the emperor's; his grandson, Charles the Bald, also had such a library. Indeed, even Einhard, who was a layman, provided himself with a valuable collection from which Lupus of Ferrières borrowed manuscripts on the basis of a catalogue continually at his disposal. But these eloquent beginnings in the formation of private libraries soon languished, for they, like many other creations of the Carolingian Renaissance, had too far outdistanced their time to develop favorably any further. One accomplishment of the Great Emperor did endure: from his time on, libraries were part of the necessary equipment of religious institutions, especially of monasteries, throughout the large Frankish Empire.

CHAPTER III. THE POST-CAROLINGIAN AGE: NINTH TO TWELFTH CENTURIES

The catalogue of a monastic library of the year 831 closes with the words: "Here, then, are the treasures of the monastery, here are riches feeding the soul with the sweetness of the heavenly life."(24) An equally high regard for the possession of books is shown by the regrets which a later chronicler appended to his account of the burning of a church library: "An inexpressible number of books perished, leaving us deprived of our spiritual weapons."(25) This feeling found probably its most pregnant expression in the saying formulated about 1170: "A monastery without a book-chest is like a castle without an armory."(26) Any of these citations might serve as a motto for the period of library history which extends from the ninth to the twelfth century. It was the period of undivided sway of church and monastic libraries. We shall turn our attention first to certain of these institutions so that out of individual characteristics noted here and there we may draw our general conclusions.

The foregoing chapter has already dealt with the very promising beginnings of the library of Fulda. This library did not attain its full importance till after 800, when Rabanus Maurus ruled at Fulda for four decades, first as head of the school, then of the entire abbey. He is rightly called the originator of the medieval method of teaching in Germany, for he continued Alcuin's work on East Frankish soil. Under his direction the <u>scriptorium</u> of Fulda became busy and active, to the special advantage of the library. Rabanus's own lines testify how rich and many-sided was its book collection in his time: "There you will find all that God has sent down to earth from heaven for the benefit of man in the pious words of the sacred scripture and all the worldly wisdom that has been made known to the world in various ages."(27)

What Fulda was to Mainfranken, Corvey was to Saxony. Its mother abbey, Corbie, itself a colony emanating from Luxeuil, maintained probably the most productive <u>scriptorium</u> in the West at the end of the eighth century. Working there at the beginning of the following century were Adelhard and Wala, relatives of Charlemagne and members of his circle, and also the great scholar, Paschasius Radbertus. It was, in fact, the first two who in 822 transplanted the Frankish tradition to the banks of the Weser. Under the favor of the ruling dynasty Corvey developed into the intellectual capital of Saxony. Very likely the groundwork of its library derived from the collections of Corbie. In 847 a chaplain of Louis the Pious presented it with a "large supply of books" (magna copia librorum). Reports of its later fortunes are quite scarce, but occasionally we can augment them by deduction. Thus we know that during the tenth century Widukind wrote his valuable chronicle at Corvey, and we are justified in assuming that he drew his rich source material chiefly from the library of the abbey. Two centuries later Wibald, the close friend of Conrad III, dwelt there as abbot. His correspondence reveals his eagerness to provide the library with worthy manuscripts, especially the works of Cicero, and his pride in the results achieved.

The Carolingian Age produced two important monastic libraries in East Francia--that at Weissenburg, the home of the religious epic poet, Otfried, and (particularly noteworthy) the library at Lorsch. None of the other abbeys of the time experienced so swift and brilliant a rise. Correspondingly there occurred a large-scale development of the Lorsch manuscript collection, which in number, textual worth, and general richness of execution, easily surpassed anything to be found in its sister institutions.

Of the Swabian abbeys, St. Gall must be named first, for it may well serve as the prototype of German monastic culture for the period from the reign of Charlemagne to the beginning of the eleventh century. It had a model school, whose students graced so many episcopal seats. Of the long line of distinguished scholars and writers from St. Gall we may name the composer of sequences, Notker Balbulus; the author of the epic Waltharius, Ekkehard I; the philologist, Notker Labeo; and finally Ekkehard IV, the author of the Casus S. Galli, which give us a clear picture of the golden age of the monastery. The scriptorium began its activity about the middle of the eight century. The true founder of the library was the abbot Grimald (841-872) along with his successor Hardmut. Right up to the eleventh century busy copyists and liberal benefectors such as Bishop Salomon of Constance saw to its growth. We know the names of the librarians, among them Notker Balbulus; we have reliable information on the richness of the collection from catalogues which have survived; we even possess a calendar, begun in the ninth and carried on during the following centuries, specifying the lives of the saints and the passions for each day which were to be found in the library. Scholars know much less that is exact about the Alsatian abbey of Murbach than they do about St. Gall. Nevertheless, a list dating from the middle of the ninth century reveals what books were already in its possession at that time and how diligent an effort was being made to acquire more.

A third center of religious life in Swabia was Reichenau, which carried on a very brisk exchange of manuscripts with neighboring St. Gall and repeatedly supplied Murbach with books. Since its founding the abbots had been industrious book collectors, but the golden age of the Reichenau library too arrived with the rule of Charlemagne. Reginbert, easily the most important librarian of his time, was active there until 846. He himself produced important texts of sacred and profane authors and supervised the work of industrious students; he garnered codices from near and far, from Italy and the West Frankish Kingdom; and in his catalogues he rendered careful accounts of the treasures assembled. In his day the library numbered over 400 volumes. That its contents resembled other monastic libraries mentioned above should not be regarded as an accident; for these libraries were built up on the plan of the emperor's palace library and with its support, and yet each shone forth in its own light, and together they reflected the spirit and the learning of Alcuin and his school. The scholarly impulse remained at high pitch for a long time at Reichenau; about the end of the tenth century, however, it began to wane, while the reputation of its school of painters became all the greater. Even though the other monasteries, especially Fulda, produced many beautiful examples of the fine art of bookmaking about the time of the Emperor Otto the Great, to the miniaturists of Reichenau went the commissions not only of princes and bishops but also of the imperial court, and even of the Pope at Rome.

With the opening of the eleventh century Regensburg assumed the leadership in illumination in Germany. We can observe how a general upswing among Bavarian monasteries set in after the terrific threat of Hungarian invasion was averted in the great Battle of the Lechfeld. One of the leading personages of the time was Bishop Wolfgang of Regensburg. To St. Emmeram as abbot he called Ramwold, who busied himself with reviving the abbey, "most of all by the cultivation of books" (maxime in librorum cultibus), so that the catalogue drawn up under his direction contained over 500 titles. A few decades later the great calligrapher Othlo worked at St. Emmeram. His unusual autobiography enumerates the long series of manuscripts which he produced, and the examples which have survived justify the recognition which his contemporaries tendered him.

From Regensburg Gozbert was sent to the monastery of Tegernsee to be abbot. There his work resembled that of

Ramwold at St. Emmeram. The correspondence of the learned master of his school, Froumund, gives us an insight into the many pains he took to acquire texts to be copied for Tegernsee; for the same purpose, in return, parts of his own library were loaned. In the following years the reputation of the monastery as a center for the production of manuscripts mounted. Even Emperor Frederick Barbarossa longed to possess a missal and a lectionary made there because the Tegernsee monks were reputed to be "fine scribes" (<u>boni scriptores</u>). We are best informed about the <u>scriptorium</u> of Michelsberg at Bamberg, as the librarian, Burchard (d. 1149), has left a kind of history of the collection entrusted to him. Here we learn what book-stock he found was to begin with and everything that was added by gift, purchase, and copying, and we are even told the names of the individual copyists and the division of work among them. Michelsberg apparently also produced manuscripts for export. What an intense intellectual life ruled at the abbey in this period can be appreciated from the diversity of the book stock and no less from the fact that the most important universal chronicle of the time originated there.

During the period which now concerns us distinguished libraries were not wanting in Germany in cathedrals but, on the whole, they lagged behind monastic libraries in importance. It is true that the cultural endeavors of Charlemagne's coworkers affected the one as well as the other: at this time Archbishop Lullus of Mainz and his colleagues, Hildebald of Cologne and Arno of Salzburg, did make very useful beginnings; nor were these collection at all neglected by their successors. But, as history shows, the German bishops of the tenth to the twelfth centuries, in addition to their religious duties, participated whole-heartedly in imperial politics. Hence they had little leisure for their special problems as leaders of cultural life. An outstanding exception was Bernward of Hildesheim (d. 1022), who made his residence a place for the cultivation of art and knowledge. He also assembled, in the words of his librarian and biographer Thangmar, "a large library of codices of the sacred authors as well as the philosophers" (<u>copiosam bibliothecam tam divinorum quam philosophicorum codicum</u>).

If we were to portray the development of collections in other countries with the same minute detail as the German, we should be merely piling up details without getting any clearer insight into the nature and structure of the library of the time. For, during this whole period Germany was the leading power in Europe, not only politically but culturally as well. It will be enough, therefore, to point out by a few characteristic examples how libraries everywhere, even far from the borders of Germany, were on the upgrade, especially where an intensive monastic life unfolded anew or revived.

To begin with the South, this is true of the mother abbey of Monte Cassino. After long decline it blossomed forth again during the eleventh century and under Abbot Desiderius regained its former renown. During this period the characteristic Cassino script and miniature work reached their highest consummation, and the bringing together of rich new manuscript collections generated scholarly activity that even acted as a model for work outside the monastery walls. At about this same time Abbot Jerome of Pomposa was attracting the attention of northern Italy by reforming his abbey and having a large number of codices made for its library.

From the tenth century on, the Order of Cluny had been giving aim and direction to ecclesiastical France.(28) Its founder, Odo, had already brought to Cluny with him 100 manuscripts, and one of his successors, Majolus, first as librarian and later as abbot, had had the monks ply their copying industrially. At the end of our period the library contained about 600 volumes. The other abbeys reformed under the influence of Cluny, for example Fleury-sur-Loire, also acquired considerable stores of books. The twelfth-century rules of the pious Order of St. Victor of Paris deserve closer attention, for they contain a separate section devoted to the duties of the librarian. Such an interest in books as appears herein was in keeping with the general scholarly zeal of the Victorines. Their institution is rightly considered one of the seeds from which grew the University of Paris.

The spirit and discipline of Cluny pressed on across the Channel to England. Under William the Conqueror, Lanfranc, Archbishop of Canterbury, led the reform movement. He revived the library of Christ Church and issued general orders for regular distribution of books in the monasteries of England. One of his relatives, Paul, abbot of St. Albans, organized the <u>scriptorium</u> there, made over to it permanent sources of income, attracted scribes from outside, and at the same time provided the library with valuable gifts. From then on to the end of the twelfth century, almost all the heads of the abbey concerned themselves with the <u>scriptorium</u> and the library. The manuscripts thus assembled were one of the conditions which made possible the great progress in the writing of history at St. Albans in the following century.

What most differentiates the medieval library from the ancient as well as the modern library is the meagerness of its book-stock. Catalogues of medieval libraries contain at most a few hundred entries.(29) In this connection, too, it must be observed that often several titles are combined in one codex. The whole literature available to the age--that is to say, the Christian writings and the surviving fragments of antiquity, together with the scholarly and devotional works brought out from the ninth to the twelfth century--could actually be contained in a number of volumes as small as this.

If a new monastery was founded, as a rule it received the basic part of its book stock, or at least the necessary liturgical manuscripts, from its mother abbey. Then the collection grew by means of gifts from the most varied sources, from religious and secular circles, as a result of which these benefactors were usually received into the brotherhood of prayer. Other material was brought by newly admitted monks or by youths who attended the monastery school. The bequests of dead brothers also proved to be quite fruitful. Purchases could be made only with great difficulty, for the value of manuscripts was extraordinarily high. Frequently we hear that whole plots of land--for example, vineyards--had to be paid as a price for manuscripts. Hence it became customary to make the necessary funds available by special endowments and by setting aside permanent taxes or rents.

Very lively exchange of manuscripts took place among the various religious institutions. For one thing, it made easier the exchange of duplicates; more often, however, it was a means of procuring texts which were then used as models for copying. Everywhere we have found firmly established the closest connection between library and scriptorium. Indeed it is not too much to assert that the contents and growth of the former depended essentially upon the industry and productivity of the latter. This activity involved not merely making copies and ornamenting them with miniatures; the monks had to provide and prepare all the necessary materials themselves--parchment and quill, ink and dye, boards and leather. That no one thought his position too exalted for such work reveals the whole monastic point of view. In hope of reward in heaven, the monks copied for weeks, months, years. In return, however, the merit of this activity was also stressed on every suitable occasion.(30)

We can now understand why the monks valued and guarded their manuscripts just as they did the treasures of the monastery. To their material worth and their importance as scholarly equipment was added the spiritual reason that they bore witness to work pleasing to God. The brothers were enjoined to use them with the greatest care and foresight; the manuscripts were proudly provided with marks of ownership, and attempts were made to guard against loss by inscribing so-called book-curses. These threats of temporal and mundane punishment can be traced far back into earlier centuries. During our period, executed sometimes in prose, sometimes in verse, they developed into a type of literature of their own.

A surer safeguard against theft than the book-curse, however, was afforded by careful and orderly administration of the library. This duty devolved upon the <u>armarius</u> or <u>librarius</u>, an important official in the abbey, who often had still other functions to discharge. In many places, for example, he held the office of <u>precentor</u> or <u>custos</u> at the same time. Quite naturally, he always had direction--or at least participated in the direction--of the <u>scriptorium</u>. The extent of his library duties proper depended upon the size of the library in his trust.

In the earliest times, and also later, manuscripts were kept together with the treasures in a safe place, for example the sacristy or one of the chapels. Sometimes they were kept with the deeds and documents of the archives. If the book stock was small, one or more chests or cupboards sufficed, of which some stood apart and others were sunk into the wall, just as we noticed in ancient times. If the number of books increased, however, they required special quarters. These have not been preserved from the Carolingian Age, but we do have the so-called architectural plan of St. Gall, a model plan for the layout of a large monastery of the time. In this plan "the library is a building which quite bespeaks the sacristy in location and size and stands against the eastern side of the presbytery. It consists of two stories. The lower is furnished as a <u>scriptorium</u>...the upper...is used for the storage of books." We know that at a later date manuscripts were stored by the Cistercians in rooms set apart near the refectory. Of Tegernsee it is reported that in the new church being erected there "the library is located above the basilica itself" (<u>super eandem basilicam armaria locatur</u>). Quite often the liturgical codices appointed for public worship were set apart from the other books; often also the books were divided into an inner collection, which was intended for the members of the monastery, and an outer collection belonging to the school; and finally a distinction was made between reference books and books for circulation.

The statutes of some orders contained strict regulations concerning the procedure for lending books. On an appointed day of the year the brothers assembled in the chapter house. There those who had borrowed books the last time were called by name and required to return them. Then the business of lending books for the next year proceeded. All this was under the direction of the librarius, who also had to keep lists of the books lent. We have been concerned here only with the lending of books to members of the monastery, but lending was not confined to these alone, as we have several times indicated above. For books lent outside, however, a receipt and a deposit were required. Reginbert of Reichenau was already admonishing the brothers that "no work was to be given to anyone to take outside unless he had first given a pledge or at least left security that he would return safe to this house what he had received."(31) Since, however, even precautions of this kind could not always prevent abuse and loss, it came to pass toward the end of our period that the rules of the monastery entirely forbade lending books outside the institution.

One of the duties of the librarius was to classify and take inventory of the books. Catalogues of the great Carolingian monastic libraries, which, as we have seen, contained very similar manuscript holdings, also show a fairly uniform subject-grouping. At the beginning stand the sacred writings; the Church Fathers, up to the "modern masters" (magistri moderni) come next, arranged by author; then comes the remainder of the sacred literature and the profane literature, including ancient pagan writers, also divided into definite subject-groups.(32) On the basis of evidence afforded by the late Middle Ages, we can assume that the arrangement of the books followed the same system and that, therefore, the Carolingian inventories can already be spoken of as shelf-lists. On the other hand, there is no trace at this time of the later custom of placing manuscripts on desks instead of keeping them in chests and then guarding against their being removed at will by the use of chains. The earliest scattered references to "chained books" (libri catenati) belong to the following centuries.

The internal arrangement of the monastic library from the tenth to the twelfth century we can sum up briefly. Surviving catalogues differ widely in quality, and often leave much to be desired in completeness and exactitude. Not infrequently the arrangement is determined simply by order of accession, or no particular order is aimed at. Whether it became customary at this time or even earlier to provide each volume with a location mark is for further research to determine. In general, one gets the impression that the post-Carolingian development of the medieval library showed no further essential progress. Such progress ensued again only when Scholasticism made its influence felt upon library matters.

CHAPTER IV. THE LATE MIDDLE AGES

We have seen how, in monasteries and other religious institutions, manuscript treasures were collected and united into libraries; how industrious monks steadily enlarged these spiritual riches, produced text after text by careful copying, and adorned them with beautiful miniatures; and how they thus saw to it that this tradition never lapsed, but rather that the heritage of ancient times was handed down to posterity. During this whole period ecclesiastical institutions were indeed the only places where the conditions favorable to intellectual pursuits could be found. The Church acquired a kind of monopoly upon education; knowledge became entirely clericalized; the Latin of the scholars held the field alone as the literary language. We can hardly even say that laymen took any independent part of their own in the great cultural activities of the day.

It was not until the later Middle Ages that a definite change came about. The laity freed themselves from the intellectual tutelage of the Church, and first to do this were naturally the nobility. They developed a characteristically aristocratic mode of life, created for themselves courtly poesy and genteel light reading. Then came the rise of the middle class in the cities. As trade and manufacture boomed, as knowledge of reading and writing became more and more widespread, there awoke in the middle class a desire for culture and instruction. This need was satisfied by a semi-scientific and popular literature which made use of the vernacular and swelled into an ever mightier stream.

The new monastic orders, Franciscans and Dominicans, settled in the cities. No longer did they lead a contemplative existence removed from the world, but instead stepped into the thick of life, made their influence felt by sermon and teaching, and gave new direction to knowledge. It was through their cooperation, in fact, that the great universities arose toward the end of the Middle Ages--foremost among them Bologna, the home of legal studies, and Paris, the stronghold of Scholastic theology and philosophy. These set a pattern for the other studia generalia in Italy, France, England, and Germany.(33) These brief remarks concerning the new orientation of Western culture should suffice to justify the division of the subject-matter of this chapter. It will attempt to answer the following questions: First, what was the later fate of the monastic library? Second, what kind of libraries do we find among the aristocracy and later among the middle class? Finally, how did the universities meet their needs in the way of books?

In many an old Benedictine abbey the religious and scholarly spirit weakened with time and with it vanished also the urge to copy and collect. Indeed, in many places we can observe a complete disintegration of monasteries and their accommodations. The library fell into neglect; the manuscripts were pledged and sold for a trifle. There was hence full justification for the loud laments we already find in Dante in the thirteenth century, for those to which Richard de Bury was giving utterance in his Philobiblon during the following century, and, finally, for those which are contained in the descriptions of the Humanists of the fifteenth century--even though the latter are exaggerated. Nevertheless we must not make these indictments too general. Let us but call to mind the great manuscript possessions acquired by religious foundations and monasteries toward the end of the Middle Ages and the magnificent choir-books which the fourteenth and fifteenth centuries have handed down to us. In this very period we have reports of the reorganizing and building of libraries, and we know also of a number of able and zealous librarians, such as Heinrich von Ligerz of Einsiedeln, treatment of whose work has recently been found worthy of a monograph.(34) As far as Germany in particular is concerned, the Council of Constance instigated a reform of Benedictine monasteries. Wherever this took effect, it led to a revival of scholarly enthusiasm. In the South, Melk operated as a model for Austria, Bavaria, and Swabia; in central and northern Germany it was the Congregation of Bursfeld,(35) founded in 1433. In the case of all these reformed monasteries we have some testimony about well-kept and well-supported libraries, and to some extent there is a justifiable presumption of their existence.

The other monastic orders must also be considered. We hear, for example, of cultivation of libraries among the Carthusians and the Augustinian Friars. The Franciscans quickly got over the dislike of the founder of their order for books and study. The scholarly activity of the English Minorites developed with particularly fruitful results. They possessed rich collections in London and Oxford. From the fifteenth century there has been preserved the Registrum librorum Angliae, a sort of union catalogue of 85 authors compiled on the basis of a general inquiry which the

Franciscan organization carried out in 160 church libraries.(36) Even more universal was the ardor of the Dominicans, who, as is well known, set up a system of scholarly instruction. If they assembled their libraries from a practical viewpoint and placed less value upon the external appearance than upon the contents of the manuscripts, this merely expressed their fundamental principle that utility should precede curiosity. The fifth master general of the order, Humbert de Romanis (1254-63) already devoted a whole section of his Instructio officialium to the librarius. This official must take care that there be appropriate space, a readily comprehensible classification, catalogues and shelf-marks and a loan-book, and he must see to yearly inventory, and finally to building up the book stock. From the fourteenth century have come down the provisions of several general chapters regarding monastic libraries; from the following century we have the library rules of various Dominican convents.

A word about Arab-Spanish library affairs must precede treatment of our second question, for western Christian libraries appear to have been influenced somewhat by them. The historical mission which Islam fulfilled in transmitting the corpus of Greek and Eastern literature to Europe is often spoken of. A goodly part of this scholarly achievement consisted, of course, in gathering and assimilating the knowledge accumulated by conquered peoples. For this reason books and writing assumed special importance there, and libraries were fitted out in the most lavish manner. Unfortunately they have not as yet been carefully studied, so that we must content ourselves with a few suggestions which carry no certainty.

The great rise of literary and scientific activity in the Islamic world set in toward the end of the eighth century. It was promoted by the manufacture of paper, introduced at that time from the Far East, which provided a cheap material for the production of books. The libraries of the Eastern Roman Empire seem to have been used as models in building. Thus we hear that Harun-al-Raschid founded a library in Bagdad and received manuscripts from Byzantium and elsewhere as tribute.(37) His son Mamun (d. 833) was an even more ardent collector. He is credited with having instigated the scholarly enterprise of translating the masterpieces of Greek and Oriental literature into Arabic. In addition to Bagdad, there were libraries at Kufa and Basra; in fact, before long all the larger mosques, as well as the universities established throughout the caliphate, acquired their own book collections. Of Persia there are similar reports. A traveler at the end of the tenth century tells of having come across a large collection in the palace of a Buyid prince at Shiraz; another traveler at the beginning of the thirteenth century, as many as twelve libraries founded in Merv.

The libraries of the Near East had competition in North Africa (e.g. Cairo and Alexandria) and above all in Spain. In the great period of Moorish culture there seem to have been about 70 public libraries on the Iberian peninsula. Caliph Hakam II (d. 976) is famous for having founded the grandest institution. He united the libraries of his father and brother with his own and had them set up in his palace at Cordova. He gathered about him scholars, copyists, and miniaturists, and sent agents to the Orient in order to get as complete as possible a collection of its literature. Even if descriptions of the number of volumes, the size of the catalogues, and the whole library structure are colored by Oriental fantasy, nevertheless they presuppose a clear idea of such an institution--and that in a time when the Christian West knew only monastic libraries. Toledo afterwards became distinguished for its abundance of libraries, just as it also became the center for the translation of Arabic literature into western languages. Later on Granada also achieved eminence. Along with public libraries there seems to have been a large number of splendid private collections. Bibliophily was fashionable among the aristocracy, and even the less well-to-do were moved by a love of books.

As is well known, the Hohenstaufen Emperor Frederick II had close relations with the Islamic world and eagerly promoted the translation of Arabic literature. Presumably he was stimulated by this to the planning of his own library. At any rate, he was one of the first western rulers to possess a large library, of which he boasted in his letter to the University of Bologna. As for the other great thirteenth-century ruler in whose reign medieval culture in France reached its highest development, his biographer says of Louis IX: "He heard it said of a certain sultan of the Saracens that he had diligent search made for all kinds of books which might be necessary to Saracen philosophers, and had these copied at his own expense and kept them in his library so that scholars could have a supply of these books whenever they needed them."(38) In accordance with this ideal the king had placed in the Sainte Chapelle a collection of the

Church Fathers which he himself diligently studied and willingly permitted others to use. We may call Louis the founder of the Bibliotheque du Roi, but a large share of the credit must go to the great scholar, Vincent of Beauvais. The king also ordered handsome Bibles and psalters. In growing number the artists engaged in producing them belonged to the lay classes. From then on there developed in Paris the craft of illuminators (<u>enlumineurs</u>), which was organized as a guild and which made the capital of France the European center of this splendid book-industry.

In his will Louis IX made over the library to four religious establishments. His successors showed little inclination to book-collecting, but a change came about with the art-loving House of Valois of the fourteenth century. Charles V inherited quite a few books from his father; others he acquired by purchase; but by far the largest number were commissioned. In this way over 900 manuscripts were assembled which Christine de Pisan might well describe as "the noble library...of all the most noteworthy volumes which have been compiled by sovereign authors... of all the sciences, most beautifully written and richly adorned."(39) Charles, too, was proud of his collection and inscribed marks of ownership in many volumes with his own hand. They satisfied his taste for luxury as well as his live desire for knowledge, for he had a large number of translations made into French--among others some of the works of Aristotle and Augustine. In 1367/8 the main part of his book treasures was moved to one of the towers of the Louvre and distributed in three rooms; the rest remained in various castles. Mallet, the <u>valet de chambre</u> so highly esteemed by Louis, undertook the direction of the library and drew up an inventory with valuable details. The king willingly lent books to others and was happy to give some as gifts. Nevertheless, the main body of the collection remained intact and even grew considerably under Charles's successors. The English occupation of the fifteenth century brought about its downfall.(40)

During the reign of Charles V, love of luxurious books spread among the French nobility; in particular the members of the royal house embraced the habit. The most brilliant patron of the <u>enlumineurs</u> was Charles's brother, Duke John of Berry. He expended tremendous sums and engaged the foremost artists, so that his splendid Gothic codices and charming books of hours are among the most beautiful produced by contemporary miniaturists. The dukes of Burgundy maintained the Valois tradition till almost the end of the fifteenth century. The third duke, Philip the Good, desired to possess "the richest and noblest library in the world" (la plus riche et noble librairie du monde), and kept continually at work a whole group of literati, translators, calligraphers, and illuminators, among them the astonishingly productive and versatile Aubert. The Burgundian library maintained a steadfast character during the entire period. Renaissance influences from Italy were slow to make themselves felt, as, for example, under Charles the Bold, who longed to vie in repute with ancient heroes.

In the fourteenth century there was in France another splendid princely library, that of the Pope at Avignon. Recent studies have made clear the cultural significance of the papal court's being situated there at the time, and have pointed out the strong concentration of scholars and writers, artists and craftsmen from all neighboring lands. We have spoken before of the beginnings of the papal library at Rome. Its later career is largely shrouded in darkness. Only the inventory which Boniface VIII had compiled in 1295 has survived, and this lists about 500 volumes, among them over 30 Greek codices. On the removal of the papacy to Avignon, however, the library remained behind in Italy and there met destruction. The founder of the new collection was Pope John XXII (1316-34), who purchased an unusually large number of items, while his two successors had more manuscripts made. A very productive source of growth was the right of escheat, in accordance with which the estate of every divine who died at the curia fell to the papal exchequer. In this way the number of volumes grew in time to 1500. They were divided into the library proper, the private library of the Pope, and the repository, which was set aside to provide for religious institutions. In many respects, for example in brilliant decoration of manuscripts, the papal collection resembled that of Charles V. But in Avignon there was less light reading and fewer translations. Because of its great wealth of scholarly, theological, and philosophical works we might compare it with the library of the Sorbonne, which will concern us further below. Still, it differed from the latter in that it contained much literature on law and church government to meet the needs of the papal court.

In those days Prague was under the influence of Paris and Avignon. King Charles IV of the house of Luxemburg, assisted by his remarkable chancellor, Johann von Neumarkt, successfully strove to make his court a rallying point of science and art. Until nearly the end of the fourteenth century the school of Prague held the leadership in manuscript illumination in central Europe. Many other German princes too, such as Ludwig III, the Elector Palatine, as well as members of the nobility, embraced the grand cult of books. In general, however, they do not bear comparison with their French compeers. To make up for this, Germany surpassed her western neighbors in developing book-collections in towns.

During the fourteenth and fifteenth centuries the prestige and influence of the German city grew steadily, so that it impressed its spirit upon the whole epoch. A new literature was written for the middle class and eagerly collected. About 1300 the poet Hugo von Trimberg, author of <u>Der Renner</u>, was already boasting of his 200 books. Toward the end of the period, we find in almost every middle-sized city libraries of varying size owned by the clergy, the aldermen, the physician, the school-master, and also by some of the patricians and their wives. At the newly established municipal schools probably only individual teachers possessed the necessary books. On the other hand, there were in many places aldermanic libraries, intended for the use of the town clerk and attorneys or of the town physician. Many of these collections originated through private initiative. Before long there even came to be institutions of a public character, although they are not comparable to those which the next chapter will point out as creations of the Italian Renaissance. Thus Canon Johann von Kirchdorff in 1399 bequeathed his home and its books to the inhabitants of Alzey; and likewise the pastor of Ulm, Neithart (d. 1439), left to the public his library, which was then, under the supervision of his family, placed in a separate room near the minster and thrown open to use.

The demands of a public avid for reading matter were filled by paid copyists. At first these were still clerics; later laymen predominated. In the fifteenth century the book-trade also spread through Germany. Books were sold from stalls near the principal church, or buyers frequented the great book-fairs, especially the one at Frankfurt.(41) In southern Germany the town of Hagenau, where Diebolt Lauber started a flourishing venture in the production of manuscripts, became especially important. In the Netherlands and North Germany the Brothers of the Common Life supplied the market with books. From the very first their founder, Gerhard Groot, focused their interest upon books. The "Broeders van de penne," as they were called, began by taking care of the needs of their own libraries, then more and more they produced books predominantly for sale in order to defray the expenses of their houses. They turned out both large and costly choir-books and also popular devotional tracts, many in the German language. In charge of the writing-room was the *scripturarius*, whose directions the *rubricator* and the *ligator* had to follow; then there was the *librarius*, whose duty it was to supervise the library. For all these the statutes contained exact instructions.

The *stationarii* occupied themselves with the manufacture and sale of scholarly literature. They were to be found in most universities--largest in number, as is easy to understand, at Paris, so that Richard de Bury was able to describe the book-mart there as a "flourishing garden of the world's books" (*virens viridarium universorum voluminum*). The Paris book-trade was under strict control of the university authorities. On the other hand--and here we come to our third question--these authorities did not bother to set up a university library, a situation partly connected with the fact that the University of Paris, like the other earliest universities, did not originate in an act establishing it, but rather grew quite slowly by the consolidation of various educational institutions.(42) The task of supplying necessary books to teachers and students was left instead to the individual colleges or student halls, those institutions of a semi-religious character which in most universities were formed on the plan of the Franciscan and Dominican religious houses.

About 1250 Robert de Sorbonne, Louis IX's chaplain, founded the college named after him, which has now become so famous. He bequeathed to it his own library, and gifts poured in thereafter so quickly and in such volume that the library of the Sorbonne soon far outdistanced the other libraries of the University of Paris. The bequests of individual scholars numbered usually about 100 volumes, once even 300, and among the benefactors were Germans, Englishmen, Italians, and Spaniards. Many authors made a practice of depositing their original manuscripts at the Sorbonne. There was also money available from legacies and the sale of duplicates with which to buy or commission manuscripts. In 1290 the library numbered over 1000 volumes, in 1338 over 1700. Theology and philosophy formed the chief contingent. The Fellows of the college were provided with keys, the remaining members of the university being allowed to enter under certain conditions, while strangers needed an introduction. There were two divisions--the great (magna) and the small (parva). In the former, codices frequently used lay chained upon 26 desks. The contents of the latter division, duplicates and material seldom used, might be loaned, and often indeed for quite a long time. A pledge was required, however, usually consisting of another book. There were several administrative posts manned by Fellows of the university. In addition to the Sorbonne there came into being in Paris up to the end of the Middle Ages about 50 more colleges. Each had its book collection, large or small.

The organization of all these libraries did not differ essentially from that of church and monastic libraries, even though the student halls, as we have already seen, were patterned on the whole after the establishments of the mendicant orders. Compared with the typical library of the preceding period, however, the tendency to practical scholarship was more pronounced. Thus the Scholastic studies which were pursued at the university and in which the Dominicans took an outstanding role, led to a better organization of the book-collection. This organization was governed by the system of scholarly instruction (liberal arts and faculties) as it had developed from ancient times through Cassiodorus and Isidore down to Alcuin and Rabanus Maurus. Even before the thirteenth century it revealed itself occasionally in the classification of books, but for the first time now it was laid down as a principle. Librarians, however, did not consider themselves inescapably tied down to the given scheme, but varied it in many ways and added new divisions whenever the accumulation of manuscripts forced them to it. The different classes were, as a rule, placed coordinately next to one another, but not yet reduced to a system of main and sub-classes, something which first came about in the seventeenth century.

It is hard to make a general statement concerning the method of keeping manuscripts, especially as differences in individual countries and orders must be reckoned with, for literary references are not clearly understandable, and though many church and college libraries have survived, their arrangement has frequently been altered. I believe this is all that may be said: along with the older practice of depositing the volumes in chests, in the later Middle Ages the new method of keeping them, namely the lectern system, seems to have entrenched itself more and more. The library, then, contained a row of desks, each having several shelves on which rested the books, chained to iron bars.(43) Desks, shelves, and codices were marked with letters or numbers, and besides this the faculties were sometimes distinguished by color. The inventory took the form of a shelf-list; to this alphabetical indexes were sometimes added. At its fullest the description of an individual volume contained the titles of the works found therein, the incipit and explicit, press-mark, provenance and price, and sometimes, in addition, details of the kind of script and general make-up.

At the Italian universities, as for example in Bologna, there were of course libraries, but apparently they had no greater significance, perhaps because there the stationarii had instituted a comprehensive lending system. It was different in Germany. At Prague the oldest university, the Collegium Carolinum, was founded by Charles IV in 1366 and was quickly well supplied with books. The College of the Bohemian Nation, created soon thereafter, immediately provided for a library. Similar libraries of student halls are to be found also at the other contemporary universities. Of their number the institution founded by the scholarly and industrious collector, Amplonius of Erfurt (d. 1434/5), deserves special mention, for even today the Amplonian manuscripts constitute the chief treasures of the library there. If, then, matters at first developed about as they had in France, the Germans, on the other hand, early took a further step and set up faculty libraries, especially that of the Faculty of Arts. This was first done at Heidelberg, and in fact soon after the year in which the university was founded (1386). At about the same time a common library was created there for all the faculties.

Thomas Cobham, Bishop of Worcester, paved the way for a general university library at Oxford as early as 1327, but as a consequence of various difficulties, it did not begin to function properly until 1412. We have reports of the general university library (communis libraria universitatis) at Cambridge from the beginning of the fifteenth century. On the other hand, there were libraries of religious orders and college libraries at both universities considerably earlier. Richard de Bury (d. 1345) planned the most ambitious enterprise for Oxford, though it went unrealized in his time. He had been the tutor of Edward III; later he rose to the rank of Bishop of Durham and Chancellor of England,

and made several trips to the continent on important diplomatic missions. De Bury is considered not one of the outstanding scholars, but one of the most passionate bibliophiles of his day. Like the French princes, he gathered about him miniaturists, copyists, revisers, and bookbinders; he dealt with sellers of manuscripts in France, Germany, and Italy, and poured out gold with a lavish hand as often as he visited the Paris book-market. In answer to numerous attacks upon his love of books, shortly before his death he composed the <u>Philobiblon,</u> which is still read with pleasure today. In it he intones a rapturous hymn of praise to the book, exalts it as the source of eternal truth, the light of the faithful soul, the weapon bestowed by God to combat all heresy. The peculiar charm of the apology consists in the fact that it contains a sound library theory--though clothed in medieval garb--and above all in its lively and original portrayal of the personality of its author and of his collector's ardor.

CHAPTER V. THE RENAISSANCE

The preceding chapter closed with Richard de Bury; at the head of this one we must put Petrarch. Although he was only slightly younger than the Englishman, and even came to know de Bury personally, he belonged to quite a different culture. While de Bury remained firmly rooted in Scholasticism, Petrarch became the founder of Italian Humanism.

Petrarch turned his back intentionally on the Middle Ages and fixed his attention on classical antiquity, which he perceived not as dead past but as living present. Consequently Cicero was the determining influence on his literary production as well as on his mode of life. He was possessed by a passionate fondness for classical authors. In order to acquire their writings he used all the means at his disposal, including wide travels and his many personal connections. Texts which could not be obtained by purchase or gift he copied himself or had copied for him. The material thus assembled was eagerly studied and provided with marginal notes. A whole dialogue in Petrarch's <u>De remediis utriusque fortunae</u>(44) rails against the mere accumulation of unread books. He placed great value upon beauty in the make-up of the manuscript, but purity of text seemed to him even more important. The library was guarded by his servants like a shrine, and he himself kept up an active acquaintance with his books, just as if they were friends capable of talking. "Books," he once wrote, "heartily delight us, speak to us, counsel us, and are joined to us, as it were, by a living and active relationship."(45) One morning he was found dead in his study, head sunk upon an open codex.

Petrarch, as has been indicated, created a new ideal for private libraries which remained a model down to the time of Machiavelli and indeed has not yet lost its influence;(46) at the same time, stimulated by a knowledge of ancient libraries, he also conceived the plan of founding a large public institution. In 1362 he bestowed his own book collection upon the Basilica of Saint Mark in Venice "for the comfort of the intelligent and noble people who may happen to take delight in such things,"(47) and in so doing expressed the wish that the Venetian government might provide for its care and growth in such a way that it would become the equal of ancient libraries. Of course this plan was not carried out, but it did point the way for posterity.

Boccaccio looked up to Petrarch as to his teacher and master. Under Petrarch's influence he became a tireless and successful hunter of manuscripts. With the exaggeration typical also of the later Humanists, he tells us that on a visit to Monte Cassino he found the venerable library there in a state of unbelievable neglect. Similar enthusiasm was developed by the Chancellor of Florence, Salutati, a man younger by about twenty years. He was already searching-- as many other scholars did in the following century--for a Livy manuscript supposed to be hidden somewhere in the far North. In this period bibliophily was already assuming occasional grotesque forms which subjected it to public scorn. In general, however, we must point out that during the whole fourteenth century these new ideas and aspirations affected only a few leading figures; it was not until the fifteenth century that they were appropriated by wider circles. What had formerly passed for a program now became fact.

The most important center of the great scholarly achievements which we owe to the fifteenth century was the Florence of Cosimo de Medici. We cannot say that he brought into being a court of the Muses on the banks of the Arno, but we can point to him as its patron in the noblest sense of the word. His literary minister was Niccoli, known for his treatise on orthography and his efforts in behalf of the new Renaissance script, and famous above all for his thoroughly systematic manuscript collecting. He raised the number of volumes in his own library to 800; and as often as his money gave out, Cosimo was obliged to come to the rescue. A modern historian aptly calls Niccoli "the 'trade list'(48) for all announcements concerning libraries and books." He sent his agents everywhere seeking out classic authors, and in this enterprise he exploited heavily the foreign trading system of the Medici. One of his instructions giving directions for thoroughly searching German monasteries has survived.

No one carried out Niccoli's commissions with greater zeal than Poggio. From the Council of Constance, to which he went as papal secretary, he visited German and French monasteries, especially St. Gall and Cluny. In the customary manner he uttered bitter complaints about the state of the libraries in these places and declared it his duty to free the treasures of antiquity from their bonds. When he could do nothing else, he copied texts, but he preferred to "save" them by thrusting them under his robe. Anyone who wishes to get a good, although historically not altogether accurate, picture of his activities should read C.F.Meyer's fine story "Plautus im Nonnenkloster."(49) It must be emphasized at this point that Poggio and his colleagues brought together the principal part of the Latin classics upon which later generations subsisted.

Just as important was the second act of the Humanistic enterprise--procuring the monuments of Greek literature at the collapse of the Byzantine Empire. At first refugees from the East brought manuscripts with them; then the Italians themselves, impelled by thirst for knowledge and love of adventure, hurried there to fetch them back. Just like Poggio in the North, Aurispa was at work here in the first decades of the fifteenth century, and he reports of himself: "I remember having given up my clothes to the Greeks in Constantinople in order to get codices--something for which I feel neither shame nor regret."(50) Many Venetian nobles, e.g. the Giustiniani, took a lively interest in these discoveries, as the city of canals, primarily because of its relations with the Orient, was the natural starting-point for such expeditions and quickly developed into a center for trade in Greek manuscripts.

During the entire fifteenth century this enthusiasm for collecting did not abate: it lasted until the time of Lorenzo de Medici and Poliziano. Toward the end of the century the rediscovery of the old codices at Bobbio caused a particular sensation, and, as one Italian has said, with this event "the heroic age of discovery came to an end," (si chiude l'età eroica delle scoperte).(51). The full value of these accumulated treasures was intensively explored, and during the entire fifteenth century there quickly ripened a powerful impetus to philological and historical research in which a whole flock of Humanists took part, among them leading thinkers like Bruni, Valla, and Biondo.

At this time, too, Petrarch's cherished project of founding a large public library, which after his death Salutati had again brought forward, became a reality. Niccoli designated 1430 manuscripts which he left behind to the public "for the common use of all," (in publico a commune utilità di ognuno), and Cosimo provided for them a worthy dwelling in the Monastery of Saint Mark, which he himself had had erected. He also gave liberally to other religious institutions, but did not as a consequence forget his own private library. Out of such beginnings developed the later Laurentian Library, (Biblioteca Mediceo-Laurenziana) which was fostered and enriched most of all by his grandson, Lorenzo. This scion of the Medici was aided first by the already-mentioned Poliziano and later by the Greek Lascaris, who undertook two separate journeys to the Orient in his employ.

Next to Venice, Florence was the great market for buying classic authors. In the Via degli Librai were housed the manuscript dealers with their employees. The most famous of these dealers was Vespasiano da Bisticci, whose shop served as a rendezvous for the literary world. He had broad bibliographical knowledge and assembled entire libraries from near and far for his noble customers. By using 45 scribes he once delivered on order to Cosimo 200 volumes in 22 months. Prices were not low, especially when classic works were dealt in. For this reason Bisticci exerted himself to get texts as correct as possible and took care that in matters of writing-material, script, miniature-decoration and binding all the demands of Renaissance taste should be satisfied.

One of his best customers was the great bibliophile, Frederick of Montefeltro, Duke of Urbino. He appears to have spent as much as 30,000 ducats upon his collection and to have kept steadily occupied 30 to 40 copyists. Place was provided for the luxurious and splendidly ornamented manuscripts in rooms specially set aside for this purpose in his newly erected castle. Frederick endeavored to achieve in his library the highest possible completeness, embracing all branches of knowledge, and he had catalogues brought from foreign libraries, even that of Oxford, in order to determine possible gaps. That the library was intended for study is shown not only by the plan of the hall, which took into consideration the most favorable lighting conditions, but also by written directions for the librarian which have come down to us. Of him it is required that he be "learned, of good appearance, good natured, proficient in both literary and common language,"(52) that he keep good order, prepare catalogues, protect his books from every injury yet make them easily and conveniently accessible to those interested, and finally, that he keep a careful record of all borrowing.

To Bisticci at Florence also came orders from foreign lands, for example, from Matthias Corvinus, King of Hungary. Married to a Neapolitan princess, Corvinus strengthened the ties already in existence between his country and Italy. He drew to his court Italian scholars and men of letters, artists and craftsmen, in order, as contemporaries said in praising him after his death, "to make Hungary another Italy"

(Pannoniam alteram Italiam reddere). For this reason his large library furnished surpassing proof of the productivity of contemporary Italy in things scholarly as well as artistic. After Corvinus's death in 1490 the collection at Buda was scattered to the four winds, so that today they are found among the treasures of very many European libraries.(53)

Just as at Florence and Urbino, distinguished libraries came into being in the fifteenth century at the courts of many Italian nobles: Naples, Pavia, Ferrara, and Venice being examples. The Aragon rulers of Naples were among the most exalted patrons of the new culture and hence took a decidedly personal interest in their books. It was different with the Visconti and the Sforza, who, to be sure, busily added to the library at Pavia, partly from the spoils of war, but considered it in the main as an ornament of their court. The Ferrara library displayed quite an individual character. The Este family ruling there still devoted themselves to the courtly manners of chivalry along with Renaissance culture. This was shown in the composition of their library, which even had a group of French manuscripts. Finally, so far as the Library of St. Mark (Biblioteca Marciana) in Venice is concerned, it was the creation of the Greek Bessarion, who rose to the rank of cardinal and became a focus of Renaissance civilization. In 1468 he bequeathed his important collection, consisting principally of Greek manuscripts, to the city of canals as "the natural link between Orient and Occident." The Library of St. Mark was made available at once in liberal manner to the public, but it was not until the fifth decade of the following century that it acquired a worthy home in the splendid edifice designed by Sansovino.

There still remains to be considered the largest and most important library of the fifteenth century--the Vatican. What had formerly been assembled as a result of the collectors' enthusiasm of the Avignon popes, was lost during the great schism. Returned to Rome, the pontiffs had to begin again right from the start. About 1432 a Humanist reported after a visit to the Vatican Library: "I found nothing whatsoever worth remembering" (nihil omnino memoria dignum inveni). Thus Nicholas V (1447-1455) really founded the papal collection anew. As a humble priest he already experienced "a certain inexplicable thirst for books" (certe inesplicabile sete di libri), and he especially searched for Greek manuscripts, often plunging himself thereby deep into debt. Like his friend Bisticci, he developed into an outstanding expert on matters pertaining to books and libraries. Because of this, Cosimo entrusted him with drawing up a canon which should contain the works necessary to a library worthy of respect, and which also, tradition has it, served as a model in the establishment of the library of Urbino and many another.(54)

In the person of Nicholas, therefore, the greatest bibliophile among the popes ascended the throne at Rome. He took over from his predecessors about 350 manuscripts; to this was added his own private library. After the jubilee year of 1450 had brought in very large sums of money, he sent agents everywhere, even to Scandinavia and the distant Orient, to track down classical authors. Assisted by his librarian, Tortelli, he planned a complete translation of Greek literature into Latin, and to this end gathered about him a whole swarm of scholars and copyists. Rome was once again to become the center of the scholarly and literary world. Part of the grand building program which aimed at the reorganization on a monumental scale of the Leonine quarter was a library "large and ample for the general convenience of learned men" (ingens et ampla pro communi doctorum virorum commodo). In this way, Nicholas hoped, his name would be honored with those of Ptolemy and Trajan. Early death brought many of his projects to an untimely end. Despite this, about 800 Latin and over 400 Greek manuscripts had been brought together. With these the Vatican was already moving into first place among the libraries of Italy.

Sixtus IV (1471-1484) continued the work of Nicholas and in some measure finished it, not so much by setting to work personally as by making available the necessary money and by selecting an excellent librarian, the Humanist Platina. The number of volumes mounted to over 3500, and now rooms worthy of them were provided, with decorations by the ranking artists of the time. The quarters were divided into a public library, which in turn was divided into Latin and Greek sections, and a reserve library set aside for the protection of rarities. Platina took care of everything-- arrangement, classification, cataloguing. The library was open to the public and there were no difficulties about lending books, as journals which have survived testify. Ariosto could say with justice: "Sixtus had ancient books gathered from all over the world for public use."(55)

The principle that libraries should be open to the public may well serve as one characteristic differentiating the Renaissance library from the library of the Middle Ages.

Were there, however, other fundamental differences between the two? The answer is in part affirmative, in part negative: what had disappeared was the specifically medieval atmosphere. The Humanists and literary men who banded together into academies at the courts of various noblemen in the manner of the ancient world looked upon the library in the old sense of a place for exchange of scholarly ideas and for esthetic enjoyment. Still dominant among them was a burning desire for the uncorrupted sources of Greek and Roman literature--a desire which Petrarch had aroused in former times, only now the enthusiasm of the fourteenth century had given way to a quieter and clearer objectivity. Because of this desire, however, medieval authors were not barred from library shelves.

In the library of Nicholas V, classical and Humanistic, Scholastic and patristic works stood peacefully side by side. This was true not only of the Vatican Library, which was primarily the collection of the Pope, but likewise of other large institutions. Indeed this universal character of the Middle Ages even found expression in paintings which decorated the walls of these buildings. Like the artists of the late Middle Ages, Melozzo da Forli chose allegories representing the liberal arts and the faculties of instruction in the universities as subjects for his frescoes in the halls of Urbino. Raphael himself adorned the private library of Julius II, the renowned Stanza della Segnatura, with such a "pictorial representation of a book catalogue."(56)

As for the individual volumes in the Renaissance library, they show a good deal of variation from medieval manuscripts. It has already been pointed out above how a Bisticci took contemporary taste into account in the whole make-up of the book. Shelving and classification, on the other hand, had remained the same. There was no pressing reason for a change in the system. Although the number of books had increased through the influx of classic and Humanist authors, this by no means made it impossible to handle them in the same old way. The products of the printing presses were, on the whole, rigidly excluded by bibliophiles such as Montefeltro. Only with the end of the century did they begin gradually to penetrate. This is what the sources say concerning the desks in the Library of Saint Mark in Florence; this is what we find in a painting of the Vatican Library; and printed books as well as chained codices have been preserved unharmed in the beautiful early Renaissance room at Cesena (Pl. III) which Malatesta Novello had erected in 1452. Even the Laurentian Library (Pl. V), built from the plans of Michelangelo, stuck to the old usage.

The library at Zutphen, which, like that at Cesena, has kept its original aspect unchanged (Pl. IV), serves to illustrate the fact that north of the Alps, too, during this entire period, the medieval system of arranging books was dominant. And why, indeed, should it be otherwise? At this time Italy led all the rest in library development, while England, France and Germany merely followed the trails she blazed.

The England of the Wars of the Roses showed, in general, little inclination to devote itself to encouraging the new culture. The bonds which Chaucer had already forged between his native land and Italy did not strengthen.(57) An exception to this rule was Humphrey, Duke of Gloucester, son of Henry IV, who was unusual in another respect also. He avidly studied the classical writers, borrowed books from Italian Humanists, and permitted them to dedicate their works to him. His truly comprehensive collections passed by gift into the possession of the Oxford University Library, and this led to the building of Duke Humphrey's Library in 1488.

France too still retained its medieval culture through the fifteenth century. Epoch-making here were the two Italian campaigns of Charles VIII and Louis XII. The former brought back to Paris in 1495 parts of the Aragon library of Naples, while five years later Louis carried off as spoils of war the Sforza library of Pavia. This made its way to the castle of Blois, which the king had already in earlier days fitted out plentifully with book-treasures. At this time there were already among the high French nobility Renaissance bibliophiles, of whom the most brilliant representative was Louis' minister, Cardinal d'Amboise. He showed a special preference for Italian manuscripts, and acquired by purchase another part of the Aragon legacy. But the new spirit first began truly to expand under Francis I. He had the Blois collections removed to his favorite seat at Fontainebleau and built there a library which compares favorably with its Italian models in every respect. As <u>maître de la librairie</u> the king appointed the great philologist and jurist Budé; furthermore we find there with him Lascaris, whom we have met before in Florence and who now looked after Greek manuscripts for Francis as he had done formerly for the Medici. Quite in the Italian manner the library was made accessible to all those interested; in fact,

Francis personally subsidized the editing of valuable texts.

From the time of Charles VIII the library contained printed books, though for a long while these continued to remain in the background as over against manuscripts. Of great importance, however, was the introduction of legal deposit by the French king. As recent investigations have shown, this arrangement developed in connection with the machinery of book-censorship and the conferring of the privilege of printing books, in that both were used as means of forcing the donation of free copies to the kings for their libraries. This was effected by laws of Francis I in 1537-1538. Later on in our story we shall see how other rulers followed his example and how today copyright forms one of the most important sources of growth for all large public libraries.

The influence of the Italian Quattrocento upon Germany was stronger and more lasting than upon England and France.(58) With the reform councils of Constance and Basel the new tendencies forced their way across the Alps. Among the pioneers were the above-mentioned manuscript-hunters, chief among them the important personage of Aeneus Silvius Piccolomini (later Pius II). The German Humanism which developed did not for a long time hence involve any break with the medieval point of view or any turning away from Scholasticism. Its primary effort was toward better formal education and more exact knowledge of the literary sources of classical antiquity. Only gradually did a more aggressive attitude set in. More vigorously than in other lands the German middle classes took part in the spreading of Humanism, linking it directly to the educational efforts we have just mentioned above.

The Humanistic doctrines also had a strong effect upon German library affairs. The improvement described in the preceding chapter, especially in the cities, proceeded as before, but with the difference that within the book collection the percentage of ancient, and later also of Italian, books slowly and gradually increased. One of the first to open his library to the new culture was Nicholas of Cusa (d. 1464), the great prince of the Church and original scholar, who competed with the Italians in collecting classical manuscripts. Of his followers I shall name the Augsburg patrician, Gossembrot, and the Frankish baron, Albrecht von Eyb. In the aldermen's library and the church libraries of Nuremberg one can observe how since the eighties classical and Humanistic literature had been gaining strength. About this time Philip, Count Palatine of the Rhine, modeled his court at Heidelberg completely on the Italian style and maintained intellectual contacts with men such as Von Dalberg, Agricola, and others of like disposition. The Palatine library took on a strongly Humanistic coloring, while the library of Heidelberg University--and this is true also of its sister universities--preserved the traditions of the Middle Ages down to the next century.

The middle-class character of German Humanism is shown by the pains taken to make Latin and Italian literature available to wider classes of people by means of translation. Nikolas von Wyle, town clerk of Esslingen, had a special enthusiasm for these translations. Very near him lived the Princess Palatine Mechthild, who built herself a library on her dowager's estate at Rottemberg on the Neckar and there busily collected older German literature.

In the meantime Gutenberg's discovery had been spread far and wide by German printers. Around the turn of the century there already flourished a lively book trade covering almost the whole of western Europe. Its most active spot was Basel, where at the time the leader of northern Humanism, Erasmus, held court--we might almost say--and gathered the Basel Group (<u>sodalitas Basiliensis</u>) about him. Within their ranks there developed an intensive cooperation between scholarship and printing: while the Humanists functioned as editors, the followers of Gutenberg, above all Froben, "the prince of German printers," took care of the publishing of classic and Humanistic works. From Basel commercial and intellectual lines of connection ran to Lyons, the chief printing city of western Europe, as well as to Venice, where Aldus Manutius had his workshop. In Basel lived also the philologist Sichardus, about whose regular visits to old monasteries in order to find basic materials fit for his editions we have detailed knowledge.

We are most interested, however, in the consequences of printing for the development of libraries. A two-fold effect can be stated. Up to this period, as we have tried to show, libraries and <u>scriptoria</u> had at all times been closely bound to one another. One need only recall the pagan academies and the Christian monasteries, or the bibliophiles of ancient times, of the Middle Ages, and again of the Italian Renaissance. In the course of the sixteenth century this close connection between the makers and the collectors of books was dissolved forever. This was one effect of the 'black art'; the other, the sharp increase in book production and the emergence of a host of hitherto unsuspected library problems in connection with it, was yet to make itself felt in the course of time. The first thing to change was the arrangement of the books, in that, as we have already observed in Italy and France, the printed book now took its place alongside the manuscript.

This held true, for example, of the library of the Nuremberg Humanist and polyhistor, Hartmann Schedel (d. 1514). Part of his collection derived from the estate of his cousin Hermann, the rest from trips to Italy or visits to German monasteries. Many of the texts had been copied in his own hand. But among nearly 600 items shown in the catalogue, up to a third were printed books. Schedel loved to decorate his books with maxims and little illustrations and to inscribe in them biographical sketches of the authors. His famous compatriot, Pirkheimer, belonged to a younger generation. Well educated and highly cultured, he embodied in his person the Italian ideal of the well-rounded man, though with German middle-class nuances. The way in which he managed his costly library, which contained among other things the complete set of Aldine Greek imprints, is revealed by the motto of his bookplate: For himself and his friends (Sibi et amicis). What Pirkheimer was to Nuremberg, Peutinger was to Augsburg. His library was held in high esteem by all the Humanists. It was well classified and catalogued and comprised over 2100 volumes--among them, however, only 170 manuscripts.

Both Pirkheimer and Peutinger were among the closest friends of Maximilian I, who rose to be the intellectual center of German Humanism and most enthusiastically promoted the art of printing. It is not correct, however, to attribute to this ruler the founding of the Court Library at Vienna. The books he collected as prince, along with those he inherited from his father, and whatever was added later, Maximilian kept partly at Wiener-Neustadt, partly at Innsbruck, and partly at other castles. Ferdinand I seems to have laid the real foundation for the Vienna library.

A whole series of important Humanist libraries could still be cited. The collector of books had now become so popular a figure in Germany that the satirist Brant included him among his types of fools. Let us point out then only Reuchlin's library, rich in Greek and Hebrew texts, the library of Beatus Rhenanus in Schlettstadt, well preserved even to this day, and finally the library at Sponheim, which the abbot Tritheim founded. Tritheim has been compared with Cassiodorus, because like him he endeavored to rescue the treasures of the past for posterity. Yet he stood at the end of a movement, while the earlier man had stood at the beginning of one. Cassiodorus, as was shown earlier, successfully bridged the gap between ancient and medieval times, and created at Vivarium the model for western monastic libraries. Tritheim, on the contrary, made the vain attempt to implant Humanism at Sponheim. The books which he had assembled there with great effort and industry were quickly scattered again by his successors. Indeed the hour was not far distant when Sponheim, like so many another monastic library throughout the length and breadth of Germany, was to vanish completely.

CHAPTER VI. THE REFORMATION AND
THE SEVENTEENTH CENTURY

The Reformation forms an epoch in the history of libraries. In this period many a medieval library ceased to exist while a large number of new libraries had their origin. Not infrequently, at the dissolution of German monasteries and religious institutions, the acquisitions resulting from many centuries of zealous collecting were carelessly disposed of or destroyed as papist literature. Revolutionary movements like the Peasants' War of 1524-25 wrought the worst havoc. From Thuringia down the Main, through the Odenwald and the Black Forest to Switzerland, ecclesiastical libraries had heavy losses to bemoan; many, such as that at Reinhardsbrunn, met total destruction. The same thing happened also outside Germany, for example in France during the Huguenot Wars. In 1562, to cite just one instance, Condé's soldiers plundered the treasures of Fleury-sur-Loire. Things seem to have gone worst in England. During the thirty years in which about 800 monasteries and convents were secularized, their book collections received the most careless treatment. In 1550 the Commissioners of Edward VI even came to Oxford and so completely emptied the library that shortly thereafter the furniture of the room was sold as useless.

If we should not pass over in silence the destructive effect of the Reformation, there is all the more reason to emphasize vigorously its constructive influence. In the circular letter of Luther in 1524 "To the Mayors and Aldermen of all the cities of Germany"(59) occurs this significant sentence: "Finally, this must also be taken into consideration... that no cost nor pains should be spared to procure good libraries in suitable buildings, especially in the large cities, which are able to afford it." Melancthon, "Germany's teacher" (praeceptor Germaniae), also worked with the same purpose. It can easily be observed in various regions that this was not merely a matter of words and exhortations, but that deeds followed words. One need only recall in this respect the beneficent activity which John Bugenhagen carried on over all northern Germany. In this activity the book collections formerly belonging to Catholic institutions generally furnished the chief materials for the institutions about to be founded.

In this way, alongside the municipal libraries dating from the fifteenth century, there arose many new ones, as in Hamburg, Nuremberg, and Augsburg, to say nothing of church libraries which served substantially the same ends, as in Bremen and Halle. In many places a collection simply passed from Catholic to Protestant hands without the slightest alterations. To these were added the many new school libraries, among which, once again, those in Saxony stood out notably. The universities founded at this time, Königsberg, Helmstedt, Jena and Marburg--we should perhaps add Leyden--acquired their needed book stock in the same way; those already in existence, e.g. Leipzig, now came to possess true university libraries. In the Catholic regions the re-establishment of libraries set in as the Counter-Reformation gathered strength. In this work the Jesuits, particularly Canisius, performed lasting services which unfortunately have to this day failed to receive any comprehensive evaluation in the literature on the subject.(60)

All these passed for public libraries, but in no way did they possess the arrangements to which we are accustomed in such institutions. Access was, as a rule, restricted to a privileged group. Administration and internal organization still left almost everything to be desired. The growth of the collection was left largely to chance, and depended upon the good will of liberal donors. Of course, Gutenberg's invention made its influence felt and caused the number of books in libraries to increase from decade to decade. But realization of the new duties which devolved upon libraries as a result of this invention seems to have dawned quite gradually. Furthermore, the need of the time for usable public institutions was materially undermined by the great abundance of private collections.

In a Meissen chronicle we read: "It is quite common for most of the nobles and burghers, even if they do not actually study, to be able at least to read and write, to bring together in their homes fine libraries of all sorts of good books of godly writings and to attract to their hearths excellent and profitable historians, physicians, and others." We may take it that among the urban patricians the number of learned bibliophiles had risen since the previous period. Two of them, members of the Fugger family, will concern us farther on. Even among artisans the joys of book collecting had spread to such an extent that Hans Sachs, with his grand collection of semi-scientific works, seems not to have been altogether an unusual phenomenon. Tradition has handed down the names of certain noble families whose libraries encompassed several thousand volumes. It can clearly be seen how movements proceeding from Humanism combined with interest in contemporary religious questions to cause large classes of the people to occupy themselves with books.

Also, in the sixteenth century many territorial princes studied at some university and continued their scholarly contacts during their reigns. Along with fitting out a library, they aimed at the same time to enhance the splendor of their courts and to provide the necessary book materials for officials with their ever-increasing administrative duties. Naturally, at times private interests prevailed and at times motives of state. At any rate, at this very time there arose a group of libraries which today are reckoned among the most important in Germany.

For example, in the thirties Duke Albert of Prussia set up in his castle at Königsberg both a public and also a private library, and Julius of Brunswick in 1568 laid the foundations of the famous collection at Wolfenbüttel. The founding of the Dresden Library by August of Saxony had occurred somewhat earlier, and a little later there came the founding of the library of Cassel by William of Hesse. Since the printing of books was now done only on a mass-production basis, so to speak, bindings alone now afforded the possibility of satisfying the individual's desire for luxury. The bounds to which this display of ostentation could go are shown by the oft-mentioned Silver Library of Königsberg. (61) As a rule, however, a leather binding with blind tooling and gilding was favored, the finest examples of which were produced by the Wittenberg bookbinders and by the Heidelberg craftsmen employed by Ott Heinrich.

Of this Elector Palatine a poet sang: "At all times he loved wisdom and art."(62) Among his most intimate friends was the distinguished Grecist and brilliant bibliophile, Ulrich Fugger. Ott Heinrich's predecessors had already brought together considerable collections of books; he enlarged them with unflagging zeal to the time of his death (1559)--to this the ancient monasteries along the Rhine, especially Lorsch, can bear witness. Ott Heinrich specialized in German manuscripts. His successors made further acquisitions, such as Ulrich Fugger's library, and took eager advantage of the Frankfurt book fairs. Extraordinarily liberal access was provided to this library, and valuable codices were often turned over to scholars for editing. In this way, until the catastrophe of 1623, the Palatine Library ranked as the most outstanding of German libraries and played the role of a kind of intellectual center for the whole Southwest.

The founding and support of libraries was by no means confined to Protestant princes, however. Proof of this is the Vienna Court Library, which at the end of the century had 9000 volumes, including 1,600 manuscripts, and was administered by the able Blotius. The best proof is the work of Duke Albert V of Bavaria. Unlike his cousin the Elector, Albert had no close association with art and knowledge: he loved ostentation and, as was later said of him, in collecting books he desired to imitate other rulers in this method of developing a splendid court. Consequently, true credit for the founding of the Munich library belongs to that John Jacob Fugger whom the Italians called "the richest and most learned man in Germany" (il primo ricco e'l più dotto di Germania). He made use of the widespread ramifications of his family's business enterprises to secure for himself, especially, Greek manuscripts and he also bought the library of Schedel, already familiar to us. First of all he induced Albert in 1558 to buy the valuable collections of the statesman and Orientalist, Widmanstetter. Somewhat later his own books came into the Duke's possession. The approximately 11,000 volumes so assembled were brought together in a new annex to the Duke's residence. In the years that followed, the collection was much enlarged, especially under Maximilian I, who himself drew up instructions for administering the library and in 1602 had the catalogue of Greek manuscripts published. Later a law was promulgated by his son favoring the Munich library with the copyright deposit of all printed books, a privilege which the Vienna library had already enjoyed for quite some time.

In Duke Albert we can observe for the first time that liking for luxury and show, that partiality for the costly and rare, which had started up among the aristocracy at the height of the Renaissance and which grew more and more to be an essential characteristic of succeeding generations. Before long every fashionable prince's court had a cabinet of art objects connected with the library as well as its cabinet of rarities. A rule of the year 1635 for "museums or libraries" (musei sive bibliothecae) held as desirable in the great hall of the library the bringing together of "some of the things which the native curiosity of a learned man is wont to delight in as food befitting, so to speak, the liberal mind, such as mathematical instruments, ancient coins, learned fragments of former times, as well as certain miracles of nature and art."(63)

What we have set forth up to this point can well be summarized in the statement that Germany in the sixteenth century was saturated with books. At this time the focus of the international book trade was also situated in Germany, and the catalogue of the Frankfurt book fair (Frankfurter Messkatalog) furnished the most complete survey of European literature. Finally, it was a German, the physician and universal scholar, Conrad Gesner, who in 1545 founded scientific bibliography with his Bibliotheca universalis.(64) Nevertheless it was denied to Germany to keep this leadership. General decline and decay, then the frightful catastrophe of the Thirty Years' War, caused Germany to be displaced by the other great powers of the West. It is clear, then, that the largest and most important collections of the seventeenth century are to be looked for outside Germany and also that in these other lands the new type, which we may refer to as the baroque library, took shape.

In the foregoing chapter it was pointed out how the Renaissance stuck to the medieval plan of arranging books, still preferring to keep them lying chained on desks. However, the more the productivity of printing presses increased, and thereby the number of books in libraries mounted, the more the inadequacies of this earlier method must have made themselves felt. Relief came first through a new device: the books were placed in rows in bookcases which ran along the walls. Soon, when it became necessary to extend the cases to the ceiling, an important advance was made by introducing galleries which made possible access to the upper shelves. Still, practical needs alone did not bring about this innovation; it expressed also the dictates of contemporary taste. As the central space was left free of books, the opportunity arose to exhibit curiosa and rarities. In this way the library took on more and more the character of a baroque exhibition room.

So far as is now known, Philip II's great architect, Herrera, was one of the first to carry out consistently the placing of books in wall cases (Pl. VI). The years 1563-84 saw the building of the majestically dark Escorial, in which the king himself lived like a scholarly monk. Under his personal supervision the library grew extraordinarily fast, by far its greatest riches coming as a legacy of the statesman De Mendoza. The librarian Montano followed unusual principles in classification: first he divided the collection by language, then separated manuscripts and printed books, and finally divided everything into 64 separate subject classes.

In France the Royal Library did not suffer neglect under the successors of Francis I. These rulers indulged in singular luxury in bindings; and, thanks to the high perfection of bookmaking in France, the king's binders (<u>relieurs du roi</u>) were capable of satisfying the most pretentious requirements. The stock of valuable manuscripts grew first through the collection of Catherine de Medici, then through that of Cardinal d'Amboise, of which we have already spoken. An important step was the transfer of the library from Fontainebleau to Paris. There it was under the direction of the librarian Rigault, who completed its first catalogue in 1622.

But despite internal and external progress the Bibliotheque du Roi was soon put completely in the shade by the library which Cardinal Mazarin fashioned. This powerful statesman interested himself no more than was customary in science and art, but at his side stood Gabriel Naudé, a scholar of rank and the <u>beau ideal</u> of library directors. His <u>Avis pour dresser une bibliothèque</u>,(65) published in 1627, set out a program for a universal library, provided with the most important books in all branches of knowledge in their original languages and in translation, along with the best commentaries and reference works. Naudé fought the prevailing partiality for rarities, desired equal consideration for older as well as more recent literature, and even wished to procure heretical writings. An unclassified collection seemed to him to deserve the name of library as little as a crowd of men deserve to be called an army. As the best classification he recommended that which is "easiest and most natural" (<u>la plus facile, la plus naturelle</u>), which was built upon the faculties and contained reasonable subdivisions. All these proposals were based upon the same idea, namely, that such a collection should not only promote the fame of its owner but should at the same time satisfy the needs of the public.

After Naudé had entered Mazarin's service in 1642, he found the opportunity to effect his program. Gifts streamed in from all sides. Generals and diplomats abroad were given commissions to carry out. Naudé himself undertook long journeys to England, Flanders, Germany, and Italy. Ultimately, some 40,000 books were brought together, all luxuriously bound in morocco and stamped in gold with the Cardinal's coat of arms. And while the Bibliothèque du Roi still kept its doors shut, Mazarin dedicated his library "to all those who desired to come there to study" (à tous ceux qui y vouloient aller estudier). But this most excellent and beautiful library, this eighth wonder of the world, as Naudé called it, fell prey to the Fronde at the opening of the fifties. Its seizure called forth from Naudé a cry of anguish, for he loved his handiwork as a father loves his only child.(66) But when his plea to the parlement, as passionate as it was proud, fell upon deaf ears, he left the place where he had accomplished so much and sought service in foreign lands. Mazarin, as we know, later returned to power and began forthwith the restoration of his library, but death overtook his librarian on the way back.

In order to understand the approach and the achievement of Naudé we must keep in mind the fact that his life coincided with the new growth of knowledge represented by such names as Scaliger and De Thou, Grotius and Hobbes, Galileo and Kepler, Bacon and Descartes. In such a period, as is easy to understand, there arose among all those who did not merely collect books, but studied them too, a desire to provide for systematic organization and expert administration of collections of books running not to hundreds but to thousands and tens of thousands. Consequently at this time the vocation of a librarian with practical training took on heightened importance, which mounted even higher during the following centuries. That in the case in point an extremely gifted representative of this profession should meet up with the most liberal of patrons was a fortunate twist of fate. Yet Naudé could already be guided by excellent examples; he himself named the Bodleian and the Ambrosian Library.

The first of these was the magnanimous work of Sir Thomas Bodley, a typical representative of Elizabethan England, in whom the common sense of the practical man was combined with a good Humanistic training. He had studied and taught at Oxford and had later come to know several courts on the continent through diplomatic service. He believed, as his autobiography reveals, that in the twilight of his life he could perform no better service than "to set up my staff at the library door" in Oxford with the purpose of restoring the university library which had been destroyed decades before, and putting it again to public use. He believed that he possessed the necessary equipment--scholarly attainments, sufficient funds, distinguished friends, and undisturbed leisure. And so, in 1598, Bodley made his offer to the Vice-Chancellor of the university and after five years of labor, during which he spared neither money nor energy, and also found the readiest support from all sides, the library was able to open in its old quarters.

It was justly called the Bodleian, for the enthusiasm of its founder never abated. He induced the Stationers' Company of London to give it free copies of all new books, and he willed his own property to the university. In accordance with the statute drawn up by Bodley, the library was open five hours each day; only graduates, however, had free access. The books were arranged in classes without subdivisions. The first printed catalogue appeared as early as 1605; the second, in 1620 testified to the great growth of the collection. In a very short time the old building proved too small. In Bodley's own lifetime a small wing was built, and in the year of his death (1613) work was begun on one considerably larger.(67) These additions had galleries with steps which led to the upper rows of bookshelves (Pl. VII). The same system had already been installed a few years earlier in the Ambrosian Library (Pl. VIII). This library may in general be pointed to as the Catholic counterpart of Bodley's creation.

Manzoni, in The Betrothed (I Promessi Sposi), has drawn us a picture of the Archbishop of Milan, Federigo Borromeo. The Archbishop followed squarely in the footsteps of his great kinsman and predecessor, Carlo. Himself an able scholar and prolific author, he strove to establish the new Catholic scholarship on a firm foundation. The founding of his library also served this purpose. Since it was to be not merely a collection of minds long dead, but rather a living center of work, he placed it under the direction of a College of Doctors, for whose own publications a special printing press was set up. To this was added an Academy of Arts with rich art collections. And to house everything a special building was erected in the years 1603-09. The Ambrosian Library contained many thousands of books and manuscripts, among them valuable treasures from the monastery of Bobbio, and it excelled in Orientalia. It was decided that it "should be open to all for study" (omnibus studiorum causa pateat).

Similar liberality prevailed at Rome in the Angelica, which the Augustinian Rocca founded in the first decade of the seventeenth century. It ruled no less at the Vatican Library just as it had as early as the Renaissance, though this was in sharp contrast to later practice. So Montaigne reports: "I saw the library without any difficulty; anybody sees it thus, and makes what extracts he pleases."(68) But

Montaigne did not know the splendid new building which Sixtus V (1585-90) had built by Fontana. The Vatican Library in this period was also fortunate in having a good administration. Among its directors was the well-known church historian, Baronius, and its valuable manuscript catalogues were prepared by the brothers Rainaldi.

The seventeenth century brought to the Vatican Library a whole series of splendid gains, of which only the three most important can be mentioned. In 1658 the Library of Urbino, which, as we know, Frederick of Montefeltro had founded, passed into the papal possession. Approximately thirty years later the books from the estate of Christina of Sweden were purchased. This learned and remarkable woman, to whom Ranke devotes a special section in his history of the Popes, succeeding her father, Gustavus Adolfus, had most enthusiastically collected books and manuscripts and had not desisted during the whole of her unsettled life. Upon her removal to Rome she took along all her treasures. But the greatest sensation in the learned world was caused by the acquisition of the Palatine Library. After the capture of Heidelberg by Tilly's troops, Maximilian of Bavaria presented the library to the Pope in 1623, presumably for reasons essentially political. The transfer of this library to the Tiber was carried out with the greatest possible care and foresight. The old bindings, which had been detached before the transfer, were replaced by new bindings of fresh vellum. Each volume then received the inscription: "I am from that library which Maximilian, Duke of Bavaria, took as a prize of war from captured Heidelberg and sent as a trophy to Gregory XV."(69)

The Duke's actions have been subjected to many bitter reproaches. It does not befit the historian to join in the chorus of moral indignation. Library history teaches just this: that from Caesar to Napoleon--and beyond--libraries have been considered valuable prizes of war. It seems more dangerous to me to use the expropriation of the Palatine Library in confessional controversies, for the hero and saviour of Protestantism, Gustavus Adolfus, made ample use of the same practice on his widespread campaigns. Libraries everywhere were systematically emptied, the Jesuit colleges drawing special attention. This occurred in 1621 in the Baltic provinces and five years later in Prussia. In 1631 a similar fate befell Würzburg, Erfurt, Eichsfeld, Mainz, and the Rheingau; in the following years Breslau, Bamberg, and Munich. After the king's death the Swedish generals enthusiastically followed his example. In particular, libraries in Silesia, Bohemia, and Moravia fell prey to them. Gustavus Adolfus had had the rightfulness of his procedures established by legal opinions; he had also used the booty brought home essentially for ideal purposes. It appeared to him a means of raising the educational level of his country. Consequently books and manuscripts were distributed among different places in Sweden. The largest share, however, went to the University Library of Upsala, founded in 1621.

In all this Germany played the sufferer's role. For three decades the dogs of war raged through her provinces. Even if fortified cities suffered less harm than the open country, spiritual impoverishment engulfed all regions. The scattering and destruction of libraries was not the greatest evil: far worse was the widespread loss--by individual and society alike--of that contact with books which had distinguished Germany a century earlier. Now it was necessary to build and create anew. And here, as in other activities, the territorial princes were among the first to recognize the demands of the hour.

The Wolfenbüttel library had been left by the grandson (Frederick Ulrich) of its founder, (Julius, Duke of Brunswick and Lüneburg) to the University of Helmstedt. Duke Augustus assembled on the old location a new and far more splendid library. He had received a careful education and as Prince, while the war raged outside, had lived in his "Ithaca," as he called it, only to collect and study books. Come to the throne in 1635, he busied himself conscientiously with the welfare of his domain. But his leisure hours belonged entirely to the Bibliotheca Augusta. Yearly he spent up to 16,000 thaler, so that at his death the library numbered some 28,000 volumes, including 2000 manuscripts. With justifiable pride the Duke boasted: "Not only have we assembled our library with great care, expense, and exertion, but with manifold unbelievable labors we have brought it into such fine order and arrangement that the like is hardly to be found in all Europe." He was his own librarian and diligently wrote out the catalogues with his own hand. In classification he did not follow the scheme of classes and sub-classes recommended by Naudé, but separated the collection, as had been done at Oxford, into twenty coordinate classes.

Motives other than those operating at Brunswick governed Ernest the Pious of Gotha (d. 1675). Dedicating all his

powers to rebuilding the duchy, which had been devastated
by war, he carried through a model administrative organization and labored so industriously in behalf of church and
school that he was called the prince among pedagogues and
the pedagogue among princes. Building the library represented only part of his educational program. The library
consisted first of the older books, then of spoils of war
which Ernest had brought home from his participation in
Swedish campaigns; to these were added many purchases.

The library which Frederick William, the Great Elector, founded at Berlin, however, stands out as the finest example of royal solicitude. "Amid the roar of battle and the
cavalcade of victories"(70) from Jutland in 1659 he gave the
necessary orders to take the first steps. The opening of the
library followed two years later, after the Peace of Oliva
had made the possession of his domain secure. There were
hardly any monastic treasures at hand to commandeer, and
what former electors had bequeathed was also very insignificant. Nevertheless, by applying himself personally to
the task, making sure that the library had a steady revenue,
and inducing the presentation of valuable gifts, Frederick
William brought the collection up to 20,000 printed books and
1,600 manuscripts. The director of the library was the
Frankfurt professor, Hendreich. Though judgments of him
differ, yet he did draw up catalogues and work out a classification which remained in use for over a hundred years.
At first the library was located in a wing of the castle where
it was at once made available to the public for use. Shortly
before the death of the Elector a separate new building was
begun, but this got only as far as the ground floor. Hendreich's eulogy extolled Frederick William's services in
behalf of the library, and another scholar said in the magniloquent style of the time that he vied for honors with the
rulers of Alexandria and Pergamum.

CHAPTER VII. THE ENLIGHTENMENT

"From the time of Leibniz to about the end of the eighteenth century there was in the realm of science, letters, and social life a uniform type of cultured individual in Europe and a société anonyme to which belonged the most diverse minds... This société anonyme no longer exists, but in libraries it lives on--and there it must continue to live."--Harnack in Zentralblatt für Bibliothekswesen, XL, p. 536.

In the period usually comprehended under the name of the Enlightenment the scientific progress which had set in during the preceding epoch pushed forward even more markedly. An optimistic urge toward research took hold, the like of which had been known only during the Renaissance. But men did not look back to the past as in that former time; on the contrary, they broke every bond of traditional authority. The autonomy of the mind working methodically was proclaimed, and men strove for rational explanation in all fields of knowledge. This new order of specialized research went hand in hand with a new systematization of the sciences, and with a new kind of organized international scholarly cooperation. In this period came the founding of most of the learned societies;(71) to this period western libraries owe their modern intellectual stamp.

We may begin our account with France, for in this age that country was not only typical of political and military power, but it also determined the style of living and held the lead in art and literature. Even if its scientific achievements were not always of first importance, it did lend the most elegant forms of expression to the intellectual productions of the time.

The second half of the seventeenth century, when Descartes was beginning to acquire followers and the skeptic Bayle was publishing his dictionary, also saw the birth of the truly scientific study of history in France. In publishing the Acta Sanctorum, the Jesuits set about systematically collecting and critically sifting source materials. A similar task was undertaken--with still better results--by the Benedictine Congregation of St. Maur, with the great scholar, Mabillon, at its head.(72) In Paris, at St. Germain-des-Prés, the Maurists created a kind of academy with a central library to which was brought the fullest possible collection of materials from the ancient monasteries of their order. After Mabillon came Montfaucon, who attempted a union catalogue of western manuscripts and is considered the father of the catalogue raisonné.

The scholarly endeavors of the Jesuits and Maurists came to have a special importance for French library history because of the lively interest which the great minister, Colbert, took in them. As bibliophile and collector he continued the tradition of Mazarin: his Naudé was the historian Baluze. Agents systematically toured the provinces for him, buying what was to be had, but also occasionally not hesitating to use somewhat objectionable methods. Yet the minister cared for the Royal Library, which had been placed under his direction in 1661, with equal enthusiasm. "Monsieur Colbert," said a contemporary, "forgets nothing that is necessary to augment and embellish the library in order to satisfy the generous inclination of his master."(73) Franch diplomats in foreign lands were called upon to buy books; special missions were sent to the Orient. For all this the necessary funds were forthcoming. And, since there was no lack of costly gifts, the library was able to quadruple its size by the time of the minister's death.

The upward trend which had begun for the library with Colbert persisted. Louis XIV supported it in every way, and his two successors on the throne did not lag behind his praiseworthy example. The whole court shared this enthusiasm for collecting, so that it was possible for one splendid private library after another to pass into the royal possession by gift or purchase. French diplomats abroad continued to be called upon frequently to perform services for the library, and scholars like the Maurists were charged with the acquisition of materials. Particularly rich was the influx of Orientalia from the Near East, and even from India and China. At the outset of the Revolution the Royal Library was rightly considered the largest and richest collection of books and manuscripts in the world.

Its internal organization kept pace with its enlargement. Of the officials involved, Clément deserves special mention, for, beginning in 1675, he undertook a re-arrangement of the collection into 23 classes, and for this purpose he completed the classed catalogue. Now also an inventory of the manuscripts was taken, a task in which the efforts of the Maurists and other scholars were enlisted once again. During this whole time the Bignon family contributed valuable services. Under the most outstanding of them, the abbé Jean Paul, new quarters were occupied in 1724, and in the following decade printing of the catalogues was begun, but this, however, was not completed. At the end of the period under consideration the library had a staff of no less than 54 people. Some measure of the high level of the demands made upon them can be gained from the lecture The Duties and Qualifications of a Librarian,(74) which the abbé Cotton des Houssayes delivered in 1780 at the Sorbonne.

The foregoing chapter has already said something about classification and cataloguing. The Enlightenment devoted itself with special energy to this task, above all in France. Bacon's division of all human knowledge(75) affected thinkers almost disastrously, for it implanted the dogma of the exhaustive classification of the fields of knowledge. One scheme followed another, a few acquiring some importance. But in practice these various successive proposals were avoided, and librarians stuck conservatively to the five divisions beloved in France (theology, jurisprudence, arts and sciences, belles lettres, and history). This division underlay Clément's classes; it was the one cultivated by Martin, the leading Parisian bookseller; and the Encyclopedists, by mentioning with praise the so-called "system of the booksellers of Paris," enhanced its reputation.

At first, public access to the library could be had only with difficulty; the abbé Bignon was the first to draw up rules making the use of the library considerably easier. In this way all the leaders of the Enlightenment were able to make use of the Royal Library, and furthermore the National Assembly of 1790 recognized its importance for French intellectual life. Its connections with historical studies never broke off. A special genealogical section was created for studying the family history of the nobility. Furthermore, the Cabinet des Chartes,(76) in whose establishment the Maurists played a prominent role, was united with the Royal Library, though at first quite informally.

Despite all this, it would be going too far to attribute to the institution as early as this a purely scientific character. As yet the conception of the library as a luxurious showplace had by no means been overthrown. When it came to buying or to soliciting gifts, precious items and rarities were much preferred. The library even had two separate divisions for prints and medals, upon which its royal owners lavished very special attention.

In England things were essentially no different. There, too, among those people who set the standards for libraries, most of the ideas which had been characteristic of the preceding period still prevailed. But progress did not occur in the same way on opposite sides of the Channel. In France it was the person of the King about whom all efforts aiming at improvement centered; in England it was the whole nation, represented by Parliament. In France, as we have seen, the impulse sprang from the historians, in England from the natural philosophers. In the movement the Bodleian Library did not play any prominent role. To be sure, it was not neglected after its splendid start: indeed it was enriched by many gifts. But during the Enlightenment the universities were not the center of English intellectual life; the capital city of London alone qualifies for consideration as such.

The plan to establish a large library in London had already made its appearance several times during the sixteenth century. About the middle of the next century, in the turbulent days of the Revolution, John Dury, keeper of the King's private collection, was occupied with library problems. This original thinker published in 1650 <u>The Reformed Librarie Keeper</u>, characterized him as "factor and trader for helps to learning," and went on to develop points of view which sound like anticipations of modern public library endeavors. The idea--not yet directly advocated by Dury--of developing the Royal Library into a public institution comes out later in Richard Bentley, who was directing this library about the turn of the century. He wrote out <u>A Proposal for building a Royal Library and establishing it by Act of Parliament</u>, and he also proposed a guarantee of a fixed yearly sum of money, one so large, in fact, that the collection could be increased to 200,000 volumes. But it was not until more than a generation later that a part of his ideas was put into operation; this was effected by the physicist Sir Hans Sloane, who was personal physician to the King.

Sloane succeeded the great Newton as President of the Royal Society. Dubbed by a satirist "the foremost toyman of his time," he collected everything which was "rare and curious," but which at the same time promoted "the enlargement of our knowledge in the works of nature," and so gathered rare animals, plants, and minerals, and also antiquities and considerable collections of books and manuscripts. In his will he created a group of trustees for his collections and consigned them to the nation in return for a sum to be paid to his heirs. In 1753 Parliament accepted the offer and united with the Sloane Collection two others--the Cottonian and Harleian Libraries. Sir Robert Bruce Cotton, a friend of Bodley's, had acquired extremely valuable materials on English history, which his grandson Robert presented to the nation in 1700, but which later suffered heavy damage by fire. Of the very valuable collection of Robert Harley (d. 1724), the books had already been sold, but now Parliament bought the manuscripts. Finally, to add to all this, George II donated his private library. The royal collection, from its inception in the Middle Ages, had had a checkered career--enrichments at the hands of the bibliophile Henry VII, losses during the period of the iconoclastic riots.(77) It owed much to Prince Henry, son of James I, and had benefitted since 1662 from the copyright system, which now applied to the national library.

After the British Museum, thus created, had acquired a worthy home by the purchase of Montagu House, it was opened in 1759. The statutes provided "free access to all studious and curious persons"; in point of fact, access was made difficult by all sorts of formalities. In general, as its very name indicates, the British Museum was to be less a place for study than for exhibition, all the more because at the time its natural history collections still formed the more important part of its holdings. Hence it is understandable too that the first three Principal Librarians should be physicians and members of the Royal Society.

During the foregoing epoch, Italy had continued to stand in the front rank along with France and England in library matters. Since the middle of the seventeenth century, however, it had rather slipped into the background. Nevertheless, even here there was no lack of scholarly movements from which libraries profited.

It was Muratori, working first in the Ambrosian Library, and after 1700 librarian and archivist for the Este in Modena, who brought the Maurist methods of study to the Italian peninsula and thus founded the great historical and antiquarian school which occupied itself with the most diverse fields of research throughout the eighteenth century. Another member of the circle represented by Muratori and the Maurists was the Tuscan court librarian, Magliabechi. An eccentric bachelor of repulsive appearance, he was the butt of Florentine jibes, yet as a scholar he enjoyed a worldwide reputation and carried on an international correspondence with the most outstanding men of the time. He was possessed by true bibliomania. In his home books were piled right up to the ceiling, and he could only find what he was looking for by virtue of a remarkable memory. Mabillon called him "a walking museum and a kind of living library" (museum inambulans et viva quaedam bibliotheca). At his death (1714) he left his collection to the Grand Duke and therewith laid the groundwork for the present-day Biblioteca Nazionale in Florence.(78)

Of other libraries which were founded, two deserve special mention: the library at Rome of Cardinal Casanate, a friend of Mabillon and Baluze, and the Brera Library at Milan, the founding of which took place in 1770 under the auspices of the Empress Maria Theresa quite in the spirit of the Enlightenment. Two exemplary accomplishments testify to the genuine scholarship then to be found in the ranks of Italian librarians--Bandini's manuscript catalogue for the Laurentian Library at Florence, and (even though it did remain unfinished), Audifreddi's catalogue of books for the aforementioned Biblioteca Casanatense.

Now if we turn our attention to Germany, we shall meet with much greater detail than in the lands just reviewed. This is conditioned, for one thing, by the plan of our book, which prescribes a closer examination of German than of other libraries. There is, however, a second reason to be adduced, which comes into play just at this point in our exposition. After 1650 Germany took a most active part in the intellectual movements of the West, even though the frightful wounds which the Thirty Years' War had inflicted upon her healed right slowly. As a consequence, up to the end of our period there prevailed in many libraries conditions little worthy of a nation great in culture, whereas during the same time other libraries whipped themselves into shape so effectively as to surpass by far in importance even what had been achieved in Paris.

There exist two accounts of German libraries: one that of Uffenbach at the beginning, the other that of Hirsching at the end of the eighteenth century. Both paint a pretty cheerless picture of the majority of institutions open to the public: insufficient space, defective classification, incomplete catalogues, bad conditions of use. These descriptions are not complete, nor do they appear free from prejudice; nevertheless, for the most part, they would seem to portray actual conditions.

Church libraries of any importance were still to be found only in the larger cities. The libraries of religious foundations and monasteries were often wholly neglected. The tendencies of the Enlightenment led to the selling of old parchment codices--for example, the treasures of the monastery of Weissenburg were in danger of being sold to goldsmiths. Only the intervention of people with insight saved them and made possible their preservation at Wolfenbüttel. But conditions were not like this everywhere. A whole series of Frankish and Bavarian monasteries, we know, took stock of their collections once more and reclassified them and even found money for acquiring new books. Also, new buildings were not lacking--I mention only the charming rococo building at Amorbach. And in the Black Forest monastery of St. Blasien there developed under the influence of the Maurists scholarly activity which under the learned Abbott Gerbert reached its climax shortly before the Revolution.

Most of the municipal libraries dragged out miserable existences; a few basked in the glory of previously acquired riches. One can credit new life only to a few cities which were then on the upgrade. At Frankfurt am Main the collections which had hitherto existed separately were merged in 1668 to form a public library, and the post of librarian was created somewhat later. Leipzig in 1677 received by private bequest a municipal library, which was later enlarged and developed. The most unusual creation was the Hamburg Commercial Library (Hamburger Kommerzbibliothek) in the year 1735. This owed its origin to the members of the merchant class, and accordingly concentrated upon important literature having to do with trade and shipping, and along with these collected local material on Hamburg.

One of the heartening phenomena in library affairs at this time was the resurgence of the private library. In this sphere the evil effects of the wars could be most swiftly remedied. Indeed, setting up such libraries expressed the general spirit of the times. In Uffenbach's account their significance already comes clearly to the fore, and Hirsching notes that they have considerably increased in number and quality. Berlin and Nuremberg had the largest number of private libraries, with Hamburg, Dresden, and Vienna not far behind. The cabinet of curiosities was not yet totally abandoned, but the scholarly character of the collections grew steadily stronger. Scientific or semi-scientific books formed the largest part of the collections, while belles-lettres were but little cultivated. As for the court libraries of the princes, they too, for the most part, preserved that typical mixture of exhibition room and study room which had come into being during the previous period.

The Court Library at Vienna developed into one of the most splendid collections of rarities in Europe. Its ascendancy began with the summoning of Lambeck, who was a native of Hamburg. He had travelled widely, made international connections in the learned world, and acquired for himself a reputation as a universal scholar. From 1663 to 1680 he labored at Vienna, and there he carried through a reclassification of the collections. Cataloguing, however, never got beyond the project stage; the descriptions of manuscripts which he gave in his <u>Commentarii</u> were too minute and in no way even comparable to Montfaucon's <u>catalogue raisonné</u>. In general Lambeck was addicted to promising more than he was in a position to carry out. The influx of books and manuscripts which had set in about the middle of the seventeenth century became even greater in the following century under the rule of the Emperor Charles VI. At that time the magnificent collections of Prince Eugene of Savoy were added, and the library acquired new and excellent quarters, the work of Master Fischer von Erlach (Pl. IX).

The library at Berlin founded by the Great Elector had its ups and downs. Under his immediate successors the collection was further enlarged and the basis of its later wealth in Orientalia established. Also, in 1699, following the example of France, the legal deposit system was put into force. Evil days arrived with the rule of the Soldier King, Frederick William of Prussia, who stopped the salaries of the staff and turned over part of the library funds to one of his generals. In fact, the book-stock was in danger of being given away to other institutions. Even Frederick the Great, for whom daily communion with books was vitally important, who set up separate libraries in his various castles, and was always accompanied by a travelling library, showed very little interest in the Royal Library for a long time. It was not until after 1770 that his attitude changed. Then large funds for buying books were provided, so that the number of volumes climbed in a short time to 150,000, and to house them a new building, the famous Kommode, was erected. But even so, the internal organization did not improve, for the staff required to administer the collection properly was lacking.

One of the admirers of Frederick the Great was Charles Eugene of Württemberg. He was a true representative of reckless, enlightened absolutism. In addition to the Karlsschule(79) he also founded a public library which, thanks to his industry as a collector, contained about 100,000 volumes when he died in 1793. The Duke made his own decisions and personally dispatched all the business of the library, working at this less in the interest of his realm than of his own personal reputation. Naturally he placed the greatest value upon rarities, and especially upon his collection of Bibles. The following incident illustrates how highly the princes of those days valued their rare books: when Professor Michaelis of Göttingen asked for the use of a Hebrew Bible codex from Cassel in 1767, the Landgrave granted him permission, but had the manuscript brought to Göttingen under the protection of a squadron of hussars.

At this point a word about the library at St. Petersburg is in order. In his efforts to assimilate Russian culture to that of the West, Peter the Great was already thinking of founding such an institution. But it was Catherine II, the admirer of Voltaire, who actually put the plan into operation. The nucleus consisted of the Warsaw collection of the brothers Zaluski. These Polish nobles had served their people well in the revival of literature and science, and had also collected a library of more than 100,000 volumes, which they turned over to public use in 1748. Thereafter, however, it fell into decline and neglect until it was carried off to St. Petersburg as a prize of war. Among the St. Petersburg library's later additions was the collection of Dubrovsky, an official of the Russian embassy in Paris, who had acquired all sorts of treasures from French monasteries during the Revolution, outstanding among them manuscripts from Corbie. During the nineteenth century the St. Petersburg library was frequently enlarged in the same way. Always the results were splendid. Today it is one of the richest and most outstanding libraries in the world.(80)

Of the reproaches which Uffenbach hurled against German libraries, the bitterest indeed concerned the incompetence of their personnel. He denounced them as ignorant, discourteous, envious, and lazy. Hirsching's characterization is equally unflattering: they have little or no knowledge of books; they are arrogant misanthropes who look upon their positions as sinecures. As a matter of fact, in this respect both commentators seem to have been not entirely unjustified. Even Lessing, when he was called to Wolfenbüttel in 1770, had it in mind to use the library rather than allow himself to be used by it. Consequently he neglected his job and, though he did initiate a reclassification, it ended in general disorder.

Nevertheless it must be stressed that not all librarians shared Lessing's point of view. The sharp criticisms which, as we have seen, often became loud, the reproachful epithets such as "Cerberus" or "Dragon of the Golden Fleece" which occur fairly often in contemporary literature, show that there was another school of thought. Indeed, on the very spot where Lessing spent his last years there had been at work two generations before the man who is looked upon as the leader of the German Enlightenment, a man who laid down excellent principles governing the duties of a librarian. This man was Gottfried Wilhelm Leibniz.

As a boy Leibniz had already taken a lively interest in his father's book-collection. When in later years he became the librarian of the learned bibliophile Von Boineburg of Mainz, he broached for the first time his favorite bibliographical project--to issue, after the fashion of the Journal des Savants, a "semi-annual selection of books" (nucleus librarius semestralis) and to cumulate these lists into "an inventory of the human knowledge contained in books" (inventarium scientiae humanae libris proditae). It was his belief that true advance of knowledge was possible only when each individual scholar could quickly and conveniently run over the sum total of previous accomplishments.

A decisive influence upon Leibniz was his stay in Paris, since this came precisely at the time of the brilliant advance of the Royal Library under Colbert. Clément and Baluze were numbered among his friends, and, along with other things, he read Naudé's Avis. From this time, too, dated Leibniz's close relations with the learned Jesuits and the Maurists. His historical studies, which inaugurated a new era in German historical research, moved entirely in the tracks which they had laid down. A real and important consequence of these researches was his steadily deepening understanding of the importance of the scholarly library.

In 1676 Leibniz was called to Hanover as librarian and historiographer, and fifteen years later he also assumed direction of the Wolfenbüttel library. Both institutions owed to him a large increase in their collections, and Wolfenbüttel in particular the creation of an alphabetical catalogue and the erection of a new building, an oval central structure with a skylight dome that aroused much admiration. But Leibniz deserves such a pre-eminent place in the history of libraries not so much for his practical accomplishments as for the principles, ideas, and projects contained in his correspondence and in his numerous proposals to the Guelphic princes.

The ideal Leibniz envisaged was a complete, well-administered book-collection, and with a continual variety of figures of speech and changing imagery he strove to delineate its importance. He compared it with a gathering of the greatest men of all ages and races who communicate to us their most select thoughts. Such a library should fulfill for state and society functions similar to church and school. He measured the value of a library, not by the number, but by the quality of its books, and desired in this respect not rarities but rather "key" works of those authors who had performed worthy services for the republic of letters. Small, "curieuse" volumes he thought more important than thick tomes with contents devoid of sense. The heaviest emphasis he laid upon regular acquisition of continuations and new books: neglect of this practice would involve the decline of the entire collection. A necessary presupposition for all this, however, was the availability of an adequate yearly appropriation. For this Leibniz never left off besieging the Guelphic princes with appeals, and kept hatching new methods for creating the necessary sources of income. In problems of classification and cataloguing, too, he showed his practical insight. Like the French librarians he preferred a strictly scholarly system, the "civil classification according to the faculties and the professions" (<u>division civile selon les facultés et les professions</u>). He favored the alphabetical catalogue, but desired also a chronological arrangement by year of publication, and recommended especially subject indexes (<u>indices materiarum</u>) arranged by catchword.

Many of Leibniz's ideas occur already in Naudé's <u>Avis</u>, others in Dury and Bentley. But this leaves undiminished the merit of his contribution, which consists in having clearly presented the importance of the large scholarly reference library and pointed out ways and means to its development.(81) It would be a pleasant task to trace in detail the effect which Leibniz had upon his contemporaries and later generations. Here, naturally, we can trace this influence only to a few places.

It is likely that with Leibniz's cooperation recommendations concerning cataloguing and acquisition were sent from Hanover to Helmstedt, but because of the inefficiency of the librarian there, they were never put into effect. In 1724 a pupil and former assistant of Leibniz, Eckhart, came to Würzburg. The Frankish university library owed to his initiative a systematic classification and cataloguing of the collection, the creation of a regular budget, as well as liberal rules for the use of the library.

Not so easy to discern is the way in which Leibniz's ideas permeated to the capital of Saxony. Dresden's wealth of private libraries has already been mentioned. At this time collecting books was fashionable, particularly among the upper classes. By far the best example was set by Count Brühl, who brought together a most valuable collection of 62,000 volumes. Among his rivals in politics as well as bibliophily was Count Bünau. In contrast to Count Brühl, his love of books arose out of no desire for ostentation, but primarily out of scholarly motives. He spent his leisure hours pursuing historical researches in the manner of Leibniz and the Maurists, and no less a figure than Winckelmann was his secretary. Bünau's great history of the German Empire and its emperors had an enthusiastic reception and earned him the reputation of a German Muratori. His book-collection arose in connection with these historical studies. It had a universal character, even though it was second to Brühl's in size.

From 1740 on Francke was in the service of the Count and, at the instigation and under the direction of his master, he published the Catalogus Bibliothecae Bunavianae. Although this work was not completed, it acquired a reputation far beyond German territories, above all for its original subdivisions, which were determined chiefly by historical and geographical principles. When, in the sixties, the collections of Bünau and Brühl were merged with the Dresden Court Library, Francke entered its service and carried through a grand reclassification according to the principles tested under Bünau. His work was continued by the historian Adelung. At this time the library received a new home in the Japanese Palace, catalogues hitherto lacking were created, and money necessary for acquiring books was readily provided.

Although Dresden at the end of this century ranked among the most important German libraries, the Göttingen University Library enjoyed a much higher reputation--and justly so, for it represented not only the most complete realization of Leibniz's program but an advance upon it by virtue of its close connection with the university, built up quite in accordance with modern principles. It was Baron Von Münchhausen, Göttingen's first curator, who "saw from the beginning what influence the library must have upon the whole nature of a university" and who "immediately laid plans to provide the university with a character of its own by means of the library."

A glance at the other university libraries of Germany reveals the unique position of Göttingen at this time. According to Hirsching, the situation was satisfactory or tolerable in only a few universities; in the majority, conditions were either permanently or temporarily downright wretched. In one the collection was not accessible because the librarian was out of town, or the librarian's sickness kept the library closed all winter. In another the rooms were dark, with broken windows covered by spider-webs, and filled with soot or mold. In a third the books were so shelved that getting at them required the agility of a tight-rope walker or a roofer. In Halle itself, where German rationalism originated, deplorable conditions existed even after the middle of the eighteenth century, primarily because there philological and historical studies were not adequately pursued, whereas they were among the most important disciplines at Göttingen.

Until his death in 1770, Von Münchhausen took personal charge of buying books, arranged to be represented at all important auctions, and kept up a steady business with foreign and domestic book-dealers. Consideration was always given to wishes of the professors. In addition, Von Münchhausen was able to induce large gifts. These activities proceeded according to the principles laid down by Leibniz, and every branch of knowledge received its due. The new books which arrived during the course of the year were placed at the disposal of the reviewers of the Göttinger Gelehrte Anzeigen, for one of the aims of Von Münchhausen was close cooperation between the library and this university publication, which speedily became known and esteemed throughout the entire learned world.

The actual director of the library was Professor Gesner. Of him his biographer says: "He was by far the first among librarians, not only in knowledge, but in most elegant civility and in the courtesy which he showed toward visitors."(82) In one of his own reports Gesner laid down the requirement that the librarian must not, like a financier, merely accumulate capital consisting of books, but must share his wealth with as many as possible. Gesner was regarded as one of the founders of Neo-Humanist philology; after him its leader was Heyne. Before his call to Göttingen in 1763 Heyne had held a position in the library of Count

Brühl, and had been on familiar terms with Winckelmann.
At Göttingen he developed into an organizer on a grand scale
who with sure penetration found the most practical solution
for every problem. He combined in his own person the productivity of both Von Münchhausen and Gesner and thereby
strengthened even more the influence of these two. The
book-collection, which amounted to about 60,000 volumes
when he took office, doubled within the next twenty years
and around the turn of the century reached the 200,000 mark.
At the outset the library had occupied a room of the lecture
building; in the course of time it took over the whole building
and made necessary the added construction of a wing.

In cataloguing a strictly scientific classification was
rejected as a matter of course and, as Leibniz had recommended, a practical scheme used. Yet the creation of the
cataloguing system did not fare well at the start: many
costly mistakes were made. It was not until after 1782,
when Heyne had found an excellent collaborator in the person
of Reuss, that they succeeded in creating a close organic
connection between the arrangement of books on the shelf
and the catalogue, and in making sure that every new book
went through a regular process in which it was entered in
the accession book and in the author and subject catalogues.

At the end of the eighteenth century the fame of the
Göttingen book-collection was on every tongue. It would be
easy to bring together a whole choir of eulogists, among
them the most illustrious minds such as Herder, Goethe and
Von Humboldt. But mean and envious people maintained
that the proud Göttingen professors owed their scholarly
successes solely to the university library.

CHAPTER VIII. THE FRENCH REVOLUTION AND THE NINETEENTH CENTURY

Since the end of the Middle Ages the development of libraries had moved with a clearly recognizable rhythm. After the Renaissance, libraries found themselves faced with the task of solving hitherto unknown problems of internal organization; and again, after the Enlightenment had produced the type of the scholarly reference library, the nineteenth century found itself harried by a series of grave new problems of organization. As the Renaissance was ushered in, large numbers of books had been transferred to new owners, and this took place at the beginning of the Enlightenment to an even greater degree. In the earlier age the Reformation had provided the impetus; now it was the French Revolution.

In November, 1789 the libraries of the Church in France were declared national property. Three years later the collections of émigrés were confiscated. It is estimated that eight million books in France parted from their owners at this time, almost two million in Paris alone. Then it became a problem to make these piles of books safe, to classify them, and to bring them into general use. The successive revolutionary governments passed a long series of laws and administrative decrees, and even planned a great French union catalogue. But times were too unsettled for action to follow upon resolve. There was much waste and destruction. In general, large quantities of books landed first in temporary storehouses, the dépôts littéraires, and from there in the new district libraries, the administration of which was entrusted to municipal officials in 1803, while the government retained supervisory powers. But for a long time the state of these communal libraries (bibliothèques communales) still left much to be desired. Not until toward the middle of the century was a general system put into effect through decrees from Paris, followed somewhat later by reorganization of the university libraries.(83)

Nine dépôts littéraires had been established in the capital. Out of them came additional book-collections for the new state institutions, the Arsenal, the Sainte Geneviève, the Mazarine Library, and, most important of all, the Bibliothèque Nationale. The holdings of the Bibliothèque Nationale increased by about 300,000 books, as well as many thousands of manuscripts, among them the treasures of St. Germain-des-Prés and the Sorbonne. The provinces also had to pay their tribute to the Bibliothèque Nationale, and when troops of the Republic and the Empire carried victorious arms to the Netherlands, Germany, Austria, and Italy, many valuable items travelled to Paris from the libraries of these countries, only part of them to return home after Napoleon's fall. A decree of 1805 had ordered that the Bibliothèque Nationale should be made as complete as possible from the resources of the remaining libraries of the land, in exchange for its own duplicates. Although this order was never fully carried out, since that time the principle has been upheld that the Bibliothèque Nationale must be the chief library of France not merely in name but in fact. With the same object, the ancient laws relating to legal deposit of copies were renewed and strengthened.(84)

This short sketch of the fortunes of the Bibliothèque Nationale would be incomplete without mention of the great services of Joseph Van Praet, who was at this time director of the Department of Printed Books. Credit is due to him first and foremost for taking advantage of all opportunities created by the events of the time. It was his leadership in the main that helped to put into effect the government's resolve to make this new state institution available to everyone. He alone--thanks to a remarkable memory--could find his way among the stored-up treasures, and he richly deserved to be called "the living catalogue" (le catalogue vivant).

The Revolution had two very important results for French library history--centralization of book-collections and the principle that books were to be accessible to the general public. Let us now see how Germany followed the example of her neighbor.

The dissolution of the Jesuit Order in Germany had already caused a noticeable transfer of large numbers of books. Now many of the other churches and monasteries began to dispose of their treasures, so that eager bibliophiles and dealers in books and manuscripts who knew their business had a profitable time. Typical of the times was the former Benedictine Maugérard, who outwitted all his colleagues by artful dodges, and moreover had no scruples about unsavory dealings.

- 77 -

From 1794 on there were visitations of libraries along the Rhine by French agents. At the start of the new century Maugérard was one of these agents, and he gleaned so thoroughly and used his knowledge and experience so unflaggingly in the service of his Parisian employers that a tablet was later erected to perpetuate his name. Only items of minor value found their way to the dépôts littéraires which had now too been set up on German soil. The regions of Germany which the defeat of Prussia first exposed to the foe suffered no such losses. Only a few collections, like that at Wolfenbüttel, saw part of their holdings temporarily removed to Paris. Göttingen, the most important library of the new kingdom of Westphalia, remained completely intact. In fact, Jerome Bonaparte planned to do with Göttingen in a small way what his brother had striven to carry out at the Bibliothèque Nationale on a large scale. But the books sent to Göttingen from abroad were hardly unpacked when the collapse of the French regime forced their return.

For the remaining libraries of Germany the Principal Decree of the Imperial Deputation in 1803 was decisive.(85) With the disappearance of a host of principalities and city republics, a good many of their libraries vanished from the scene or changed masters. Most important of all, just as in France, seizure of church libraries was now effected.

Secularization achieved its best results in Bavaria, and Munich benefitted especially. A short time before, when the crown had passed to the Palatine line, the very large holdings of the Mannheim library had been transferred to Munich. Now, under the prudent and (despite certain errors) unexceptionable direction of Von Aretin, about 150 church and monastic collections found their way to the capital. As a result the Hofbibliothek at Munich held the leadership among court libraries for a long time, and its wealth in medieval manuscripts and incunabula may well remain forever unsurpassed. In addition to Munich, the Bavarian government provided especially handsomely for Bamberg and Würzburg. Things went correspondingly well, though on a more modest scale, in Württemberg and Baden, where the collections of Stuttgart and Karlsruhe enjoyed considerable growth. The same was true, finally, of Hessen-Darmstadt, while in Nassau, for the most part, resources were squandered in criminal fashion.

For Prussia secularization was no such epoch-making event because the Catholic domain formed but the smaller part of her territory. Moreover, there was no plan of any kind for centralization which would benefit Berlin: only a few of the duplicates which were sent out by the provinces reached that city. More worthy of notice is the growth of resources at Münster and Königsberg and, above all, Breslau. The university was moved from Frankfurt an der Oder to Breslau, and along with it came its book-collection. Thereupon it was planned to make Breslau into a central library like those at Munich and Paris. The transfer of church collections to this library, it is true, was soon stopped, yet the Breslau library received about 70,000 volumes, among them a large number of incunabula.

The changes which have been described produced the problem of making usable these institutions, some of them newly born, some importantly enriched. This task shaped up all the harder because at the same time demands upon libraries had grown heavier--for the following reasons. In the first place, in Germany deepening national consciousness and change in social organization caused libraries generally to be looked upon as public institutions. Then again, the new century brought an increase in scholarly activities by which libraries could not remain unaffected. But they showed themselves quite unprepared for it, as can be understood from the points made in the last chapter. There was practically no such thing as a class of trained librarians. Still, there were two libraries whose organization served as useful models--Dresden and Göttingen.

The Göttingen system now swept triumphantly through Germany. It was carried over into the Prussian university libraries, and so into the newly founded libraries of Bonn and Breslau. That it was put into operation in Berlin, too was due to Wilhelm von Humboldt, who as a student at Göttingen had eagerly cultivated the friendship of Heyne, and who now, in the rebirth of Prussia, assumed decisive leadership of the educational system, even if only for a year. The University of Berlin was founded at this time, and as a consequence the responsibilities of the Royal Library expanded greatly.(86) Through Humboldt's initiative the yearly budget increased, the organizational structure improved, and more liberal arrangements for using the library went into effect. The new alphabetical catalogue stuck close to the Göttingen model. On the other hand, a couple of decades later Schrader used his own methods in setting up a classed catalogue. Since that time the Prussian State Library has had an administrative tool which neither the British Museum nor the Bibliothèque Nationale yet possesses.(87)

At Berlin conditions were relatively simple. But how was the sister institution at Munich to overcome its much stiffer problems?

At first there was an attempt to group by subject the manuscripts which had been acquired, but this track was fortunately abandoned in time. It was Schmeller's great contribution not only to have insured continuation of the historical tradition by re-establishing the principle of provenance, but also to have carried out the cataloguing and shelving according to this principle during the years from 1829 to 1852. Treading in his footsteps, his students and followers could then publish the monumental Munich catalogue of manuscripts.(88)

The same thing happened with the newly acquired books. Here too a few unlucky experiments were made at first until there appeared in Schrettinger just the person to come to the rescue. A keen practical mind, Schrettinger derived from an unsuccessful trial of the Göttingen system the realization that imitation would not lead him to his goal and that the special problem which he faced required a solution of its own. Consequently he classified his mass of books in coordinated groups which he then combined into a few main classes, and completed the alphabetical catalogue up to the year 1818. His other plans were far ahead of his time; some were blocked by the opposition of colleagues and others were never carried out completely. But Schrettinger left them to posterity in his theoretical writings. In them we find also the fundamental theme: "to dispel the chimaera of detailed technique is to lay the foundation of a genuine library science."

Among the opponents of this point of view was F. A. Ebert. He had been trained at Dresden, had steeped himself thoroughly in the system of Francke, and had made it his ideal. Consequently, appointed to head the Wolfenbüttel collection in 1823, he began to reclassify without proper regard to local conditions; then, before the work was done, he returned to Dresden and there--though barely forty-- met his death by falling from a ladder. If, in the light of the above, Ebert's practical accomplishments were of little value, his literary achievements deserve all the greater consideration. We can only mention here his history of the Dresden library, based scrupulously upon reliable sources, his bibliographical dictionary, worked out with careful scholarship,(89) and his original treatise on manuscripts, which grew out of his work with the Wolfenbüttel treasures.

We must glance for a moment at his youthful essay <u>On Public Libraries</u>.(90) Here he waxes sarcastic over university library conditions which were still the rule at the beginning of the nineteenth century, describing the libraries as "dusty, desolate, and unfrequented rooms in which the librarian must spend a few hours weekly to discharge his duties--so that during this time he can be alone!" From this he passes on to proposals for reform, of which the most important asserts: "The hitherto existing practice of librarianship as a part-time affair must be done away with. The proper direction of a public library requires persons endowed with the finest qualities of mind and character, who will bring their abilities to bear on the task before them." These ideas are found again in a more profound and expanded form in a later work, <u>The Training of the Librarian</u>.(91)

"I spend my own energies serving others" (<u>aliis inserviendo consumor</u>) was to be the motto of every capable library worker, according to Ebert, and Schrettinger furnished a public example of this point of view. Where these two differed was in their working methods. Schrettinger, pre-eminently a practical man, had derived new principles from a great new problem; Ebert, the theorizer, remaining for the most part steeped in the ideas of the past century, held fast to the ideals of Francke.

Both Schrettinger and Ebert, however, struggled virtually alone in their day. It would be incorrect to deny altogether in this epoch of poets and thinkers any true interest in the internal organization of libraries: the efforts of Goethe in behalf of the institutions at Jena and Weimar which had been placed under his supervision argue just to the contrary.(92) But it appears in general as if the orientation of knowledge at the time actually made difficult a true understanding of the situation on the part of the educated classes from which the library officials were usually recruited. Even if we consider as an exception the notion of Hoffmann von Fallersleben, curator of the University of Breslau Library, who saw in his office only a sinecure and declared the rigorous demands for service made upon him oppressive and worse than the worst corporal punishment of eighteenth century army discipline, it still remains significant on the whole that the new professional periodical, the <u>Serapeum</u>, ventured to publish his opinions in 1840.

The all-powerful library committee was a disastrous creation, for it led mostly to the already meager funds' being earmarked for the use of special faculties, or indeed of individual professors.(93) At Tübingen the Professor of Constitutional Law, Robert von Mohl, came up against especially bad conditions of this kind. He waged a sturdy fight against them, and in 1836 took over the direction of the library himself. His words show the conception of the duties of the new office which animated him: "The chief librarian, whatever else he may be, must think and plan night and day for his library; in its behalf he must buy and exchange, beg and--one might almost add--steal." But he met strong opposition from his colleagues and the administration, and failed in his attempt to eliminate the influence of the library committee and to regulate the expenditure of funds by uniform and reasonable principles.

The next decades brought the Revolution and then the Reaction. The times were not suitable for fundamental library reforms, which came only after conditions in general had changed. In order to evaluate them properly, however, it is necessary to have some acquaintance with contemporary events in England and France, more particularly with the development of the British Museum and the Bibliothèque Nationale.

The great reform of the British Museum is bound up with the personality of the Italian, Sir Anthony Panizzi. He was not a scholar, though we do have valuable works from his hand, such as the editions of Bojardo, but he devoted himself wholly to public life and took a most active part in politics. Passionate by nature--he had been forced to flee his native land as a Carbonaro--and faced with opposition from many sides in his new position in a foreign land, he loved a fight, yet carried it on not from any personal motives but only in the interests of the institution to which he had dedicated his powers and which he believed himself alone capable of leading to the desired eminence. His contemporaries called him the second founder of the British Museum, the Napoleon of librarians. Garnett, his successor, said of him: "Panizzi governed the library as his friend Cavour governed his country, and in a spirit and with objectives nearly similar, perfecting its internal organization with the one hand while he extended its frontiers with the other."

Panizzi's steady rise--in 1831 he became Extra-Assistant, in 1837 Keeper of Printed Books, finally in 1856 Principal Librarian--only signifies a steady extension of the range of his influence. In reports to the trustees, in oral and written transactions with government commissions, even in social contacts with friends and acquaintances, he fought for his principles, which he had early in his career summarized in the following three sentences: "The (British) Museum is not a show, but an institution for the diffusion of culture. It is a department of the civil service, and should be conducted in the spirit of other public departments. It should be managed with the utmost possible liberality." What this meant for his time is shown by the remark of the contemporary member of Parliament, Cobbett: The British Museum is a place where the rich and the aristocrats go to amuse themselves by reading. Let them pay for their own amusement.(94)

Since its origin, the British Museum's holdings in books and manuscripts had been expanding on a large scale, thanks especially to large and frequent gifts, such as the King's Library, the favorite project of George III. Also, from time to time, Parliament had approved additional appropriations. System and continuity, however, were lacking. Panizzi took the position that the British Museum was called upon to become a national library worthy of a nation like England. It should preserve all English books and the most important foreign literature. Consequently he made sure of a large and regular yearly budget, the appropriation of which was not contingent upon conditions of any kind. The result was that the book-collection quickly doubled, and about 1870 it had already reached 1,000,000 volumes. At the same time he was instrumental in obtaining valuable gifts, notably that of his friend Grenville. Finally, entirely through his personal insistence and despite all opposition, he brought about strict enforcement of the copyright provisions, which had hitherto been administered very negligently.(95)

Panizzi applied himself with similar industry to the problem of cataloguing, which was pressing for solution just at the time he entered the Museum. He opposed the classed catalogue which had already been begun and succeeded in getting an alphabetical catalogue started. For this he drew up rules which before long came to be regarded as canons in the Anglo-Saxon library world. Publication of the catalogue had to be discontinued at first after a premature attempt had been made in deference to the wishes of the trustees, and work under Panizzi's direction was completed only in manuscript; nevertheless printing of the catalogue in later years (1881-1900) was carried through entirely in the spirit of its creator.

Panizzi has a special claim to high repute because of the building changes and additions made to the British Museum in his day. At a time when the continent stuck to the old hall-with-gallery type of building and exerted itself only to increase its dimensions, as the fantastic creations of the Frenchman Horeau illustrate (Pl. XI), when even America could not bring herself to abandon this tradition, Panizzi took the step required by circumstances and separated the rooms used for shelving books and the rooms used by readers. Strongly impressed, in all probability, by the recently completed Crystal Palace, which had shown the dazzling possibilities of iron construction, in 1852 he himself drew up the plan for the reading room. When the building was finished five years later (Pl. XII), the height of its dome and its spaciousness aroused universal admiration: it fell short of the Roman Pantheon by only a very little, and it provided accommodation for several hundred readers.
    The new stack space surrounded the reading room. The principle on which the stacks were constructed had already been enunciated by a writer in Frankfurt, but had attracted no real attention at the time. Gärtner's beautiful building for the Munich library had gone only as far as constructing the galleries low enough to enable the impractical ladders to be dispensed with. In the British Museum the sections of stack had removable shelves, and fireproofing was achieved by the use of iron exclusively. The greatest efforts, however, were expended upon saving space by setting the sections of shelf back to back. The New Library thus constructed (Pl. XIII), represents an epoch in the history of library buildings.
    The first imitation of this British Museum model came in Paris with the extensive enlargement of the Bibliothèque Nationale. This had become a crying need, since the enormous number of books which the Revolution had brought into the library and which had then grown slowly but steadily could now for the first time be arranged so as to form a view of the whole collection. First, after Van Praet's death in 1837, the old and already catalogued parts of the collection were grouped into a fonds porté; the uncatalogued books which had accrued since 1789 and the later acquisitions were gathered into a fonds non porté; both fonds were then divided into the classes of the shelving scheme, which had descended essentially intact from Clément. Then the labor of cataloguing went forward and at first, just as across the Channel, there was an attempt at a classed catalogue.

Some sections were completed and even got into print. But here too the path which had been entered upon did not lead to the desired goal. And what Panizzi had been for London and Schrettinger for Munich, Delisle became for Paris at this fateful moment.

Léopold Delisle was one of the most brilliant representatives of nineteenth-century French scholarship and, without ever occupying a professor's chair, he became the leader of a historical school. As a pupil at the École des Chartes he carried on, as it were, the traditions of the Maurists. Quite naturally, therefore, he devoted himself at first to the Department of Manuscripts, the cataloguing and classification of which is essentially his work. Probably to him even more than to Schmeller belongs the honor of being called the creator of the modern manuscript catalogue. Placed at the head of the library in 1847, Delisle demonstrated his ability as an organizer on a grand scale. He had already shown his determination a short time before by defending the collections against the attacks of the Commune. How well he combined scholarly acuteness with diplomatic skill is shown in the notorious case of Libri. That Italian scholar and adventurer, after having attained a high position in France, had used it to carry to astonishing lengths a plundering of the libraries of Paris and the provinces. The action brought against him became entangled with the political controversies of the year of the Revolution, 1848, and consequently resulted unsatisfactorily. It was not until some decades later that Delisle was able to produce indisputable proofs of the larceny and even to retrieve for France an important part of the stolen treasures.

As head of the library Delisle was to do for the Department of Printed Books what had already been done for the manuscripts. First, within each class he placed the new acquisitions in a special group, the <u>fonds nouveau</u>, within which the books were shelved simply by a running number (<u>numerus currens</u>). At the same time a list of new books--at first written, a bit later printed--began to be issued to the public. Then the still untouched parts of the <u>fonds non porté</u> were worked on, so that by 1893 everything in the library was recorded on cards. Three years later printing of the alphabetical catalogue began. Since then, despite many obstacles, it has been pressing forward steadily, even though the time of its completion is not yet in prospect.(96)

Now if we turn our attention back to Germany, the question forces itself upon us: was what occurred in Germany at the end of the nineteenth century influenced from abroad by the examples of Paris or London? As for Paris, the answer must be negative. Delisle, to be sure, had very active contacts with his colleagues across the Vosges, but Germany already had the completely adequate example of Munich, and (most important of all) the reorganization of the Bibliothèque Nationale came too late to be seriously considered as a model. It was different with regard to Panizzi. That striking personality embodied the ideal which Ebert and Von Mohl had once championed. We know today that those in authority in Germany were in touch with him; systematic research, in my opinion, will make clear the details of these relations. As a result, the new type of building created by Panizzi formed an essential part of the German program of reform, as we shall see.

At the head of this movement stood the philologist, Friedrich Ritschl of Bonn. His biographer has nothing but praise for his term as library director, comprising the years 1854-1865. The recent historian of the library of the University of Bonn, on the other hand, takes obvious pains to depreciate his merits. There is little doubt that he had many truly unpleasant characteristics. Nor do we owe to him any really trail-blazing innovations. But, fired by the example of the Alexandrian Library, which his own investigations had for the first time placed in its true light, he transformed the hitherto badly and rigidly administered Bonn library into a "well managed instrument of ready liberality."

Even more important, however, was the influence of Ritschl's personality. From the ranks of his subordinates and a host of volunteer assistants developed that school of librarians whose effectiveness revealed itself in the seventies. One of them was Klette, whose pamphlet The Autonomy of the Profession of Librarianship(97) contributed in no small measure to a break with the previous system. Another was Dziatzko, who, as Prussia's first professional librarian, reorganized the ill-managed Breslau library wholly in the spirit of his teacher, drew up the exemplary Instructions for the alphabetical card catalogue, and, transferred to Göttingen in 1886, occupied there the newly created chair of Library Science.

Barack, founder and for many years director of the great new Strassburg collection, was a professional librarian. So, too, was Hartwig at Halle. Like Ritschl and Dziatzko he directed his attention chiefly to complete and up-to-date cataloguing of the collection. The fruits of his labors, the scheme of the Halle classed catalogue, won universal approval. His regime is important in another respect. In the years 1878-1880 came the new library building, which made use of the Anglo-French stack system for the first time in Germany. A whole series of additional new buildings followed, bringing into being the new and ever more practical type of lay-out: stack, administrative rooms, reading room, and periodical room. Attempts were made to combine esthetic with practical aims until finally in the Deutsche Bücherei at Leipzig, completed in 1916, the most fortunate answer to the problem was found (Pl. XIV & XV).

But let us not hasten too far ahead of our period! The reform movement laid hold of ever-widening circles and even found strong support within the scholarly world. Realism had replaced idealism. Now the effort was to make sure of single facts by exact methods. In order to master such masses of subject-matter, large-scale organizations were created and progressive differentiation of research carried through. Each individual discipline provided itself with one or more special journals. In all this the library attained a much higher importance than ever before. To administer the collection efficiently and make it ready for use was, so to speak, a necessary element of the whole business of scholarship.

To this we must add that after the formation of the German Empire, with the consequent political and economic prosperity, considerably larger funds had been made available. Moreover, the development of trade and technology increased the possibilities of taking care of the expansion of book-collections just as far as the need of them grew. Finally, the government now also awoke to its obligations toward libraries.

No one was more aware of the importance of the library as a public institution than Althoff, who had been the moving spirit of the Prussian Ministry of Education since the eighties. In his still unwritten biography his efforts in behalf of libraries will take up a good deal of space.(98) We may even speak of an Althoff era. He fought most earnestly for the adequate financing of the institutions under his control. His next concern was for the library staff, its enlargement, improvement of its economic and social status, and finally for adequate training and regular employment. These efforts of the Ministry found support in the new professional journal founded by Hartwig (Zentralblatt für Bibliothekswesen) and in the library association (Verein Deutscher Bibliothekare) founded in 1900, with its annual meetings.

Naturally Althoff's actions especially benefitted the Royal Library at Berlin. The year 1885 brought a reorganization in which its functions as a national institution were greatly expanded. Even if the desired end was not nearly attained, as we shall later see, yet the Royal Library now took a deserved first place among its German sister institutions. And that an occasional violation of the principle ordinarily followed of appointing professional librarians exclusively can lead only to good results is shown in the case of Harnack, who took over direction of the collection in 1905 and supervised its transfer to the splendid new building.(99)

Althoff worked for organic cooperation among all libraries no less industriously than for the welfare of the Royal Library. To this end decree followed upon decree. In 1885 publication was begun in Berlin of yearly catalogues of German university publications,(100) and soon thereafter a catalogue of school program dissertations.(101) From 1892 on, the Berlin library printed lists of newly acquired titles, at first alone, then six years later in conjunction with all the Prussian university libraries.(102) An additional undertaking was the inventory of all the older books up to 1898 in an alphabetical union catalogue. The idea was not new: it had been aired already in several countries. In Germany it had emerged in the forties. Urged on by Althoff, Treitschke brought the matter to a head in an essay in the Preussische Jahrbücher. In the middle of the nineties the work began, and today it is complete in preliminary form. Since the first World War and its consequences made impossible for the time being the printing of the catalogue, the Berlin Information Bureau (Auskunftsbüro Deutscher Bibliotheken) has assumed special importance.(103) It was opened in 1905 and developed into a center of bibliographical research. Finally, all these organizations became useful on a wide scale through the system of interlibrary loan (Deutscher Leihverkehr), which since 1892 has bound German libraries to one another in ever-widening scope.

The other events of Althoff's regime--I call to mind the creation of a German music collection in Berlin and the catalogue of incunabula(104) can only be mentioned in passing. From them all emanates the same spirit. Basically it is Leibniz's plan of organization made real by Althoff and his circle with modern methods and adapted to modern needs.

CHAPTER IX. FROM THE NINETEENTH TO THE TWENTIETH CENTURY

The past fifty years have seen more developments in the library world than any previous period of equal length. Many of them are still in the making, and it is possible to judge them only tentatively. To do justice to them all would require a lengthier and more detailed treatment by far than can be given here. We shall try to sketch the more important of them, concentrating upon three large topics: national and scholarly libraries, the evolution of the public library, and the problems more or less common to all libraries during the current era.

. . .

Many of the great libraries of Europe can now look back upon a long past through which they have developed distinctive characteristics. But in the course of this historic development they have also fallen into groups, usually defined by national boundaries, and these groups possess traits whose explanation is to be found in the history of their respective nations. The history of the great national libraries of France and Great Britain has already been presented. They have gone along their accustomed paths steadily, with some interruption by wars and economic crises, but in essential continuity with their past.(105) These libraries have now been joined by a third, the Library of Congress, which in the past fifty years has taken a place among the first national libraries of the world.

Founded in 1800, the Library of Congress grew rather slowly for the first century of its existence.(106) Thomas Jefferson took a keen interest in the library from the start; in fact its purchases during the first decade were made largely according to his recommendations. In 1814, when the invading British army set fire to Washington, the Library was completely destroyed. Shortly thereafter, Jefferson offered to Congress his distinguished personal collection, which became the nucleus of the new library. Two subsequent fires in 1825 and 1851 wrought no small havoc upon the collections, but their growth went forward steadily. In 1897, when the books were moved into a magnificent new building, there were some 800,000 printed volumes and 200,000 pamphlets. Transfer to the Library of Congress of the Registry of Copyright in 1870 had appreciably accelerated its growth.

In 1899 Herbert Putnam, then librarian of the Boston Public Library, was appointed Librarian of Congress. His administration was truly epoch-making.(107) By the time of his retirement in 1939 the library had grown to some 6,000,000 volumes, and it had become necessary to build a gigantic annex capable of housing over 7,000,000 volumes in addition to reading rooms and work-space for many of the library's processing operations. But physical growth merely reflects the expanding influence of the library, for it has become a center of national culture, and in its encouragement of scholarship and the arts has developed into a kind of national university. Always strong in Americana, the library has built up special fields such as Slavic and Oriental languages, has acquired outstanding collections of music, maps, and prints, and has added impressively to its manuscript holdings. It is impossible to survey here in a brief space the many diverse highlights of its collections,(108) but special note must be made of the attention paid in recent years to Hispanic literature and history.

In 1927 a generous endowment made it possible to create the Hispanic Foundation, and the following year another gift provided for a consultant in Hispanic literature. A beautiful Hispanic Reading Room has been created, and the work of the Foundation, which has grown in cultural importance with the years, is now centered in one section of the building.

The Hispanic Foundation represents the archetype of a scholarly service that has evolved in a number of fields. The library has added to its permanent staff a group of specialists holding endowed chairs and a further group of consultants and fellows, some of the latter being in residence for short terms. Thus the special collections are under constant scrutiny, and in many of the leading fields of learning users of the library may have expert advice.

To add to these notable advances in book-holdings and personnel the Library of Congress has steadily expanded a number of special services which it fulfills as a national institution. Of these perhaps the most widely influential has been distribution of printed catalogue cards. Over 100 libraries in the United States and other countries until recently received depository sets; many of these libraries will now substitute the printed catalogue and its supplements. The possibility of purchasing catalogue cards prepared by experts has revolutionized the cataloguing procedures of American libraries, large and small. A number of the larger reference libraries contribute copy for certain classes of books, thus putting cataloguing in the United States to some extent on a cooperative basis and presenting recurrent inducements to standardize cataloguing practices. With the printing of A Catalog of Books Represented by Library of Congress Printed Cards Issued to July 31, 1942, and the supplements,(109) libraries throughout the world will have a most helpful bibliographical aid. Subject Headings Used in the Dictionary Catalogs of The Library of Congress (5th ed., Washington, 1948), with its cumulative supplements, provides an outstanding cataloguing tool. The library has also published a large number of bibliographies, some highly specialized and exhibiting accomplished scholarship. Particularly useful is the monthly checklist of state documents compiled by the Documents Division.

Another service which grows in importance each year is the Union Catalog, in which some 14,000,000 cards had been filed by 1946 and from which inquiries regularly are sent for books not already recorded which have been requested by readers. Working closely with the Union Catalog is the Photoduplication Service, which has become more and more active with the rapid development of methods of photoduplication in recent years.

Very much more might be said about other outstanding activities of the Library of Congress such as its promotion of music through the Coolidge and Whittall Foundations, but here it may be enough to close with mention of Dr. Putnam's successors. Archibald MacLeish, like Adolf von Harnack, was not a trained librarian, but he quickly acquired a firm grasp of technical problems, while his acknowledged eminence as a literary figure gave the library added impetus as a center of national culture. His impact upon the technical operations of the library is described in his own essay, "The Reorganization of the Library of Congress, 1939-44,"(110) but even more important than organizational reforms were the vision and spirit which he brought with him and infused into the library and its staff. MacLeish's successor, Luther Evans, is distinguished by inexhaustible energy and the vast scope of his interests. Within the first year or two of his tenure he has already put the Library of Congress more firmly at the head of the American library profession than ever before. Some idea of this leadership can be gleaned from the Annual Reports from 1945 to 1947.

Apart from the Library of Congress there are many research libraries scattered through the United States and

Canada. Some are private institutions like the Huntington Library in California. Others are public libraries like the New York Public Library, which, with some 4,500,000 volumes (in 1947), is one of the greatest research libraries in the world. The majority, however, are university libraries. A few have long histories and great collections. The Harvard University Library, for example, is just over 300 years old and now (1947) contains just under 5,000,000 volumes; the Yale University Library, dating from 1701, now (1947) owns over 3,600,000 volumes. But many are fairly young. This is particularly true in the Midwest, where collections to be reckoned with, sometimes running to a million volumes or more, have been built up in less than a century. It is characteristic of all these institutions, whatever their structure and financial support, that they are liberally open to any serious student with little formality.

The continuing influence of regional and particularistic forces has long been characteristic of Germany. Political unification of the numerous small states and principalities is comparatively recent, and even the intense and comprehensive measures of unification undertaken by the Third Reich did not obliterate differences of tradition and practice rooted deep in the history of institutions. In the individual states of Germany there are state, provincial, and university libraries quite dissimilar in structure. Along with these are to be found municipal libraries in each of which a distinctive local character persists. Taking prewar statistics, Berlin far surpassed any other German city in book-holdings. The Prussian State Library alone contained nearly 3,000,000 volumes,(111) and the other Berlin libraries, including those of the numerous government agencies, together had about 8,000,000 volumes. But the Bavarian State Library at Munich had over 2,000,000 volumes, and the annexation of Austria acquired temporarily for Germany two very large institutions with over a million volumes--the Vienna National Library and the Vienna University Library. Moreover Germany had five state and municipal libraries with about a million volumes, and five with about half a million volumes. The recent war has wrought havoc upon practically all the great libraries of Germany.(112) So serious has been the damage that Germany may never regain its centuries-long eminence in library matters.

For years efforts to create a German national library were frustrated by the problem of depository copies. In

1848 the publisher Hahn of Hanover presented his stock of publications to the Frankfurt Parliament as the nucleus of a national library. About forty colleagues followed his example, and a librarian was appointed to take charge. Several years later the books of this new institution were removed to the Germanic Museum at Nüremburg. Not until after the Empire was established did Hahn's plan revive. Then the publisher Brockhaus took it up; Treitschke discussed it in the Preussische Jahrbücher; and the librarians Dziatzko, Hartwig, and Wilmanns addressed a memorandum to the Ministry of Education. Among other things the plan at this time called for building up the Royal Library at Berlin into a great national institution. But now, when political conditions were not unfavorable, the publishers balked at being called upon by a law of the Reich to deposit copies of their books. Opposition came also from special groups: for example, not long afterwards several attempts were made to establish a separate Catholic central library.

Despite all obstacles the project did not bog down. For this credit is due first and foremost to Althoff, who saw in its consummation the crowning of his efforts in behalf of libraries. To him can be traced the proposal to create a separate library of the Association of German Publishers and Book-dealers (Börsenverein der Deutschen Buchhändler) and he did not insist that it should be located in Berlin. In 1912 an agreement was signed by the State of Saxony, the City of Leipzig, and the Börsenverein creating the Deutsche Bücherei. According to its statutes the function of the Deutsche Bücherei is "beginning with January 1, 1913 to collect all literature which appears in German and in foreign languages within Germany, to preserve it, to make it available, and to record it by scientific principles." Heroic efforts were exerted to induce all publishers, associations, official bodies, and those who issued works outside the trade to submit deposit copies to the Deutsche Bücherei. By 1916 a high degree of success had been achieved.

Not only does the Deutsche Bücherei serve as a German book archive; it also performs extensive reference services, maintains public reading rooms, and lends books when they cannot be obtained from another German library. By far its most important function aside from collecting is its bibliographical publishing. In 1921 it began to issue three trade bibliographies--a daily and a weekly list of new books and a list of new periodical and serial publications. The preparation of a monthly list of official publications began in 1928. The greatest bibliographical undertaking is the Deutsche Nationalbibliographie, begun in 1931. Four years later the Deutsche Bücherei took over publication of the Jahresverzeichnis der deutschen Hochschulschriften, which was assigned to it by the Ministry for Science, Education, and Popular Enlightenment. Urged on by the same ministry, in 1937 the Deutsche Bücherei entered upon a project that had been desired since 1920--centralized cataloguing. Special library issues of the trade bibliography have been printed on one side of the sheet for some years and used by some 200 libraries; in 1937 printed cards began to appear which are now used by over 150 libraries.(113)

Severe economic stringency, particularly the postwar inflation of the early twenties, seriously threatened the very existence of the Deutsche Bücherei: indeed in 1920 it was even proposed to close the institution. But support rallied around the library from all sides. The most encouraging move came from the Reich, which recognized the library as an institution of national significance and became a regular contributor to its income. The seizure of power by the National Socialists gradually led to the assumption by the Third Reich of the leading role in the control of the library. Revision of the copyright laws of the several German states in 1935 removed the deposit of copies from the status of voluntary contributions and achieved in effect a national law of legal deposit. In 1940 a government decree changed the legal basis of the library, making it a public institution under the supervision of the Minister of Folk Enlightenment and Propaganda. The Deutsche Bücherei came through the war with only slight damage; of all the major libraries in Germany, it is in the best position to carry on its normal functions in the postwar period.

In contrast to Germany, France has long been considered the example par excellence of strong central government and this tendency is reflected in the organization of French library service.(114) The Bibliothèque Nationale is by far the largest library in the country, with about 4,500,000 volumes. The remaining libraries of Paris together have some 8,000,000. Administratively, furthermore, several of the more important Parisian libraries, such as the Arsenal, the Sainte Geneviève, and the Mazarine, are under the aegis of the Bibliothèque Nationale. The National and University Library of Strasbourg (Bibliothèque Nationale et Universitaire de Strasbourg) possessed a fine collection of 1,700,000 volumes, of which some 500,000 were lost during the war.(115) Aside from all these there are only three other libraries in France which approach or exceed 500,000 volumes. As was pointed out in the previous chapter, the Revolution inaugurated a movement toward uniformity which affected chiefly the large state libraries and university libraries. The Ministry of Education, by virtue of a series of decrees over a long span of years, has produced a good deal of uniformity in staff and administration. Even municipal libraries, though left to local authority, are subject to ministerial supervision.(116) What such impressive organization can accomplish is shown by the printing of the Catalogue général des manuscrits des bibliothèques publiques de France which, begun in 1885, is now virtually complete. Germany, by contrast, had to labor for some forty years before similar nationwide undertakings such as the German Union Catalogue could reach the printing stage.

In its library organization Italy holds a position halfway, as it were, between France and Germany. It has many great old collections which grew up individually over a long period. With the political unification of Italy these libraries were taken under the wing of the new kingdom and a high degree of uniformity was introduced into their organization, a process which was continued and perhaps intensified under the Fascist regime.

There are thirty-two state libraries in Italy, many of them formerly old and famous private libraries whose history we have already traced.(117) Of these, two (at Florence and Rome) are national central libraries entitled to a copy of every book published in the republic. The National Central Library at Florence (Biblioteca Nazionale Centrale di Firenze), formerly the Magliabechi Library, is the largest in Italy, with over 2,500,000 volumes and pamphlets. Since 1886 it has published the official national bibliography, the Bollettino delle pubblicazioni italiane. The Victor Emmanuel National Central Library (Biblioteca Nazionale Centrale Vittorio Emmanuele II) at Rome concentrates on collecting foreign books, and publishes a list of foreign publications acquired by Italian state libraries, the Bollettino delle opere moderne straniere acquisitate delle biblioteche pubbliche governative del Regno d'Italia. Five other libraries on the peninsula are designated "national" libraries; each is located in the chief city of a province, and exercises general supervision over the libraries of the province. There are still many fine private libraries in Italy and a large number of church libraries, headed by the two great papal institutions, the Ambrosian Library at Milan and the Vatican Library.

Italy can boast of one of the great libraries of the world in the Vatican. After a period of relative quiescence this library took a new lease on life late in the nineteenth century and transformed itself into one of the most progressive and efficiently administered libraries in Europe. This progress has been accomplished under the leadership of a succession of extraordinarily brilliant directors: Father (later Cardinal) Franz Ehrle, 1895-1913; Mgr. Achille Ratti, 1913-1922 (before this he had been librarian of the Ambrosian, and later became Pope Pius XI); Mgr. (later Cardinal) Giovanni Mercati, 1922-1936; and the present incumbent, Mgr. Anselmo Albareda; in addition, Cardinal Eugene Tisserant was Curator of Oriental Manuscripts from 1908-1930, and Acting Director from 1930-1936. Many notable collections have been acquired by the Vatican Library in the past few decades: among them might be mentioned the collections of the Borghese and Barberini families, the Chigi Library, the Caetani Archives, and many others of high distinction. Numerous improvements in buildings and administration, begun under Father Ehrle, culminated in the grandiose reorganization effected under the sponsorship of Pius XI. In 1888, under Leo XIII, the Vatican Library had been thrown open to the public, a reference room created, and added space provided for readers. As new collections streamed in with the passing years, more space was urgently needed. Various make-shifts only postponed the inevitable readjustments and enlargements which, begun in 1927 and completed in 1933, have greatly increased the book capacity, partly by the use of Snead stacks, and provided excellent quarters for staff and readers.

The building program undertaken in 1927 coincided with a wholesale reorganization of the administrative procedures of the library, in particular with a notable reform of its cataloguing. After preliminary negotiations carried on in 1926 and 1927, a group of leading American librarians, headed by William Warner Bishop, librarian of the University of Michigan, and sponsored by the Carnegie Endowment for International Peace, arrived at the Vatican in February, 1928. In the meantime four members of the library staff had been sent to the United States to study American methods. As a result of the work of the visiting commission, a complete new cataloguing system for printed books, very similar to the American system, was adopted. The Library of Congress made the Vatican Library one of its depositories for card sets, and the library, in turn, adopted Library of Congress printed cards in cataloguing its books. Cards are printed for books not represented by Library of Congress cards, and are sold to other libraries. A classified catalogue of Library of Congress cards is also maintained. A manual of cataloguing rules based upon Library of Congress practice has been published, and is now in its second edition.(118) This manual, along with the successful demonstration of a dictionary catalogue in use, has already had some effect upon other European libraries. The Vatican Library still retains its hereditary character as a great manuscript collection, and consequently close attention was paid to the cataloguing of manuscripts. A card index was decided upon as the most useful approach to the collection.(119)

The influence of the Vatican Library upon other libraries and upon the world of scholarship is strengthened not only by its cataloguing but also by publications of great scholarly value. The latest expansion of its scope is the creation of a library school designed primarily to train personnel for ecclesiastical and parochial libraries. With all these activities the Vatican Library has moved into the very front rank of European libraries.

Only brief notice can be taken here of other European nations. The Scandinavian countries have flourishing national libraries, and have given special effort to building public library service around their national libraries. One of the youngest European national libraries is the Swiss National Library at Bern. Founded in 1895, it has grown quite rapidly, and now has over 700,000 volumes. In 1931 it formally opened a new building which is one of the leading examples of modern functional library architecture. New books are deposited by the great majority of Swiss publishers on a voluntary basis, in return for which the publisher receives a copy of the monthly bulletin of new books, Das Schweizer Buch (Le livre Suisse), published by the library. Other current bibliographies are also issued, and a union catalogue listing the holdings of over a hundred Swiss libraries is maintained.(120)

In Russia the Leningrad Public Library, historically the great national library, has made tremendous strides since the Revolution. In the past thirty years the number of volumes has just about trebled, partly as a result of government confiscation of private libraries. All modern improvements in library practice have been eagerly investigated, and many adopted. For example, the library prints some 50,000 card sets each year and exchanges them with such diverse institutions as the Vatican Library and the Library of Congress. Much too little is known as yet to the Western world of Russian libraries, but two other developments may be pointed out. One is the Lenin Memorial Library in Moscow, for which a vast new modern building has just been completed, and which is today possibly the largest library in the world. The other is the great number of large collections constituting libraries of academies, institutes, and universities, as well as regional and provincial libraries scattered over the vast expanse of the Soviet Union. We shall have more to say about these in discussing popular libraries further along in this chapter.

. . .

We have seen how one of the forces determining the recent development of libraries has been nationalism, how the character of a single library or of a group of libraries is conditioned by the size and organization of the social order to which it belongs. But there are even wider determining forces--the general historical conditions of an age, in the broadest sense of the term. The period from 1815 to the present has been characterized historically by nationalism. But there has been another movement which has swept across national boundaries and been united by common ties all over the world. If we wish to assign specific dates, we might say that the century beginning with 1848 has been the century of the common man. Enlargement of political franchise and spread of education have been paralleled by the development of the public library. Aside from formal education there has been what might be called general popularization of knowledge. In the United States the Lyceum movement and Chatauqua were really forms of the adult education movement which is so strong today. Similar activities are to be found in other countries. In this century one of the striking phenomena in the publishing world has been the success of popularizations of scientific and scholarly advances. Since it is the United States which has made the most progress in this respect, we shall sketch the American movement before going on to Europe.

Limitless faith in education has grown to be part of the American idea. That acute observer, Alexis de Tocqueville, wrote in 1835: "In the United States the whole education of the people is directed toward politics."(121) Only education can make people capable of governing themselves wisely, and only education can cause one great united nation to distill out of the heterogeneous elements poured into the melting pot. Everyone, regardless of birth or position, must be educated to be a worthy citizen of what Münsterberg has called "ethical democracy." In this educational process the library has acquired a place alongside the school. Much of the success of the American public library arises from the early realization that it must continue the educational work of the school and provide further opportunities for those whose formal schooling has ended. Consequently the library aims to broaden the interests of its readers, to help them with their vocational problems, and to supply good recreational reading. Every effort is made to attract all classes of people, to remove all hindrances, and thus to make the widest possible use of books. Something of the enthusiasm and technique of American business has slipped into American library practice: the library tries to "sell" the worth-whileness of its wares to the user. Publicity devices such as exhibitions, newspaper articles, and radio broadcasts are actively exploited, and suggestions from the public welcomed. The library often sponsors lectures or musical programs, and thus takes its place as the cultural and intellectual center of the city. These attempts to improve educational facilities in the widest sense have caused the American public library to be referred to as "the people's university."

But the so-called American idea itself was something which developed in the eighteenth century and became articulate with the Revolution; then there arose the vast problem of implementing the idea by practical measures. Faith in education was but a corollary of the notion of the indefinite perfectibility of man, a leading idea of the Enlightenment which found its way via the French philosophes into the mental furniture of such men as Franklin and Jefferson. Achievement of a comprehensive educational system took years. The earliest colonial tradition was to provide schooling for the children of those who could afford it. The first American universities, such as Harvard, William and Mary, and Yale, were designed essentially to train new members of the ministry. Only gradually was free education provided by the community for those children whose parents could not afford to furnish it at their own expense, and even then these common schools smacked of charity and were often not attended by children of more prosperous families. Not until the middle of the nineteenth century did the concept of free common schools for all children gain ascendancy, and the first state law making education compulsory was not passed until 1852.

The typical American public library as we now know it, a free, tax-supported institution, likewise did not come into being until the middle of the nineteenth century.(122) In the two hundred years preceding it, several other kinds of libraries supplied reading matter to the public. We shall pass over private libraries and early college libraries as not being really public. Among the earliest public libraries were those established in some of the southern states, notably Maryland, Virginia, and the Carolinas, by the Rev. Thomas Bray, the eminent divine and missionary. There were also some parish libraries in existence in northern states. Dr. Bray, entrusted with supervision of Anglican churches in Maryland, saw that one of the conditions which would attract young clergymen of ability to the colony was assurance of having books at their disposal. Consequently he set about providing parish libraries "for the clergy and gentry." The basic collection for these libraries was carefully supervised by Dr. Bray, catalogues were drawn up, and provisions made for lending books.(123)

The next important step was instigated by no less a personage than Benjamin Franklin. This was the organization in 1731 of the first subscription library in America, the Free Library Company of Philadelphia. The next hundred years saw the founding of similar libraries in many other cities, the best known being the Boston Athenaeum, the New York Society Library, and the Charleston (S.C.) Library Society. Some of the subscription libraries have retained their independence to the present day. A larger number, however, were either forced out of existence by the subsequent emergence of public libraries, or evolved into public libraries.

Membership in a subscription library, however, was possible only for those of better-than-average means, and even so it was not long before many subscription libraries found it expedient to admit readers on the basis of an annual subscription without enforcing the condition of an initial purchase of shares. Meanwhile other strata of the populace began to organize libraries to serve their needs. The first decades of the nineteenth century saw the beginnings of mechanics' and mercantile libraries, the desirability and general character of which had already been outlined by Franklin. These libraries were motivated primarily by the needs of young men--artisans, mechanics, clerks--to improve themselves in their vocations and to spend their leisure to good advantage: in this way they hoped to acquire broader culture and to rise in their careers.

None of these libraries was yet a public library in the present connotation of the term. The bridge between the "social" libraries we have been describing and the true public library was the school-district library. In 1835 the New York state legislature passed a law authorizing each school-district to lay a tax for the purchase of libraries. Subsequent legislation and grants of money enabled the school-district libraries to blossom rapidly. Other states imitated the system; by 1876 nineteen additional states had passed similar laws. But the school-district was not a practicable unit, and administrative difficulties and political abuses caused the New York school-district library movement to pass its peak and start downhill within twenty years. A similar fate befell these libraries in other states. A relic of the school-district movement remains today in about half a dozen states, with forty cities having public libraries organized on the basis of the school-district as the governmental unit, and even here, as Joeckel has been able to show, the looser the connection between school and library, the better the library service.(124) The school-district movement in the two decades after 1835 had acted nevertheless as an entering wedge: taxes had been authorized by state legislatures for the support of public libraries.

A true public library, supported by public taxation but still without a state enabling act, was established by the town of Peterborough, New Hampshire, in 1833. To the state of New Hampshire also goes credit for having passed the first general library law in 1849. But leadership in the movement was soon taken over by the state of Massachusetts and its capital city, Boston. During the first half of the nineteenth century some sixty laws relating to libraries had been passed by Massachusetts. In 1848 the city of Boston was authorized to establish a tax-supported public library. In 1851 a general law extended the privilege to other towns throughout the state. At first limits were set to tax increases for library purposes, but these were later abolished. Since 1890 the state has provided funds for the promotion of libraries and has created a library commission which has served as a model for other states. In 1939

Massachusetts had 405 public libraries, 77 of them in communities with less than 1000 inhabitants.

There had been lively interest in a public library in Boston for some time before the legislative act made it possible to go ahead with its creation. One of its most enthusiastic proponents was the Harvard professor, George Ticknor, who had studied at Göttingen in 1815 and been profoundly impressed by the richness and liberality of the university library. During the years when the proposal to establish the library was being pushed, Ticknor wrote in one of his letters: "The public library should come in at the end of our system of free instruction, and be fitted to continue and increase the effects of that system by the self-culture that results from reading"--this in contrast to Prussia, where one had no such opportunity after leaving school. Ticknor's program, supported by a group of eminent Bostonians, became realized in 1854 with the opening of the Boston Public Library. The library has grown steadily, has twice acquired a new building, has established branch libraries and deposit stations throughout the city, and in 1939 possessed about 1,750,000 volumes, including some splendid special collections.

The greatest of American public libraries, the New York Public Library, developed out of three large endowments. In 1848 the merchant prince, John Jacob Astor, left $400,000 for the purpose of founding a library, which was incorporated in 1849. Its director, Joseph Green Cogswell, once a fellow-student of Ticknor's at Göttingen, had spent some years before Astor's death buying books for the library on Astor's commission. A second independent foundation, established in 1870, was the Lenox Foundation, containing a distinguished collection. The will of Samuel J. Tilden, a prominent citizen and man of affairs, who died in 1886, left a large bequest to be used for establishing and maintaining a free public library in New York City, but litigation delayed execution of the will for some years. These three separate endowments were merged in 1895. In 1896 a great organizer, John Shaw Billings, became Director of the New York Public Library.(125) Under his leadership, and speeded by a munificent gift in 1901 from Andrew Carnegie, which created 65 branches at one stroke, there took place a merger of a number of circulating libraries, which had been operating independently, with the New York Public Library. Today the library has a Reference Department with a massive building in the center of the city containing a superb collection of some 3,000,000 volumes and a Circulation Department with about 1,500,000 volumes and 60-odd branches.

In general the progress of the American public library movement was slow until the last quarter of the nineteenth century. The year 1876--something of a wonder year in American cultural history--witnessed a number of developments which measurably accelerated the movement. In that year the American Library Association was founded, and the first number of the Library Journal appeared. The American Catalogue and the special report of the United States Bureau of Education on public libraries were published. The Library Bureau was established to supply libraries with the various kinds of equipment they require. Melvil Dewey published the first edition of his Decimal Classification and took a leading part in creating the American Library Association. From this year on Dewey's influence in the library world was strong up to the end of the century. It was he who headed the first library school in the United States, opened in 1887. Since that time a number of library schools have been founded, concerning which we shall have more to say later.

Certain characteristics and traditional services have come to be recognized as part of the essence of the American public library. These we shall try to outline, with the one precautionary reservation that what is being portrayed is a type and that variations from this type are very great among American public libraries. In general a large public library will have all the features menioned, and more,(126) whereas the smaller libraries will not provide all these services. A typical, well-organized public library, then, is open long hours, usually well into the evening and often on Sundays. An open stack, giving readers direct access to the books, is one of the important American contributions to public library practice. In addition, book lists showing new accessions are often published, and a readers' advisory service is maintained. Efforts are made to display the library's facilities in connection with contemporary problems such as proposed legislation, or political and social questions, or with historic occasions such as national holidays. Various other publicity devices already mentioned are freely used. Not infrequently there is a lecture room in the library building. In addition to circulating books practically all American libraries consider it part of their function to maintain reference service which will provide information with speed and efficiency. This service is a kind of bridge between public and scholarly libraries in the United States, for as a public library grows in size and its reference service expands, it takes on some of the functions performed by university and special research libraries. A recent, but fast developing service, of which the Library of Congress is now the center, is provision of books for the blind.

Among the finest activities of American public libraries are their provisions for children. Separate rooms are opened with collections of juvenile literature graded according to age, and librarians have paid much attention to the psychology of children and their use of books. Children's librarians work closely with schools, sending special collections to the classroom on loan, and in return teachers encourage and instruct children, beginning in the lowest grades, in the use of the library. Here is a close and fruitful relation between school and library operating to lay a firm foundation for the great educational achievement envisioned in the American idea.

American public libraries owe their existence, for the most part, to local initiative abetted by private philanthropy. The greatest individual benefactor of public libraries, Andrew Carnegie, who gave over $40,000,000 for public library buildings, insisted on preserving local responsibility by making his grants contingent upon the guarantee of minimal support of the library by the community. Under these conditions, and considering also the differences in geography, economic resources, date of settlement, and other cultural factors throughout this vast and various continent, it is not surprising that the quality of library service should vary widely from place to place. Particularly inadequate have been services to rural communities which fall outside the governmental limits of municipalities. Following the example set by Massachusetts, state library commissions were created, and in a number of states such as New York, Ohio, Indiana, and particularly California, with its system of free county libraries, much was done to eliminate the condition. But the depression of the thirties and social analyses which came in its wake forced a painful awakening to the fact that some forty million people in the United States were still without library service.

Much of this is due to the complex and irrational governmental structure of the American public library, which puts artificial obstacles in the way of regional library service. To the problem C. B. Joeckel has devoted a masterly study, and one of his suggestions, library service on the basis of municipal trading areas, may be a practicable solution, though it will involve difficulties in political, legislative, and administrative readjustment. Many of the areas are so poor--and are furthermore sections of larger areas, such as counties or states, suffering from financial distress-- that nothing short of federal subsidy similar to that advanced for agricultural extension and vocational education would be effective at present. The federal government is conscious of this problem. In 1938 a Division of Library Service was created in the Office of Education, and while it is yet too early to pass judgment, the Division gives every promise of worth-while achievement. At any rate, experiments with regional library service made possibly by new conditions, such as those in the Tennessee Valley, demonstrate what can be done by basing library service upon regions which have natural geographic and economic unity.

The British public library system shows marked likeness to the American in many respects, yet there are interesting differences. The average British public library is perhaps not so highly developed as its American counterpart: in particular, certain techniques such as library publicity have not been carried through so thoroughly because of differences of tradition. Other long-established American developments, for example county libraries and library schools, came fairly late to Great Britain. On the other hand, as will appear, planning for library service on a nationwide basis has been carried farther in Great Britain than in the United States.

The question of priority and of influence in historical development cannot be fully answered.(127) That each country has influenced the other continuously is hardly to be doubted. Aside from the constant traditional cultural interchange, there are such specific instances as the early affiliation of the American Library Association and the Library Association of the United Kingdom, and in general the parallel evolution of so many features of the institution in both countries. For example, open stack, Dewey Decimal Classification, and reference service are to be found in most British and American public libraries. Most significant historically is the fact that the great initial impetus to the development of the public library system came at exactly the same time in both countries. Unquestionably we have here a case of the simultaneous operation of the same large social force, the Industrial Revolution with its attendant phenomena--emergence of large cities, growth of a laboring class needing improved technical education, enlargement of the franchise, and growing political consciousness of the people, along with spread of education.

In Great Britain tentative attempts to provide public libraries quite similar to those in the United States can be traced back well over two centuries before the start of true public libraries. There were a few instances of libraries established by individual municipalities as early as the first decade of the seventeenth century. The Rev. Thomas Bray founded parish libraries in Great Britain also, some of them still being maintained. There were likewise the familiar subscription libraries (probably the most illustrious survivor of this type is the famous London Library, which was founded in 1841), and mechanics' libraries were especially numerous.

The parliamentary committee appointed in 1835 to inquire into the reform of the British Museum turned up a good deal of information concerning the state of other libraries throughout the realm. This marked the beginning of agitation for improved public libraries, in the forefront of which was Edward Edwards, whose efforts have entitled him to be considered the spiritual father of the English public library movement. He combined theoretical insight with practical ability and unceasing industry. In 1849, when a parliamentary committee began to take evidence concerning public libraries, Edwards played a leading role in supplying it. He worked closely with the chairman, William Ewart, who was to be found in the front rank of every fight for public education. Through Ewart, Edwards furnished the committee with detailed data he had been collecting for some years, and sponsored a number of general principles which eventually found their way into the committee's report. The account which Edwards has written of the public library movement in his country is still a classic.

In 1845 Parliament had passed a law empowering town councils to levy taxes for the purpose of establishing public museums. The town of Warrington had taken advantage of this law to establish a museum and a library. Now, in 1850, Parliament extended the taxing power of the town councils to the establishment of public libraries in boroughs of over 10,000 population. Further legislation in succeeding years culminated in the Public Libraries Act of 1892, providing that every urban district, and every parish in England and Wales not within an urban district, shall be a library district. Similar laws were passed for Scotland and Ireland about the same time. With some modifications, these are still the main library laws under which British libraries operate.(128)

The Library Act of 1850 was permissive: it still left the founding of libraries to local initiative. A few cities were quick to take advantage of the act and, as the years passed, more and more cities were added to their number. Yet, on the whole, progress was slow. Extension of school legislation in the seventies caused a quickening of tempo, as did also the founding of the Library Association in 1877. The Jubilee Year of Queen Victoria, 1887, was widely celebrated by the founding of libraries. But perhaps the most important impetus came from the benefactions of J. Passmore Edwards and of Andrew Carnegie, culminating in creation of the Carnegie United Kingdom Trust in 1913. The large industrial city of Manchester has played in England a role of analagous to that of Boston in the United States. Its public library was opened in 1852 and directed for six years by Edward Edwards in exemplary manner. To the present day it continues to be a leader among British public libraries. Metropolitan London, however, has always lagged behind, partly because of the complexity of its governmental structure.

Great Britain has been ahead of the United States in at least one very important aspect of its public library system -- nationwide coverage. Legally this can be accomplished with comparative ease. In the United States permissive measures for local library units have had to be passed in each of the 48 states, which has meant a good deal of variety in library laws. In Great Britain, Parliament has been able from the beginning to pass laws providing for all the United Kingdom. This effects greater unity from the start. The first World War resulted in the necessity of economic reconstruction for the nation. Among the comprehensive measures for reconstruction was the Library Act of 1919, which removed hitherto obstructive limits to library taxation and created county library authorities.

The most important single factor making for nationwide coverage, however, is the development of the National Central Library. Chiefly as a result of demands made by educators, this was established in 1916 with a Carnegie grant as the Central Library for Students to act as a center of bibliographical information and as a central lending agency. It has steadily expanded its functions, with constant support of the Carnegie United Kingdom Trust. In 1930 the name was changed to the National Central Library, and in 1937 it occupied new large, modern quarters. The National Central Library has had vast influence in inducing library cooperation throughout Britain, as well as British cooperation with other countries. It has affiliated with it a number of general and special libraries known as "outliers" which agree to lend books from their collections upon request. The university libraries too, after an abortive attempt at a cooperative system of their own, joined the National Central Library system. During the past fifteen years regional bureaus have been built up to act as intermediaries between the individual student and the National Central Library. It is thus possible for a reader who wishes a particular title to apply directly to the National Central Library (if he lives in one of the comparatively few British areas without library service) or to his public library, which, if it does not have the book, will apply to the regional bureau or, if there is no regional bureau, directly to the National Central Library. By means of union catalogues or other bibliographical aids either the regional bureau or the central library will supply the book, borrowing it, perhaps, from an affiliated library, or buying it if other methods fail. The service given by the National Central Library has steadily expanded, and appreciation of its usefulness has increased.

The economic depression of the thirties and the outbreak of the second World War combined to bring the problem of nationwide library service to the fore. After the first World War study of this problem continued. In 1927 the Report on Public Libraries aroused considerable interest, but was rather indeterminate. It was followed in 1929-30 by the Final Report of the Royal Commission on National Museums and Galleries, which made recommendations for libraries. The McColvin report,(129) which appeared during the war, analyzes the current state of affairs and makes courageous and far-flung plans for the reorganization of British library service. The report faces squarely the several inadequacies of present-day conditions and advances detailed proposals to reconstruct the library system, if possible, in conjunction with changes in government and taxation, but if not, by a reform within the organization of library service itself which will be based upon geographic and economic regional units naturally suited to provide the service. Whatever happens to the specific recommendations of this report, its penetration, courage, and idealism augur well for British libraries in the postwar era.

In turning from American and British public libraries to those of continental Europe one must be careful to make certain definitions and distinctions. The term "public library" has come to be used for a library specifically and avowedly open for free general public use and financed by public taxation. Many "public" libraries in Europe are open to a fairly restricted clientele; a much smaller proportion than in the United States or Great Britain are publicly financed; and many of the libraries opened specially for popular reading charge small fees. Europe has always been-- and still is--outstanding for its large number of fine private libraries. In some measure the very existence of these private libraries has militated against the establishment of public libraries, for often they have been liberally opened to the serious student. The public libraries of Europe fall into two large classes: the so-called "learned," "scholarly," or "scientific" libraries (wissenschaftliche Bibliotheken) and the popular libraries (Volksbibliotheken). In the first group are to be found the great reference libraries belonging to the nation, to universities, to learned societies and institutions, and in some cases to private individuals who place little obstruction in the way of their use by the general public. These libraries we have already examined in some detail. The libraries of the second group vary considerably from country to country. In general the popular library serves primarily as a lending center. Little or no attempt is made to give reference service or gradually to build up a more serious background collection, a process which occurs naturally, so to speak, in British and American libraries. The popular library performs roughly the circulation functions of an American public library without offering to its users the adjoining potentialities for reference work or more serious study.

One exception to these generalizations must be made at the outset--the popular libraries of the Scandinavian countries. The development of the Scandinavian public library systems occurred at the turn of this century, when the American public library movement was already vigorous enough to exert strong influence. Norway was the first to adopt American methods such as open access, dictionary catalogue, and simplified charging systems. A number of Norwegians visited and studied in the United States and returned to pioneer in the transmission of American methods to their own country, from which these methods radiated to Denmark and Sweden. Two of the Norwegian pioneers, H. Tambs Lyche and Haakon Nyhuus, deserve special mention.(130) In Denmark the educator A. S. Steenberg, learning of American methods from a publication by the Austrian professor Eduard Reyer, enthusiastically propagandized for them. In all three Scandinavian countries the central government exercises careful supervision over libraries, largely by means of grants which reward good local library service. Technical aid in book-selection, purchase, and cataloguing is also given by the government. Nationwide coverage is very good; indeed Denmark has been pointed to as ideal in this respect.

Germany has long been famous for its scholarly libraries and also for its many private libraries. But the development of popular libraries has been rather halting. Its first stage came between the wars of liberation (1813-15) and the middle of the century, which brought widespread social revolutions. Many small libraries belonging to associations of artisans and to educational association, and also a number of travelling libraries in rural districts sprang into existence. Worthy of note here is the work of the revenue official Karl Preusker, who propagandized for libraries for the community, brought about creation of a municipal library at Grossenhain in Saxony, and stimulated the Saxon Economic Society (Sächsische Ökonomische Gesellschaft) to establish village libraries.

Much of this progress failed to survive the mid-century revolution and the reaction which followed. A happy exception is to be seen in the public libraries of Berlin, which originated through the efforts of the historian Friedrich von Raumer, who, as Ranke says, "was on the side of every moment of his time that could be called progressive." Motivated by impressions of a trip to America, he founded the Association for Scientific Lectures (Verein für Wissenschaftliche Vorträge) in 1841, and made over its large proceeds to the city of Berlin, so that in 1850 the first four popular libraries could be opened. After almost two decades of continuous support from the association, the city took over sole financial responsibility. In the 1890's there was a reorganization: the book-collections were brought up to date, funds increased, and more convenient hours of opening adopted. In 1907 a central library was created, and the organization of Berlin public library service has been suggested as a type toward which other municipalities should tend.(131) Before the war the central scholarly library had some 350,000 volumes. Under its control were some 130 popular libraries and special reading rooms. These were scattered through the 20 administrative districts of Berlin and the director of the Berlin Municipal Library had final control on technical and cultural policies and practices.

Progress outside Berlin had to wait until after the Empire was founded. In the last decade of the nineteenth century the larger cities made considerable gains. Two individuals must be singled out as leaders in the movement: Constantin Nörrenberg, librarian at Kiel, who had become acquainted with American practices on a trip to the Chicago Exposition in 1896, and Eduard Reyer, a Viennese professor who had also travelled in the United States and England, and who created a noteworthy organization of popular libraries (the Verein Zentralbibliothek) in his homeland. One result of this awakening interest in popular libraries was the founding of a professional journal, the Blätter fur Volksbibliotheken und Lesehallen, in 1900.(132) Several societies also served the cause well: the Society for Ethical Culture (Gesellschaft für Ethische Kultur), with its establishment of public reading rooms, the Comenius Society (Comenius-Gesellschaft), and the Society for the Spread of Popular Education (Gesellschaft zur Verbreitung der Volksbildung), whose activities were especially beneficial for rural districts and small communities.

In agricultural districts several German states encouraged the creation of regional organizations with travelling libraries. Saxony and Württemberg were the first to provide modest state aid, and Prussia has a long history of state sponsorship. In the frontier regions specially strong efforts were made to provide books. In 1896 a Union of Upper Silesian Popular Libraries (Verband Oberschlesischer Volksbibliotheken) was founded, and by 1914 it had made appreciable progress. The Kaiser Wilhelm Library in Posen became the center for town and rural popular libraries in its region. It operated a travelling library and united the institutions of the whole province under one administration. After the first World War the Frontier Library Service (Grenzbüchereidienst) was founded to supply literature that would strengthen nationalist feeling among those in areas removed from German control or threatened with removal by plebiscite. This organization was most successful, and indeed the Grenzbücherdienst may be looked upon as a prototype for other organizations created by the Third Reich to reclaim for Germany large numbers of its former inhabitants and to enlist the loyalty of people of German ancestry throughout the world.(133)

When it had got well under way, the German popular library movement could be seen to be moving clearly in the direction of separating the popular library from the scholarly library. Its early proponents aimed not only at creating new libraries but at transforming those already in existence. They induced most of the older municipal libraries to

abandon competition with state and other scholarly libraries
and to adopt the aims and policies of the new popular libraries. A separate professional association was even organized,
the Association of German Popular Librarians (Verband
Deutscher Volkbibliothekare). In the past twenty-five years,
however, there has been some reversal of this tendency.(134)
The feeling is still fairly widespread in Germany that popular
libraries suffice for small communities, and that large cities
which can afford it should have both a scholarly municipal
library and a popular library system, separately administered.
(In a few large cities, such as Berlin, administration of the
two has been combined.) For middle-sized cities, however,
a central library system combining the two types is being
adopted. A new kind of library, the so-called "Einheitsbibliothek,"(135) has thus come into being in recent years. The
widespread destruction of the war and consequent economic
difficulties appear to be encouraging a trend in Germany to
the consolidation of libraries, particularly in those large or
middle-sized cities which had both municipal and university
libraries.

In both France and Italy popular libraries are still
badly underdeveloped by comparison with other countries.
While centralized administration resulting from the Revolution worked to the progressive advantage of French scholarly libraries (university libraries having made notable advances in recent times) municipal libraries have languished.
France has a few noteworthy municipal libraries, but they
resemble scholarly German libraries much more than the
public library of a good-sized American or British city.
There has been neither adequate local initiative nor sufficient
encouragement by the central government to provide satisfactory free lending libraries in the majority of French cities
and towns. Just when interest was heightening--partly
through the example set by the American Library in Paris--
the severe economic distress of the 1930's made it impossible to get anything done. In the reconstitution of France
after the recent war, organization of flourishing public libraries will present a major challenge and a great opportunity.

After political unification Italy had to take the preliminary step of eliminating widespread illiteracy. The popular
libraries which came into being were largely sponsored by
partisan groups: there were religious libraries or workingmen's libraries with their own particular bias and with
mutual antagonism. After the turn of the century the most
important popular libraries were maintained by societies

whose object was to improve the lot of the workers. In 1917 a law was passed making it obligatory for every commune to maintain a library, but conformity with this law was lax. The Fascist government took steps to stimulate the public library movement. Two Italian library associations (Associazione Italiana per le Biblioteche and Ente Nazionale per le Biblioteche Populari e Scholastiche) were founded, and training courses for librarians were started. It is still too early to forecast the future development of popular libraries in Italy, but much remains to be done before facilities will be adequate.

Striking progress in developing public libraries has been made in Soviet Russia. It has been an integral part of determined efforts made by the government to eliminate the high rate of illiteracy which existed in 1917 and to raise the educational and cultural level of the people. The amazing growth and distribution of new libraries was made possible partly, as in France, by confiscation of rich private collections, and partly also by fundamental government reorganization which provided an administrative basis for nationwide library service.

The most obvious evidence of this activity is the existence of so many large libraries. Spread throughout the expanse of the Union are many collections of hundreds of thousands--and sometimes a million or more--volumes which came into existence after the Revolution. Each of the constituent republics has a large and flourishing state library, and many municipal and regional libraries are of impressive proportions. The two greatest libraries in Russia are the Leningrad Public Library, which has a long and illustrious history, and the Lenin Memorial Library in Moscow, which has a recently completed wing making its capacity about 10,000,000 volumes, and which seems to be on its way toward outstripping all other libraries in the world in total number of volumes. Both these libraries now number about 7,000,000 volumes. Some idea of the size of state libraries can be gained from the Kharkov State Library, with over 1,000,000 volumes and the White Russian State Library at Minsk, with over 1,500,000 volumes.(136) Then there are university, school, and military libraries with sizable collections.(137) In addition, many institutions or associations have large libraries. By far the most important of these is the library of the Academy of Sciences, which, with its branches in Moscow and Leningrad combined, will contain some 7,000,000 volumes. The government has provided for building up the most important of these large libraries by granting deposit privileges to a number of them throughout the union. Part of their growth is attributable to the large number of books published in Russia, which just before the war exceeded the combined production of the United States and Germany in one year.

Throughout Russia there is the familiar European distinction between scholarly and popular libraries. But Russian librarians contend, probably with some justice, that the difference is merely one of function. Large scholarly libraries maintain close contacts with popular (or, as they are called, mass) libraries, either by administering them as branches or by exercising what is called patronage--that is, providing advice and supervision. The collections of scholarly libraries are drawn upon heavily and regularly. Popular, or mass, libraries are exceedingly numerous, and are to be found scattered through municipal districts and in factories and workers' clubs and dormitories. Regional service for rural districts is supervised generally by the large state libraries. In setting up a system to provide library service for its far-flung peoples, the Soviet government solicited the advice of Harriet Eddy, formerly county library organizer in California, and sent one of its own librarians to the United States to study current practices.

In general Russian libraries have been influenced more by American than by European libraries. The Dewey Decimal Classification is widely used. Some of the larger libraries have adopted the Brussels Expansion, and a few are using the Library of Congress classification. At present a Marxist library classification is being worked out. Anglo-American cataloguing practice, with some natural modifications, is followed, and the Central Book Chamber in Moscow does central cataloguing, issuing card sets to Russian libraries. Open access is still infrequent, but there is a tendency to adopt it more widely.

Bibliographical work of good quality is now being done in Russia. In addition to numerous national and special bibliographies prepared by the Central Book Chamber and the Leningrad Public Library,(138) all libraries pay a great deal of attention to promoting reading by preparing lists, and much work is done with individual readers, like that carried on at Leipzig under the leadership of Walter Hofmann. Taken all in all, the picture presented by Russian libraries is one of vigorous growth.

. . .

Looking back over the history of libraries we find certain problems with which all libraries are faced in any given historical period. Partly these are produced by the general historical climate, and partly they arise out of the evolution of the library. At present this is no less true than in the past. For some time now libraries have been beset by common problems on the solution of which depends their future progress, and today, when the whole of society is in convulsion, clear analysis of these problems and full awareness of possible solutions is imperative. Although it is not given unto men to see the present in nearly as adequate perspective as the past, some attempt must be made to come to an understanding of contemporary problems.

One of the gravest of these is space. Only a little more than a century after printing had been invented, Leibniz said: "If the world goes on this way for a thousand years and as many books are written as today, I am afraid that whole cities will be made up of libraries."(139) Two centuries later we find a similar flight of the imagination in America: the libraries of Cambridge (that is, of Harvard University) were to grow toward Boston, those of Boston toward Cambridge, until in the intervening space everything was to be submerged and drowned out in a sea of books. Things are not yet so bad as that, but how serious the problem is can be appreciated from the fact that since 1876 large research libraries in America have approximately doubled in size each twenty years.(140) Since the adoption of steel stacks, which made it possible to use space more efficiently in storing books, there has been no important architectural innovation: architectural improvements have been confined to attempts to do away with space-wasting monumental structures and to plan functional buildings.(141) But even relatively satisfactory buildings erected in this century are crammed to capacity with constantly growing collections. This has made it necessary to examine the implications of future growth and to reconsider the principles governing storage and preservation of printed materials.

It has long been generally recognized that the use of books in libraries varies widely, that a few books are intensively used, some frequently, some occasionally, and a considerable proportion very rarely.(142) There have been radical proposals to divide large collections into living and dead parts and to weed out the latter by discarding or selling volumes periodically. A more carefully thought-out proposal was made by President Eliot of Harvard in 1902: storage of

little-used books in a separate place where they could be
shelved by size, two or three deep, and thus inexpensively
preserved apart from the central collection. Similar proposals for depositories outside large cities were advanced
in America, Italy, and Germany. In 1931 the Association
of German Librarians aired the whole question of storing
so-called "dead" literature, but no practical steps were
taken.(143) Meanwhile, however, several large libraries
were adopting measures of this kind. In 1906 the British
Museum built a special depository for newspapers at Hendon,
a London suburb. By 1921 the building was full, and in 1932
it was enlarged and reopened as the Newspaper Library at
Colindale.(144) The New York Public Library acquired an
empty commercial loft about a mile from its central building in 1933 and fitted it out as a storehouse. Now all its
newspaper files have been moved to the storehouse, along
with other bulky and little-used materials. In 1932-1934
the Bibliothèque Nationale constructed an annex for newspapers and journals at Versailles. All these measures gave
genuine relief, but this relief is admittedly only temporary.

    A more direct attack on the problem, stemming from
President Eliot's proposals, has lately been made in Boston.
Here twelve research libraries--among them the two largest in the metropolitan area, the Harvard University Library
and the Boston Public Library--have joined to form a corporation which controls a recently constructed, inexpensive
block building with a small reading room, but with the greatest part of its space given over to shelves for about 1,000,000
volumes. Since storage is the main objective, the height of
the stack level has been increased and the width of the aisles
decreased. Space may be rented by any library, which uses
its own space as it sees fit.(145) By 1947 the Harvard University Library had moved over 200,000 volumes into the
New England Deposit Library. Similar depositories are being
planned by other large libraries.

    New developments and new problems in classification
and cataloguing have not been lacking. During the Enlightment tendencies in classification and cataloguing which had
been developing for years came, as it were, to maturity.
One school of librarians acquired a passion for classification and insisted that books on the shelf ought to be arranged
to parallel the classed catalogue. This theory still has its
adherents; indeed one contemporary librarian writes: "The
German view is definitely that the arrangement of the catalog
is the primary factor to which the arrangement of the books

on the shelves must then be adapted, in so far as the library in question provides for classified or systematic shelving."(146) The last qualifying phrase is significant, however. Even during the Enlightenment, other librarians contended that consideration of space and physical convenience ought to determine the way in which books were shelved. In Europe faith in classification has gradually been undermined. The great-hall structure, which united all the library's books into a kind of intellectual cosmos, has disappeared, and with the separation of reading rooms and stack, which means that the shelves are no longer open to readers in many research libraries, one of the incentives has been removed. We have seen how in the early nineteenth century new systems of shelving books were adopted, notably at the Bibliothèque Nationale. Today many European libraries, especially within Germany, divide their books into a few large groups within which they are arranged by size, and then in accession order. Subject catalogues have been started to accompany such changes, and in many libraries the classed catalogue, if not displaced, has come to be primarily a tool for staff use.(147)

In America, where access to the shelves is common, even in large research libraries, much effort has been expended upon classification. The Dewey Decimal Classification, first published in 1876, has gone through 14 editions, and is used by the great majority of American public libraries, and also by some research libraries. College and research libraries, however, have shown a tendency to abandon the Dewey Classification as their collections grow beyond 100,000 volumes. A few large libraries in Europe have adopted the Universal Decimal Classification, an expansion of the Dewey scheme prepared by the International Federation for Documentation, but this is used less for library classification than for scientific documentation. In the United States another great scheme of classification was developed for the collections of the Library of Congress. The schedules have been printed, and there is a noticeable trend among college and research libraries toward adoption of the Library of Congress scheme. Printing of both Dewey and Library of Congress class numbers on Library of Congress catalogue cards is an added inducement to use one of the two schemes which have now become more or less standard in America.

In cataloguing, the great development of the past fifty years has been the emergence of the dictionary catalogue in English-speaking countries, and also in a few European libraries. Here America has led the way. Printing of cards by the Library of Congress and their use by other libraries have produced in American catalogues a greater degree of uniformity than can be found in any other country. Subject cataloguing is unified by the printing of Library of Congress guides (of which the fifth edition was published in 1948) and of guides sponsored by the H. W. Wilson Co. primarily for small libraries, but in close correlation with Library of Congress practice.

At the present time much serious thought is being given to general cataloguing policies, especially to the cost of cataloguing. Publication of the Anglo-American code in 1908 was a milestone in cataloguing history, and produced highly beneficial results in raising the quality and unifying the practices of cataloguing in American and British libraries.(148) Gradually, over a period of forty years, supplementary rules have mushroomed in the catalogue departments of individual libraries. This is particularly so in large libraries, of which the Library of Congress is perhaps the best example. At the same time the cost of cataloguing has mounted alarmingly. Publication of a preliminary edition of the revised American Library Association code has provided the occasion for American librarians to re-examine their policies.(149) A movement toward simplification in cataloguing is gaining strength, and impetus will undoubtedly be lent by the Library of Congress adoption of simplified rules.(150)

Segregation of ephemeral and little-used material, which reaches its climax in storage in a special depository, will also have inevitable repercussions upon classification and cataloguing. For some time there has been a growing fear that many classes of books were growing so large that the purposes of classification itself were being defeated: even with open access it was becoming impossible to see the forest for the trees. Restriction of material which goes onto the classified shelves will help somewhat. It will also reduce library expenditures for the technical processes of classifying, and even more for cataloguing.(151)

Next to the emergence of the dictionary catalogue, it is the production of gigantic printed catalogues which has recently held the spotlight. We have already traced the history of the printed catalogues of the Bibliothèque Nationale and the British Museum. The latter, completed at the end of the last century, proved so valuable a bibliographical aid to libraries all over the world that the trustees decided to print a second, enlarged edition. Printing began in 1931, and volumes have continued to appear each year, though the war has slowed down their rate. Completion of the Bibliothèque Nationale catalogue was only prevented by the war. We have already mentioned the printing of A Catalog of Books Represented by Library of Congress Printed Cards Issued to July 31, 1942. Reproduced by photo-offset with a reduction in card size, this catalogue runs to 167 volumes and represents some 2,000,000 volumes in the Library of Congress for which cards have been printed up to the terminal date. Supplements are appearing regularly.(152)

The greatest project of its kind, however, is the printing of the German Union Catalogue (Deutscher Gesamtkatalog). At the end of the nineteenth century a union catalogue of Prussian libraries was begun on cards at the (then) Royal Library in Berlin. Shortly before the first World War plans were under way to begin printing, but the outbreak of hostilities put an end to them. The plans were revived in 1925 and after a vast amount of preliminary work the first volume appeared in 1931 as the Union Catalogue of Prussian Libraries (Gesamtkatalog der preussischen Bibliotheken). It listed the books printed before January 1, 1930 held by the Prussian State Library, the ten Prussian university libraries, the libraries of the four technical colleges, and the Academy of Braunsberg, and also by the Bavarian State Library at Munich and the National Library at Vienna. It was recognized from the beginning that the work ought to be expanded to include the holdings of more libraries. This was made possible by the advent of the Third Reich and subsequent political developments. Beginning with the ninth volume (1936) the work became the German Union Catalogue. It then listed the holdings of about 100 libraries throughout greater Germany. The fourteen volumes published between 1931 and 1939 constitute a bibliographical tool of world-wide importance, and proved of great aid to the work of the German Loan Exchange (Deutscher Leihverkehr).(153) Books published after January 1, 1930 are listed in the Berlin Accessions (Berliner Titeldrucke), which thus becomes a supplement to the Gesamtkatalog.(154) In Germany some libraries are making use of the Gesamtkatalog as a printed catalogue of their collections by writing in their call numbers. Such a practice may very well become widespread as the scope and comprehensiveness of other printed catalogues increase, but it is too early yet to do more than to watch this tendency closely.

Provision of so thoroughgoing an inventory as the German Union Catalogue is one of the highlights of efforts made by scholars and librarians to take stock of their resources. No single library--and no group of libraries in any one nation--can fulfill all demands in this age of intensive scholarly research. A natural first recourse is the creation of union catalogues. Here Germany, as we have seen, was formerly ahead of other nations. The Library of Congress, however, is pushing its Union Catalog toward much greater inclusiveness. A large number of American libraries have agreed to submit to the Union Catalog titles which they have and which are not to be found in the new Library of Congress printed cafalogue. This should provide a large proportion of titles now unlisted in the Union Catalog, which is estimated to be about forty per cent of all titles held in American libraries. A movement which has gained impetus and no lack of enthusiastic protagonists in the United States of late is the building up of regional--and even municipal--union catalogues. Many librarians have looked askance, however, at the money and energy expended upon such projects and have urged rather that the Union Catalog in Washington be enlarged. When that has been accomplished, it may very well remove much of the incentive to compiling smaller union catalogues.

Of equal value, perhaps, has been the publication of a number of special bibliographies and inventories--many of them cooperative enterprises. Before the first World War, for example, there was the International Catalogue of Scientific Literature, published by the Royal Society. In 1927 a vast cooperative project of American and Canadian libraries culminated in publication of the Union List of Serials. So valuable did this prove that two supplements were presently called for, and in 1943 a greatly enlarged edition with careful bibliographical recension appeared, containing about 150,000 titles and listing the holdings of some 600 libraries. By 1945 publication of a supplement was necessary. Another great bibliographical enterprise is the Union Catalogue of Incunabula (Gesamtkatalog der Wiegendrucke), the first volume of which was published in 1925 and which, when completed, aims to list all known incunabula.(155) We have already referred to the Inventaire général des manuscrits des bibliothèques publiques de France. Similar inventories are in preparation in other countries: for example, the Verzeichnis der Handschriften im Deutschen Reich and the Catalogue général des manuscrits des bibliothèques de

Belgique. It would be a task in itself to enumerate the important specialized works in various fields that have appeared since 1900.

The vast multiplication of research materials which has led to union catalogues and special bibliographies has brought to the fore the general problem of scholarly resources. At present this problem is seen most clearly in its national form: how to insure that all needed books shall be provided and that adequate collections shall be reasonably well distributed geographically. Such a problem is particularly acute for a large nation like the United States with its regional differences in culture and its heavy concentration of books in the northeast and southwest. In Germany a far-sighted move was taken during Althoff's regime in the Prussian Ministry of Education. The ten Prussian universities were assigned special fields in which to concentrate. As a result they have built up special collections of high calibre while no one library has had to undergo the strain of trying to cover all fields thoroughly. Efficient operation of the German Loan Exchange in conjunction with this acquisition policy has gone far toward meeting Germany's needs. In smaller countries, or in restricted regions, a number of cooperative arrangements have been made. Thus in Denmark the Royal Library and the University Library in Copenhagen have an agreement whereby the former specializes in history, literature, and the humanities, and the latter in science, medicine, and technology. There is a similar arrangement between the Swedish Royal Library and the Library of the Royal Academy of Sciences. In the United States several local agreements have been made--for example, between Duke University and the University of North Carolina, and between libraries in metropolitan centers, such as New York and Chicago.

In the United States growing awareness of the problem has led to recent surveys of library resources. Several studies have been produced under the editorship of R. B. Downs, and the Special Libraries Association is publishing a series of guides to selected special collections in the United States and Canada. Several years of war during which the main sources of foreign publications have gradually gone dry have also served to make librarians and scholars acutely conscious of how important it is to have adequate coverage of this literature by American libraries. At the present moment a program for cooperative acquisition of the important scholarly literature of the world is being started in the United

States. It calls for voluntary assumption by libraries of carefully delimited fields in which they would take the responsibility of collecting exhaustively. In connection with comprehensive acquisition a classed catalogue is also being proposed as a great inventory of scholarly materials.(156)

A staggering amount of work will have to be done to put such a scheme into effect, but it is heartening that plans should be going forward enthusiastically in such trying times. Enabling scholars throughout the nation to get at research materials quickly and efficiently will no doubt be facilitated by comprehensive inventories of resources, augmented perhaps by improved interlibrary loan arrangements. American libraries might well study the British and German systems. Already such new technical devices as microfilm are making it possible to achieve broad distribution of scholarly materials, though it is too much to expect a complete solution by these means alone. Along with collecting materials systematically, we shall have to see to it that they are scientifically recorded and thus brought to the notice of potential users, and that readers of all classes and interests, no matter where they happen to live, shall be able to obtain them conveniently. Here greater cooperation among all kinds of libraries is devoutly to be wished.

To achieve such objectives requires not only marshalling resources and improving organization, but also maintaining competent personnel. It will be recalled that during the last century there was a growing conviction of the importance of making librarianship a profession, culminating in moves to establish formal training for librarianship. Formal courses in librarianship were started at the University of Göttingen in 1886, being given by the eminent librarian Karl Dziatzko. A year later Melvil Dewey established the first library school in the United States.(157) Formal training for librarianship is over half a century old, and it is possible to make some evaluation of it.(158) In fact it is one of the matters in the library world that is being most seriously pondered at the moment.

As might be expected from their general library structure, Europe and America have differed in the kind of training devised for librarians. In Europe much emphasis is still put upon auxiliary sciences such as paleography, and in general upon the scholarly elements of the librarian's profession. In America more attention has been paid to methods and technical processes, especially for public libraries. The École des Chartes in Paris probably represents the extreme

of European training; indeed France has done very little to
provide training for assistants in popular libraries. Germany has worked out a program compounded of theoretical
instruction and practical apprenticeship. Althoff early recognized the necessity of setting standards, and the government has organized examinations and grants certificates
for two types of library work, the scholarly grade (wissenschaftlicher Dienst) for those who occupy the higher administrative posts in scholarly libraries, and the middle grade
(mittlerer Dienst) for professional assistants in scholarly
libraries and in popular libraries. Germany has been most
successful in attracting men of considerable scholarly ability
into the profession, but attention to personnel for popular libraries has increased only recently, largely through the efforts of men like Walter Hofmann, whose German School for
Popular Libraries (Deutsche Volksbüchereischule) at
Leipzig was the leading institution of its kind, and Wilhelm
Krabbe at Berlin. The Third Reich supported training of
personnel for popular libraries, recognizing their importance in influencing the culture of the great masses of the
people.

    Many trained librarians in the Scandinavian countries
have gone to the United States--or lately to Britain--for
their training. In most of the other European countries formal library training is either so little organized or so recent that we shall pass them over. Russia, however, seems
to be developing long and intensive courses for her librarians, in which American and German methods have both been
adopted.

    In Great Britain there was much reluctance for years
to inaugurate formal courses. The Library Association tried
to set certain minimum standards by giving examinations
and granting certificates indicating various degrees of professional achievement. But British librarians themselves
admit that the system was not satisfactory. In 1919 the London University School for Librarianship was opened and
courses were given in following years by several other universities, for example the National University of Wales. The
British curriculum is a compromise between the German
and American, with considerable emphasis upon auxiliary
sciences. As yet the London School has not found acceptance
in the profession such as is enjoyed by German or American
schools. The whole British system of training for librarianship is in an unsettled state which greatly troubles leaders of
the profession, and thoroughgoing changes may well take place.

In America library schools have grown fairly steadily in influence since their inception. There has been substantial agreement upon basic elements of the curriculum and general objectives, though not always upon adequacy of the achievement. The American Library Association has encouraged a certain amount of uniformity, yet schools have varied greatly in standards, in the quality of their instructors, and in the type of student who has come for study. The critical Williamson report for the Carnegie Corporation(159) gave voice to dissatisfaction shared by many librarians. The Board of Education for Librarianship, and the Carnegie Corporation both put their weight behind certain recommendations of the report. Library schools were accredited according to definite professional criteria, and several new and excellent schools (among them California, Columbia, Michigan and Chicago) were founded. There is little doubt that a few good library schools have had a salutary influence upon the profession. But after twenty years signs of discontent are again cropping up. It is usually admitted that a fairly satisfactory job has been done in raising the professional level of assistants in the average public library; this is probably the finest accomplishment of American library schools. But there is also criticism--much of it justified-- of the lack of scholarship among American librarians and of the failure of library schools to improve the situation. The complaint comes largely from reference libraries, which need people with scholarly equipment and administrative ability in key positions.

The source of the trouble may well lie in conditions much more general than library training. At present severe strictures upon the whole of higher education are common. As for administration, the dearth of young librarians capable of stepping into positions with large administrative responsibility is due to a complicated set of circumstances in which both administrators and young assistants have failed to work out a satisfactory system of gradual professional advancement during which the necessary experience will be acquired. A larger theoretical aspect of the problem can also be seen in the interminable current discussions of public administration in general, which are ineffective largely because in order to administer well it is necessary to know what one is administering _for_. Thoroughgoing analyses of library needs and objectives like those by Joeckel and McColvin may well do more to improve library administration than a host of formal courses. It is likely that in the future, however, American library training will be organized on a more specialized basis, with different training beyond common fundamentals for those desiring to go into smaller libraries and those preparing to work in larger or research libraries.

. . .

The course of library history in various countries has been conditioned by a number of factors, which we have tried to point out. Of these nationalism has been one of the most important in the past hundred years. Unless our civilization disintegrates completely, the coming years will sound the death-knell of extreme nationalism. Scientific and economic changes have produced a situation in which peaceful intercourse and mutual cooperation among nations are beginning to be considered necessary for the survival of our civilization. In the world of scholarship, which knows no national boundaries, such cooperation has a long history. In the library world we have had to wait until the antecedent development of national library systems had reached the stage at which the advantages of international cooperation should become manifest. It is not surprising, therefore, that international library organizations are comparatively young.

Cordial relations among individuals, groups, and nations have not been wanting. Panizzi's relations with German librarians of his generation have already been noted, and many European librarians have visited America with mutual profit. Close cooperation between Great Britain and the United States has been a boon to the libraries of both countries. The reorganization of the Vatican Library with the advice and cooperation of the American commission has had repercussions upon the entire library world. And no librarian ever thinks of such beneficent organizations as the Carnegie and Rockefeller foundations without deep thankfulness.

The first international organization to achieve any influence was the International Federation for Documentation. This was founded in 1895 as the International Institute of Bibliography, and has several times undergone changes of name and structural reorganization.(160) It undertook the ambitious project of compiling author and subject catalogues of the world's literature, but this has been fulfilled only on a small scale. Much more successful has been its work with the Dewey Decimal Classification. The so-called

Brussels Expansion has been published in several languages, and is used somewhat for library classification, and more widely for scientific, governmental (administrative), and commercial documentation. In microfilming the Federation was a real pioneer, foreseeing the importance of the new technique long before it became generally recognized. Microfilming has enabled libraries to preserve materials threatened with deterioration, to conserve space by filming bulky materials such as newspapers, and to acquire textual reproductions of rare or valuable works. Its greatest value has been in documentation, as the experience of the National Archives in Washington already proves. The first World War dealt the Federation a staggering blow, from which it had not fully recovered when the second holocaust swept over Europe. But in the interim between wars the Federation patiently pursued its path and performed its function as a coordinating body by centralizing and distributing information about developments in scientific bibliography and documentation all over the world.

The League of Nations was responsible for the International Institute of Intellectual Cooperation. Its object is broad: to bring into contact intellectual workers of all kinds and in all countries. It has stimulated exchange of information among national library bodies, sponsored meetings of librarians and bibliographers, and produced a number of valuable publications, among them the Index Translationum and studies of professional training(161) and popular libraries.(162)

In 1927, after several years of preliminary soundings, the International Federation of Library Associations was founded.(163) Despite subsequent world-wide economic depression the Federation kept functioning up to the outbreak of war, and has resumed activity after the war. It has to its credit the working out of standard regulations for international library loans and the intangible but real benefits accruing from regular personal contacts between librarians of different nations, which, it is hoped, will be renewed after the war. Valuable information on current library developments in various countries is to be found in its publication, Actes du Comité Internationale des Bibliothèques.

One of the more significant trends of our time is improvement of relations among the nations of the Western Hemisphere. This the war has speeded, and cultural interchange, with better mutual understanding, is proceeding apace. The Library of Congress and the American Library

Association have been important agents in maintaining good relations. American librarians are being invited to South America to give library instruction or to aid with such libraries as the Biblioteca Benjamin Franklin in Mexico City. Establishment of the Inter-American Library Association, which held its first convention in 1938, gives evidence of the growth and seriousness of hemispheric cooperation.

. . .

What will happen to international cooperation among libraries depends very much upon the structure of the postwar world. Despite ominous possibilities of a complete political and cultural split between groups of nations, a good deal of solid progress is quietly being made in restoring and improving international cultural cooperation.(164) The value of the American Book Center and the Inter-Allied Book Center became so clear during the war that plans are being made to carry on the work. The mere existence of UNESCO demonstrates faith in the future of intellectual cooperation, and the ably-edited UNESCO Bulletin for Libraries gives evidence of solid achievement. Libraries played a great wartime rôle in meeting national crises; they can play an even greater rôle in averting future crises and helping to build a better world. Just how much of this rôle they will be permitted to play is the concern and the responsibility of every intelligent citizen. What is accomplished remains for the future historian to record.

FOOTNOTES*

[1] Fritz Milkau, Geschichte der Bibliotheken im alten Orient (Leipzig, 1935), a scholarly survey of pre-Alexandrian libraries with copious bibliographical notes giving an evaluation of the literature, is unfortunately not available in English translation. J. W. Thompson, Ancient Libraries (Berkeley, 1940) is useful chiefly for bibliography. Frederick Kenyon, Books and Readers in Ancient Greece and Rome (London, 1935) is short, authoritative, and stimulating.

[2] "Die Bibliothek. . . war nach sachlichen Gruppen wohl geordnet und mit Orientierungsmarken versehen." J. Menant, La bibliothèque du palais de Ninève (Paris, 1880), p. 32 states flatly: "A careful examination of the inscriptions shows that they were arranged in the library in a methodical order easy to reconstruct." Carl Bezold, however, after painstaking study, contents himself, in the Catalogue of the Cuneiform Tablets in the Kouyunjik Collection of the British Museum, V (London, 1889), p. xxix, with: "We have no knowledge as to the way in which the tablets were arranged in Ashur-bani-pal's Library." That there was some sort of systematic arrangement is a matter of general agreement. Many of the tablets clearly belong to series; the order of each tablet within the series is often indicated at its beginning by a repetition of the last line of the preceding tablet, and, at the end, of the first line of the tablet which follows. There are also tablets bearing series titles, and references to the series or group to which a tablet belongs sometimes appear in the colophon. The study of this library is still far from complete. Cf. R.C. Thompson and R.W. Hutchinson, A Century of Exploration at Nineveh (London, 1929) for a brief but expert survey. Edward Chiera, They Wrote on Clay (Chicago, 1938) is a sprightly general introduction to cuneiform tablets and their historical significance.

[3] The term used in most Western languages derives from the compounding of two Greek words: biblos, book, and theke, container or repository.

[4] Aristophanes, Frogs, 943, 1409. Cf. also Athenaeus, Deipnosophistae, I, 3: "Euripides possessed one of the largest libraries in the ancient world."

[5] For descriptions and illustrations of the layout of ancient libraries see Bernt Götze, "Antike Bibliotheken," Jahrbuch des deutschen archaologischen Institutes, LII (1937), 225-247.

[6] Graecia capta ferum victorem cepit. Horace, Epistles, II, i, 156.

[7] See Felix Reichmann, "The Book Trade at the Time of the Roman Empire," Library Quarterly, VIII (1938), 40-76.

[8] Primus ingenia hominum rem publicam fecit. Pliny, Naturalis Historia, XXXV, 10.

[9] For a sketch of the libraries of Rome see C.E. Boyd, Public Libraries and Literary Culture in Ancient Rome (Chicago, 1916).

[10] For a description of such a library see H.F. Pfeiffer, "Roman Library at Timgad," Memoirs of the American Academy in Rome IX (1931), 157-165.

*Note: No italics are used in the footnotes or bibliography.

[11] Iam enim inter balnearia et thermas bibliotheca quoque ut necessarium domus ornamentum expolitur. - Seneca, De tranquillitate animi IX, 4.

[12] Quo innumerabiles libros et bibliothecas, quorum dominus vix tota vita indices perlegit. - Ibid. IX, 7.

[13] See Götze, op. cit.

[14] The period covered in the next four chapters is dealt with in great detail in J.W. Thompson, The Medieval Library (Chicago, 1939). This is the latest and most comprehensive treatment in English, but it must be read with some caution. C.P. Farrar and A.P. Evans, Bibliography of Engligh Translations from Medieval Sources (New York, 1946) provides a useful guide to the literature of the period. Falconer Madan, Books in Manuscript (2nd ed. London, 1927) is a little classic in its field.

[15] Ammianus Marcellinus, XIV, 6, 18.

[16] Si quem sancta tenet meditandi in lege voluntas
Hic poterit residens sacris intendere libris.

[17] See Cardinal Gasquet's translation, The Rule of Saint Benedict (London, 1925).

[18] Isidori Opera Omnia (Rome, 1803), VII, 179. Quoted in J.W. Clark, The Care of Books (Cambridge, 1909), p. 46.

[19] Bibliothecarius omnium librorum curam habeat, lectionum et scriptorum. Cf. C. Cipolla, Codice diplomatico del monasterio di S. Columbano di Bobbio, I (Rome, 1918), p. 140.

[20] For an account of Bede and the monasteries of Wearmouth and Jarrow see Bede: His Life, Times, and Writings; Essays in Commemoration of the Twelfth Centenary of his Death, ed. by Alexander H. Thompson (Oxford, 1935).

[21] Emil Lesne, Les livres, "scriptoria," et bibliotheques du commencement du viii^e a la fin du xi^e siecle (Lille, 1938) is an admirable study, chiefly of France, but including also some libraries now within the national boundaries of Germany and Switzerland.

[22] A helpful little study of Alcuin and his work is A.F. West, Alcuin and the Rise of Christian Schools (New York, 1892).

[23] Quis saltem poterit seriem enumerare librorum
Quos tua de multis copulat sententia terris.--Monumenta Germaniae historica. Poetae latini medii aevi, I, 96.

[24] Hae ergo divitiae claustrales, hae sunt opulentiae caelestis vitae dulcedine animam saginantes.--From the catalogue of the monastery of St. Riquier, reprinted in E. Edwards, Memoirs of Libraries...I, 297-301.

[25] Inexplicabilis librorum copia periit, nosque spiritualium nostri armorum inarmes reliquit.--I have been unable to identify this passage.

[26] Claustrum sine armario quasi castrum sine armentario.-- Geoffrey of St. Barbe in Thesaurus novus anecdotorum, ed. E. Martène and U. Durand (Paris, 1717), I, 511.

[27] Quidquid ab arce deus coeli direxit in orbem
  Scripturae sanctae per pia verba viris,
  Illic invenies, quidquid sapientia mundi,
  Protulit in mundum temporibus variis. -- "Hrabani Mauri Carmina XXIII: Ad Gerhohum Prestiberum," in Monumenta Germaniae historica. Poetae latini medii aevi, II, 187.

[28] See Joan Evans, Monastic Life at Cluny, 910-1157 (London, 1931). For France in general, see Lesne, op. cit.

[29] See J.S. Beddie, "The Ancient Classics in the Medieval Libraries," Speculum, V (1930), 3-20, and his "Libraries in the 12th Century, their Catalogues and Contents," in Anniversary Essays in Medieval History by Students of Charles Homer Haskins (Boston, 1929).

[30] In this connection see the informative and entertaining chapter by Florence E. de Roover, "The Scriptorium," in J.W. Thompson, The Medieval Library.

[31] Hoc ut nullus opus cuiquam concesserit extra,
  Ni prius ille fidem dederit vel denique pignus,
  Donec ad has aedes, quae accepit, salva remittat. -- Quoted by W. Wattenbach, Das Schriftwesen im Mittelalter (3rd. ed. Leipzig, 1896), p. 572.

[32] See Dorothy M. Norris, A History of Cataloguing and Cataloguing Methods (London, 1939).

[33] The standard work in English on medieval universities is Hastings Rashdall, The Universities of Europe in the Middle Ages (New ed. Oxford, 1936). A shorter and more popular account is Nathan Schachner, The Mediaeval Universities (New York and London, 1938).

[34] The reference is apparently to Gabriel Meier, Heinrich von Ligerz, Bibliothekar von Einsiedeln im 14. Jahrhundert (Leipzig, 1896).

[35] An association of reformed Benedictine Monks.

[36] See Norris, op. cit., 30-34.

[37] See Ruth S. Mackensen, "Four Great Libraries of Medieval Baghdad," Library Quarterly, II (1932), 279-299. See also the chapter contributed by S.K. Padover to J.W. Thompson's The Medieval Library, which gives additional references.

[38] "Audivit...de quodam Sarracenorum soldano quod omnia librorum genera, quae necessaria esse poterant philosophis Sarracenis diligenter faciebat inquiri, et sumptibus suis scribi, et in armario suo recondi, ut litterati eorum liborum copiam possent habere, quoties indigerent." Geoffroy de Beaulieu, Vita Ludovici Noni, XXIII (Recueil des historiens des Gaules et de la France, XX (1840), 15).

[39] La belle librairie...de tous les plus notables volumes, qui par souverains auteurs aient estés compilés...de toutes sciences, moult bien escrips et richment adornez. -- Quoted in Léopold Delisle, Recherches sur la librairie de Charles V (Paris, 1907), I, 2.

[40] The library was bought by the Duke of Bedford in 1424 and removed to England.

[41] See the historical introduction by J.W. Thompson to The Frankfort Book Fair (Chicago, 1911), a translation of Henri Estienne's Francofordiense Emporium.

[42] See the works by Rashdall and Schachner already cited.

[43] A detailed study of this arrangement, with helpful illustrations, is B.H. Streeter, The Chained Library (London, 1931).

[44] So far as I can discover there exists no complete English translation of this work other than an early one by Thomas Twyne, Phisicke against Fortune, as well prosperous as adverse (London, 1579).

[45] Libri medullitus delectant, colloquuntur, consulunt et viva quandam nobis atque arguta familiaritate iunguntur. - Letter to Giovanni d'Incisa. See Petrarca, Le Familiare, ed. Vittorio Rossi (Florence, 1932-1941), I, 139.

[46] One of the greatest of fifteenth-century private libraries is described in Pearl Kibre, The Library of Pico della Mirandola (New York, 1936).

[47] ad ingeniosorum et nobilium, quos continget in talibus delectari, consolationem. The legacy is printed in P. Nolhac, Pétrarque et l'humanisme (new ed. Paris, 1907), I, 94.

[48] It is impossible to reproduce in English the allusion so neatly struck off by the German "Börsenblatt." The Börsenblatt is the regular organ of the German book trade. The nearest American analogy is Publishers' Weekly.

[49] A translation, "Plautus in the Convent," has been published in v. 14 of the collection German Classics of the Nineteenth Century, ed. by Kuno Francke.

[50] "Memini Constantinopoli Graeculis illis vestimenta dedisse, ut codices acciperem, cuius rei nec pudet nec poenitat." Carteggio di Giovanni Aurispa, a cura di Remigio Sabbadini (Rome, 1931), p. 91.

[51] R. Sabbadini, Le scoperte dei codici latini e greci ne secoli xiv e xv, I, 164.

[52] "docto, de bono aspecto, de bona natura, et bona et expedita lingua." C. Stornajolo, Codices Urbinates Graeci Bibliothecae Vaticanae (Rome, 1895), I, Praef. XX.

[53] For a sketch of this library's history see Geza Schütz, Bibliotheca Corvina," Library Quarterly IV (1934), 552-564.

[54] "When Cosimo de Medici wanted to provide the Monastery of Saint Mark in Florence, which he had built, with a library, he prevailed upon the then highly regarded book expert, Tomaso de Sarzana, to draw up a standard catalogue from which purchases could begin to be made. Later, when Tomaso himself had become Pope, his catalogue spread far and wide under the title, The Inventory of Pope Nicholas V, Which he Composed at the Request of Cosimo de Medici himself, and in scope and arrangement it served as a model for the setting up of new libraries. It began with the Bible as the comprehensive and the most important work on theology, followed by the Church Fathers. After the theologians, as a second division, come the philosophers, beginning, as

is proper, with Aristotle. The humanities form the third division, and the classic poets occupy the chief place. The fourth division, jurisprudence, as chance would have it, is missing in the copy of the inventory that has come down to us, but as we have seen from the foregoing description of the Library of Urbino, which was arranged according to this inventory, that section was originally present in the inventory."-- Translated from Franz Wickhoff, "Die Bibliothek Julius' II," Jahrbuch der preussischen Kunstsammlungen XIV (1893), 53-54. A copy of the inventory is published in G. Sforza, La patria, la famiglia e la giovinezza di Papa Niccolo V (Lucca, 1884), Appendix A.

[55] Di libri antiqui... per public' uso, Sisto da tutto il mondo fe' raccorre. Ariosto, "Satira VI (VII)," 139-141 in his Opere Minori, ed. Giuseppe Fatini (Florence, 1915). For an archaic translation see Ariosto's Satyres in Seven Famous Discourses... in English by Garius Markham (London, 1708).

[56] "The paintings in the Stanza della Segnatura, then, provide us with a pictorial representation of a book catalogue, a project which is rather remarkable in a room designed to be used for everyday purposes... The allegorical figures which sit enthroned on high have books in their hands; only Justice has her hands full with sword and scales. The Gospels, the books most revered by Christians, are being brought down to the faithful by angels; and four Holy Fathers gathered about the sacrament are writing and reading books; books are scattered about the ground, and saints and laymen in the company are distinguished by possessing them; those who rejoice in the mysterious presence of the Muse hold rolls and manuscripts; books and tablets are in everybody's hands in the School of Athens. Composing, copying, reading, expounding books goes on in all corners, so that hardly any conceivable relation to books fails to find here a sensible expression. Even the two greatest of the philosophers are only indicated by their two most famous books; the Pope holds a book along with the laws of the Church, and Justinian is seated with his famous Corpus before him. On the cameos below the Parnassus, on one side books are found in a marble sarcophagus, on the other, books are being burned. There exists no other work of painting in which books play so large a role, in which everything starts from and returns to books." -- Translated from Franz Wickhoff, loc. cit.

[57] There is a considerable body of literature on Italy's influence on Chaucer, but little is known, apparently, about his use of Italian libraries. See R.A. Pratt, "Chaucer and the Visconti Libraries," ELH; A Journal of English Literary History, VI (1939), 191-200.

[58] There is a thoroughgoing study of this influence in German: Heinrich Kramm, Deutsche Bibliotheken unter dem Einfluss von Humanismus und Reformation (Leipzig, 1938).

[59] "An die Ratherren aller Stadte deutsches Lands." The letter is translated in Chapter IX of F.V.N. Painter's Luther on Education (Philadelphia, 1890). I have used Painter's translation of this passage.

[60] James Brodrick has now given us a detailed account of these activities in his St. Peter Canisius (London, 1935). The concluding chapter contains a resume of Canisius' accomplishments in education.

[61] So called from the collection of books bound in silver which came from Anna Marie, the second wife of Duke Albert of Prussia.

[62] Ist auch allzeit gewesen Weisheit und Kunst geneigt. Quoted by Hans Rott, Ott Heinrich und die Kunst (Heidelberg, 1905), p. 173. (Mitteilungen zur Geschichte des Heidelberger Schlosses V, 1/2).

[63] nonulla quibus ingenua curiositas hominis eruditi delectari solet, tanquam proprio pastu animi liberalis, als da seien instrumenta mathematica, numismata antiqua, erudita rudera prisci temporis sowie quaedam naturae et artis miracula. -- Cf. C. Clément, Musei sive bibliothecae tam privatae quam publicae extructio, instruction, cura, usus (Lyon, 1635), p. 376.

[64] For an account of Gesner which amiably denies to him the honor of founder see T. Besterman, The Beginnings of Systematic Bibliography (2nd. ed. London, 1936). Archer Taylor, in his useful little Renaissance Guides to Books (Berkeley, 1945), agrees with Besterman in dating modern bibliography from Johannes Tritheim (1462-1516).

[65] There is an English translation by John Evelyn, Instructions Concerning Erecting of a Library (London, 1661) reprinted Cambridge, 1903. See also J.V. Rice, Gabriel Naudé, 1600-1653 (Baltimore, 1939).

[66] See Gabriel Naudé, News from France, or a Description of the Library of Cardinal Mazarin, preceded by The Surrender of the Library (Chicago, 1907). Cf. Also, J.V. Rice, Gabriel Naudé, 1600-1653 (Baltimore, 1939).

[67] See Trecentale Bodleianum; a Memorial Volume for the Three Hundredth Anniversary of the Public Funeral of Sir Thomas Bodley (Oxford, 1913).

[68] Je vis la bibliothèque sans nulle difficulté, chacun la voit einsin et en extrait ce qu'il veut. -- Montaigne, Journal de voyage en Italie par la Suisse et l'Allemagne en 1580 et 1581, ed. Maurice Rat (Paris, 1942), p. 114. There are several English translations.

[69] Sum de bibliotheca quam Heidelberga capta spolium fecit et Gregorio XV trophaeum misit Maximilianus dux Bavariae.

[70] Medios inter praeliorum strepitus, victoriarum curcum. Quoted by A. Hortzschansky, Die Königliche Bibliothek zu Berlin (Berlin, 1908), p. 19.

[71] See Martha Ornstein, The Role of Scientific Societies in the Seventeenth Century (Chicago, 1928).

[72] See J.N. Bergkamp, Dom Jean Mabillon and the Benedictine Historical School of Saint-Maur (Washington, D. C., 1928).

[73] Monsieur Colbert n'oublie rien de ce qu'il faut pour augmenter et embellir la bibliothèque afin de contenter la genereuse inclination de son maître. -- I have been unable to verify this quotation.

[74] Des Devoirs et des qualités du bibliothecaire. The English translation (Chicago, 1906) has a brief bibliographical introduction.

[75] partitio universalis doctrinae humanae. It is interesting to note that after the War of 1812, when the Library of Congress was reconstituted out of Jefferson's private collection, the classification it used was Jefferson's adaptation of Bacon's scheme.

[76] A great collection of archives and historical documents now known as the Collection Moreau from the name of the Parisian lawyer who instigated it. See Henri Omont, La Collection Moreau (Paris, 1891)

[77] Not only religious images, but many books too, were destroyed as a result of religious controversy in seventeenth-century England. See C.R. Gillett, Burned Books (New York, 1932).

[78] Cf. W.E. Axon, "An Italian Librarian of the XVII and XVIII Centuries, Antonio Magliabechi," Library Association Record V (1903), 59-76.

[79] Founded in 1770. At first a military academy only, it developed into a general university. In 1794 it was dissolved by Duke Louis Eugene of Wurttemberg.

[80] The Communist revolution was epoch-making for this, as for all Russian libraries. For a brief account, see Chapter IX.

[81] See further A.L. Clarke, "Leibnitz as a Librarian," The Library III, ser. 5 (1914), 140-154.

[82] Non modo scientia bibliothecariorum omnium longe princeps erat, sed etiam elegentissima humanitate et exprompta adversus hospites facilitate. J.A. Ernesti, Narratio de Ionne Matthia Gesnero... (Leipzig, 1826), p. 30.

[83] See Charles Mortet, "The Public Libraries of France, National, Communal, and University," Library Association Record, n.s. vol. III (1925), 145-159. Important French library laws of the eighteenth and nineteenth centuries will be found in Ulysse Robert, Recueil de lois, décrets, ordonnances, arrêtés, circulaires, etc. concernant les bibliothèques publiques, communales, universitaires, scolaires et populaires (Paris, 1883). See also Christian de Serres de Mesplès, Les bibliothèques publiques francaises--leur organization--leur reform (Montpellier, 1933).

[84] See Henri Lemaître, Histoire du dépôt légal. Ire partie (Paris, 1910); Robert Crouzel, Le dépôt légal (Toulouse, 1936).

[85] The Imperial Deputation, composed of eight influential political leaders of the German Empire, effected a drastic territorial redistribution which greatly reduced the number of autonomous units within the Empire and abolished almost all the ecclesiastical states, imperial villages, and free cities. "The net result of the redistribution was to build up a number of medium-sized states with some approach to geographical homogeneity." -- C.T. Atkinson, A History of Germany, 1715-1815 (London, 1908), p. 460.

[86] Although the university library has a considerable reference collection of its own, it has always been able to fall back upon the vast scholarly resources of the Prussian State Library, with which it therefore does not try to compete.

[87] Attention should be called, however, to the printed subject indexes of the British Museum: Subject Index of the Modern Works Added to the Library, 1881 - London, 1902-); and Subject Index of Books Published up to and including 1880. Series 1-3 (London, 1933-1939).

[88] Catalogus codicum manuscriptorum Bibliothecae regiae monacensis. Tom. I-III. (Munich, 1858-1915).

[89] This has been translated into English by Arthur Browne with the title A General Bibliographical Dictionary, from the German of Frederic Adolphus Ebert. (Oxford, 1837).

[90] Ueber öffentliche Bibliotheken. I have been unable to find an English translation. The term "public library" here should be taken to mean "library open to public use" as over against the private library. More will be said further on concerning the kinds of public libraries in Germany. For the titles of Ebert's other works mentioned here, consult the bibliography.

[91] Die Bildung des Bibliothekars. There is an English translation (Woodstock, Vt., 1916).

[92] See C.F. Gosnell and Geza Schütz, "Goethe the Librarian," Library Quarterly II (1932), 367-374. A fuller account can be found in Otto Lerche, Goethe und die Weimarer Bibliothek (Leipzig, 1929).

[93] Control of German university libraries in the nineteenth century was commonly in the hands of a committee composed of officials such as the rector and the deans and members of the several faculties of instruction. In order to achieve recognition and true responsibility the professional librarian had to emancipate himself from overly rigid supervision by this committee.

[94] Cobbett's words are worth quoting at some length: "Let those who lounged in it, and made it a place of amusement, contribute to its support. Why should tradesmen and farmers be called upon to pay for the support of a place which was intended only for the amusement of the curious and the rich, and not for the benefit or the instruction of the poor? If the aristocracy wanted the Museum as a lounging place, let them pay for it." Hansard's Parliamentary Debates, ser. 3, vol. XVI (March 1 - April 1, 1833), p. 1003.

[95] Cf. R.C.B. Partridge, The History of the Legal Deposit of Books Throughout the British Empire (London, 1938).

[96] The printing of this catalogue continues. It was expected that it would be completed shortly after 1940, but the outbreak of war in 1939 upset this plan. E.G. Ledos, Histoire des catalogues des livres imprimés de la Bibliothèque Nationale (Paris, 1936) provides a detailed expert account of the various catalogues of printed books of this great library, and the admirable preface by M. Julien Cain, administrateur général of the library, gives a brief historical survey of its cataloguing procedures.

[97] Die Selbstandigkeit des bibliothekarischen Berufes. The pamphlet has not been translated.

[98] Arnold Sachse, Friedrich Althoff und sein Werk (Berlin, 1928) now fills the gap which existed when this sentence was written. Out of some 350 pages it devotes some 10 to Althoff's library activities, but many of these activities connect with, and flow from, wider educational accomplishments, to which a good deal of space is given. See also Friedrich Schmidt-Ott, "Althoff und die Bibliotheken," Zentralblatt für Bibliothekswesen LVI (1939), 101-103.

[99] See F.E. Hirsch, "The Scholar as Librarian; to the Memory of Adolf von Harnack," Library Quarterly IX (1939), 299-320.

[100] Jahresverzeichnis der an den deutschen Universitäten erschienenen Schriften.

[101] Bibliographischer Monatsbericht über neu erschienenen Schul-, Universitäts- und Hochschulschriften.

[102]Berliner Titeldrucke. For a brief sketch of the history of this publication, see the introduction to The Prussian Instructions... Translated by Andrew D. Osborn (Ann Arbor, 1938).

[103]The Deutscher Gesamtkatalog, begun in 1931 as the Gesamtkatalog der preussischen Bibliotheken, was designed to give this information in printed form. So far only 14 volumes (carrying the alphabet as far as the middle of the letter B) have appeared.

[104]E.H. Vouilléme, Die Inkunabeln der Königlichen Bibliothek und der anderen Berliner Sammlungen (Leipzig, 1906).

[105]For the more recent history of these institutions see Arundell Esdaile, "Between Two Wars in the British Museum," Library Quarterly XII (1942), 794-804; and José Meyer, "The Bibliothèque Nationale During the Last Decade," ibid, 805-826. It is probably too early to assess the effects of World War II on these libraries.

[106]See the painstaking account by David C. Mearns, The Story up to Now (Washington, 1948).

[107]Cf. Essays Offered to Herbert Putnam by his Colleagues and Friends on his Thirtieth Anniversary as Librarian of Congress, 5 April 1929 (New Haven, 1929).

[108]For further details see Lucy Salamanca, Fortress of Freedom (Philadelphia, 1942).

[109]The first supplement, published in 1948, contains printed cards issued from August 1, 1942 through December 31, 1947. Cards printed after that date are contained in the Cumulative Catalog of Library of Congress Printed Cards (Washington, 1947-).

[110]First printed in the Library Quarterly XIV (1944), 277-315, and reprinted in the Annual Report of the Librarian of Congress for...1945 (Washington, D. C.), p. 107-142.

[111]What happened to this library during, and immediately after, the war is described in Richard S. Hill, "The Former Prussian State Library," Music Library Association Notes III (1945-46), 327-350, 404-410.

[112]For a preliminary estimate of the destruction see George Leyh, "Die Lage der deutschen wissenschaftlichen Bibliotheken nach dem Kriege," Zentralblatt für Bibliothekswesen LXI (1947), 19-32.

[113]For a list of the more important bibliographical publications of the Deutsche Bücherei see Otto Neuburger, Official Publications of Present-Day Germany (Washington, D. C., 1942), p. 61-62. The Soviet Military Administration has granted permission for resumption of publication of these bibliographies. In 1946 the Deutsche Nationalbibliographie reappeared, and preparations are being made to produce some of the other titles as soon as possible. A new post-war bibliography resembling the Deutsche Nationalbibliographie and listing primarily publications of the British, French, and American zones of occupied Germany is the Bibliographie der Deutschen Bibliothek, Frankfurt a.M.

[114]Central control has been strengthened after the recent war by decrees appointing M. Julien Cain director of the libraries of France, and giving to the director wide powers. See Journal officiel de la République française, 24 August 1945, p. 5293 and 13 March 1946, p. 2119.

[115] See the Survey of Losses and Needs of Libraries in Some European Countries put out by the Preparatory Commission of the United Nations Educational, Scientific and Cultural Organization (UNESCO Prep. Com/L&M/13. App. I. Paris, November 14, 1946. Mimeographed).

[116] This has been asserted on a very small scale, however, with the result that there is still much variety among French municipal libraries.

[117] See I. Giordani, "The Work of Italian Libraries," Library Quarterly VIII (1938), 145-155.

[118] Norme per il catalogo degli stampati, 2nd ed. (Città del Vaticano, 1939). An English edition, Rules for the Catalog of Printed Books, translated by T. J. Shanahan, V. A. Shaefer, and C. T. Vesselowsky, and edited by W. E. Wright, was published in 1948.

[119] See E. Tisserant, "The Preparation of a Main Index for the Vatican Library Manuscripts," in William Warner Bishop; a Tribute, 1941, p. 176-185.

[120] See Fünfzig Jahre Schweizerische Landesbibliothek, 1895-1945, (Bern, 1945).

[121] Dans les Etats-Unis l'ensemble de l'éducation des hommes est dirigé vers la politique.

[122] Sidney Ditzion, Arsenals of a Democratic Culture; A Social History of the American Public Library Movement in New England and the Middle States from 1850 to 1900 (Chicago, 1947) makes a good beginning in this field. A major contribution to the history of the public library movement in New England is: Jesse H. Shera, Foundations of the Public Library (Chicago, 1949).

[123] See B.C. Steiner, ed., Rev. Thomas Bray; his Life and Selected Works Relating to Maryland (Baltimore, 1901); W.D. Houlette, "Parish Libraries and the Work of the Reverend Thomas Bray," Library Quarterly IV (1934), 588-609.

[124] C.B. Joeckel, The Government of the American Public Library (Chicago, 1935), p. 111-150 et passim.

[125] For a sketch of Billings' qualities and manifold achievements see H.M. Lydenberg, John Shaw Billings (Chicago, 1924).

[126] A good idea of the complex functions of a large public library can be obtained from the annual report of the New York Public Library. For a detailed description of the Chicago Public Library see C.B. Joeckel and L. Carnovsky, A Metropolitan Library in Action (Chicago, 1940). The clearest picture of the role played in the community by the average American public library will be found in R.S. and H.M. Lynd, Middletown (New York, 1929) and Middletown in Transition (New York, 1937).

[127] Cf. Sidney Ditzion, "The Anglo-American Library Scene: A Contribution to the Social History of the Library Movement," Library Quarterly XVI (1946), 281-301.

[128] For further details see J. Minto, A History of the Public Library Movement in Great Britain and Ireland (London, 1932).

[129]L. R. McColvin, The Public Library System of Great Britain (London, 1942).

[130]See further, A. Arnesen, "How Norway Became the Focus of American Library Methods in Europe," Library Quarterly IV (1934), 148-155. It is also worth noting that one of the most acute works on American libraries has been written by a Norwegian: W. Munthe, American Librarianship from a European Angle, (Chicago, 1939).

[131]W. Schuster, "Die Zusammenarbeit der Stadtbibliothek mit den Volksbüchereien," Zentralblatt für Bibliothekswesen LV (1938), 457-467.

[132]There have been several changes of title. Its last title was Die Bücherei and it was published by the Government Bureau for Popular Library Affairs (Reichsstelle fur Volksbüchereiwesen). It ceased publication shortly before the end of World War II.

[133]See W. Scheffen, "Zwanzig Jahre 'Grenzbuchereidienst'," Die Bücherei VII (1940), 254-263.

[134]It is interesting to note, however, that the first library journal to be published in Germany after the war was devoted to popular libraries: Der Volksbibliothekar (Berlin, I, No. 1, Oct., 1946-). Publication was aided and encouraged by the Soviet Military Administration.

[135]There is no English term which exactly gives the sense of the German. "Einheitsbibliothek," as nearly as we can translate it, means "unified library," that is, a library in which a number of functions are now performed in a central place which formerly were performed in disparate libraries of a special type--either scholarly or popular.

[136]These figures are, of course, pre-war. Both libraries may well have been demolished during the fighting.

[137]The Handbook of Medical Library Practice, (Chicago, 1943), produced by The Medical Library Association, lists the largest medical libraries in the world in Chapter I, Appendix I. From the figures there presented it transpires that the three largest medical libraries--and twelve of the thirty-six largest--are in the Soviet Union.

[138]See D. M. Krassovsky, "Bibliographical Work in Russia," Library Quarterly IV (1934), 449-466; A. B. Berthold, "Survey of Recent Russian Library Literature," Library Quarterly XVII (1947), 138-147; N. Delougaz, "Some Problems of Soviet Librarianship as Reflected in Russian Library Periodicals," Library Quarterly XV (1945), 213-223.

[139]Sic mundus adhuc mille annos durabit, et tot libri, ut hodie, conscribentur, vereor, ne e bibliothecis integrae civitates fient.--Quoted by Hessel. I have been unable to identify the passage.

[140]See the two illuminating articles by K. D. Metcalf: "Some Trends in Research Libraries," in William Warner Bishop; a Tribute, 1941, p. 145-166; and "Spatial Growth in University Libraries," Harvard Library Bulletin I (1947), 133-154. For an imaginative projection of the problem and a daring solution see Fremont Rider, The Scholar and the Future of the Research Library (New York, 1944).

[141]The most comprehensive historical study of library architecture is Georg Leyh, "Das Haus und seine Einrichtung," in Handbuch der Bibliothekswissenschaft, II, 1-115. A most thoroughgoing and informative

treatment, with emphasis on modern buildings, is J. L. Wheeler and
A. M. Githens, The American Public Library Building (New York, 1941).
Plans of modern European popular libraries will be found in M. Wieser
and E. Ackernecht, Der Volksbüchereibau (Stettin, 1930). For large
libraries see the special number "Bibliothèques" of L'Architecture
d'aujourd'hui (Vol. IX, no. 3, March 1938).

[142] "Some books are to be tasted, others to be swallowed, and some
few to be chewed and digested..." Francis Bacon, "Of Studies," in his
Essays (numerous editions).

[143] Cf. Fritz Juntke, "Magazinierung der toten Literatur," Zentralblatt für Bibliothekswesen XLVIII (1931), 391-421; 565.

[144] The building was bombed during the war, with loss of priceless
files of provincial newspapers.

[145] For more exact details see K. D. Metcalf, "The New England
Deposit Library," Library Quarterly XII (1942), 622-628.

[146] Sigismund Runge, "Some Recent Developments in Subject Cataloging in Germany," Library Quarterly XI (1941), 49-50.

[147] It must be remembered that the classed catalogue is perfectly
feasible even with a completely unclassified collection. Weakening of
the instinct for classification is not responsible in itself for the adoption of other types of catalogues.

[148] For an outline of the production of catalogue codes and of recent developments in cataloguing history see the "Report of the Sub-Committee on Uniform Catalog Rules," Actes du Comité International
des Bibliotheques X (1938), 55-69. See also J. C. M. Hanson, A Comparative Study of Cataloguing Rules Based on the Anglo-American Code
of 1908 (Chicago, 1939).

[149] Cf. A. D. Osborn, "The Crisis in Cataloging," Library Quarterly XI (1941), 393-411.

[150] Rules for Descriptive Cataloguing in the Library of Congress
(Washington, 1947). The principles underlying these rules are revealed
in two other publications of the Library of Congress: the brilliant
Studies of Descriptive Cataloging (Washington, 1946) and the Report of
the Advisory Committee on Descriptive Cataloging to the Librarian of
Congress (Washington, 1946).

[151] For policies, and a preliminary estimate of reduction of cost,
in handling this type of material see A. D. Osborn, "Books for the Deposit Library," Harvard University Library Notes IV (1942), 80-83.

[152] See p. 163, note 5.

[153] The war put a stop to publication of the Deutscher Gesamtkatalog. When, if, and how it will be resumed, it is as yet impossible to
say.

[154] See H. Fuchs, "The Gesamtkatalog of the Prussian Libraries,"
Library Quarterly IV (1934), 36-49; and the Translator's Introduction
by A. D. Osborn to The Prussian Instructions. The Berliner Titeldrucke
continued to be published during the war, though on a reduced scale.

[155] In a manuscript report prepared at the request of the Library of Congress Mission the Kommission für der Gesamtkatalog der Wiegendrucke reported that the reference library used in preparing the Gesamtkatalog had been totally lost. The Library of Congress Information Bulletin, December 30, 1947—January 5, 1948 states, nevertheless, that the manuscript was undamaged and that the work is going forward.

[156] Beginning January 1, 1948 the so-called "Farmington Plan" is being operated on an experimental basis in three countries: Sweden, Switzerland, and France. The plan is described in K. D. Metcalf and E. E. Williams, "Proposals for a Division of Responsibility Among American Libraries in the Acquisition and Recording of Library Materials," College and Research Libraries VI (1944), 105-109. The inadequate representation of foreign research materials in American libraries is pointed out in E. E. Williams, "Research Library Acquisitions from Eight Countries," Library Quarterly XV (1945), 313-323.

[157] Cf. Columbia University School of Library Service, School of Library Economy of Columbia College, 1887-1778; Documents for a History (New York, 1937).

[158] See the special number of the Library Quarterly (VII, no. 2, April, 1937) devoted to education for librarianship. For a general evaluation, see K. D. Metcalf, J. D. Russell, and A. D. Osborn, The Program of Instruction in Library Schools (Urbana, Ill,, 1943). A brief but perceptive analysis is J. P. Danton, Education for Librarianship; Criticisms, Dilemmas, and Proposals (New York, 1946).

[159] C. C. Williamson, Training for Library Service (New York, 1923).

[160] See F. Donker Duyvis, "The International Federation for Documentation," Journal of Documentary Reproduction III (1940), 176-191.

[161] Le rôle et la formation du bibliothécaire (Paris, 1935).

[162] Mission sociale et intellectuelle des bibliothèques populaires (Paris, 1937).

[163] See A. C. de Breycha-Vauthier, "The Federation of Library Associations," in William Warner Bishop: a Tribute, 1941, p. 34-49.

[164] For a survey of some of the problems--and an excellent bibliography--see E. E. Williams, ed., Conference on International Cultural, Educational, and Scientific Exchanges, Princeton University, November 25-26, 1946 (Chicago, 1947).

BIBLIOGRAPHY

Translator's Note

The list of references which follows consists of Hessel's bibliography, which I have expanded to about twice its original size by the addition of (1) older works--preponderantly though not exclusively in English--published before Hessel's book appeared but not cited by him, and cited by me as being useful chiefly to English-speaking readers; and (2) newer works published after the appearance of Hessel's book. These additions have been chosen with some care. The fact that a book or article deals with the subject of this work has not automatically qualified it for inclusion in the bibliography. I have tried to cite only useful and qualitatively good materials. This has sometimes been difficult because certain books or articles have few or no competitors. I make no claim to having produced an authoritative bibliography in any sense: the specialists will undoubtedly find much with which to quarrel. I trust, however, that the bibliography will be useful to the general reader.

Hessel's citations were of the catchword type, almost always abbreviated, and sometimes sufficiently inaccurate to make identification quite difficult. I have checked all his citations and brought them into conformity with approved modern bibliographical practice. Those few items which I have not been able to examine or to verify in a reliable catalogue or bibliography--and hence cannot vouch for--are preceded by an asterisk. In all cases the latest, or the best, edition known to me has been cited, and I have used English translations, if satisfactory, to replace the original works in other languages.

Hessel's original bibliography was classified. My additions have produced a bibliography so large as to make classification too complicated and too expensive to print. William Warner Bishop has commented on the instruction to be had from examining the backs of books; I trust some of my readers will experience the edification to be had from the exercise of reading straight through an alphabetical bibliography.

To save space the following familiar abbreviations have been used:

LJ -- Library Journal

LQ -- Library Quarterly

ZfB -- Zentralblatt für Bibliothekswesen

Abel, Sigurd. Jahrbücher des fränkischen Reichs unter Karl dem Grossen. Leipzig, 1866-1883.

Ackerknecht, Erwin. "Das schwedische Bücherei- und Vortragswesen," Bücherei und Bildungspflege III (1923), 135-144.

------ and Fritz, Gottlieb. Büchereifragen; Aufsätze zur Bildungsaufgabe und Organisation der modernen Bücherei. Berlin, 1914.

Adriani, Gert. Die Klosterbibliotheken der Spätbarock in Österreich und Süddeutschland; ein Beitrag zur Bau- und Kunstgeschichte des 17. und 18. Jahrhunderts. Graz, 1935.

Akademie der Wissenschaften, Munich. Mittelalterliche Bibliothekskataloge Deutschlands und der Schweiz. Munich, 1918-

Akademie der Wissenschaften, Vienna. Mittelalterliche Bibliothekskataloge Österreichs. Vienna, 1915-

American Library Association. Manual of Library Economy. Preprints. Various eds. Chicago, 1911-

------ A Survey of Libraries in the United States. Chicago, 1920-1927.

------ Committee on Post-War Planning. A National Plan for Public Library Service. Chicago, 1948.

Apolloni, Ettore. Guida alle biblioteche italiane. Milan, 1939.

------ and Circamone, Guido. Le biblioteche d'Italia fuore di Roma; storia, classificazione, funzionamento, contenuto, cataloghi, bibliografia. Rome, 1934-1939. (Bibliothèque des "Annales institutorum," III)

Arnesen, Arne. "How Norway Became the Focus of American Library Methods in Europe," LQ IV (1934), 148-155.

Association of Research Libraries. A Catalog of Books Represented by Library of Congress Printed Cards Issued to July 31, 1942. Ann Arbor, 1942-1946.

Aufsätze Fritz Milkau gewidmet. Leipzig, 1921.

*Aus den Tagen eines erloschenen Regentenhauses in seiner ehemaligen Residenz. Hessische Nachrichten aus alter und neuer Zeit. Aus dem grösseren Nachlass eines kürzlich verstorbenen Staatsdieners. Hannover, 1878.

Axon, William E. A. "An Italian Librarian of the XVII and XVIII Centuries. Antonio Magliabechi," Library Association Record V (1903), 59-76.

Baasch, Ernst. "Die Kommerzbibliothek in Hamburg," ZfB XXXVI (1919), 147-157.

Bähr, J.C.F. "Die Entführung der Heidelberger Bibliothek nach Rom im Jahre 1623," Serapeum VI (1845), 113-127, 129-144, 145-159.

Baker, Ernest A. The Public Library. London, 1922.

------ ed. The Uses of Libraries. London, 1920.

Balcke, Curt. Bibliographie zur Geschichte der Preussischen Staatsbibliothek. Leipzig, 1925. (Mitteilungen aus der Preussischen Staatsbibliothek, VI)

------"Fünfzig Jahre Jahresverzeichnis der deutschen Universitäts- und Hochschulschriften," ZfB LII (1935), 308-312.

------"The German Library World and its System," Library Association Record, n.s. V (1927), 101-121.

Bartholomew, Augustus T. Richard Bentley, D.D.; a Bibliography of his Works and of all the Literature Called Forth by his Acts or Writings. Cambridge, 1908.

Barwick, George F. The Reading Room of the British Museum. London, 1929.

Batiffol, Pierre. La Vaticane de Paul III à Paul V, d'après des documents nouveaux. Paris, 1890. (Petite bibliothèque d'art et d'archéologie, II)

Beck, Richard. "Die Beziehungen des Florentiners Antonio Magliabechi zu Christian Daum, Rektor zu Zwickau," ZfB XV (1898), 97-111, 145-176.

Becker, Gustav H. Catalogi bibliothecarum antiqui. Bonn, 1885.

Beddie, James S. "The Ancient Classics in the Medieval Libraries," Speculum V (1930), 3-20.

------"Libraries in the 12th Century. Their Catalogues and Contents," in Anniversary Essays in Medieval History by Students of Charles Homer Haskins (Boston, 1929), p. 1-23.

Beer, Rudolf. "Bemerkungen über den ältesten Handschriftenbestand des Klosters Bobbio," Anzeiger der K. Akademie der Wissenschaften in Wien, Philosophisch-historische Klasse XLVIII (1911), 78-104.

------"Bobbienser Mischhandschrift: patristische und grammatische Schriften, zum Teil auf reskribierten Blättern mit klassischen, biblischen und apokryphen Texten," in Monumenta palaeographica Vindobonensia II (Leipzig, 1913), 1-54.

Beeson, Charles H. Isidor-Studien. Munich, 1913. (Quellen und Untersuchungen zur lateinischen Philologie des Mittelalters, IV, 2)

Behrend, Fritz. "Corveys elfhundertjährige Geschichte im Spiegel seiner Büchersammlungen," Zeitschrift für Bücherfreunde, n.s. XV (1928), 11-21.

Beiträge zum Bibliotheks- und Buchwesen Paul Schwenke zum 20. März 1913 gewidmet. Berlin, 1913.

Beltrami, Luca. La Biblioteca Ambrosiana. Milan, 1896.

Benedictus, Saint. The Rule of Saint Benedict, translated with an introduction by Abbot Gasquet. London, 1909.

Bergkamp, Joseph U. Dom Jean Mabillon and the Benedictine Historical School of Saint-Maur. Washington, 1928.

Berlin. Preussische Staatsbibliothek. Fünfzehn Jahre Königliche und Staatsbibliothek. Dem scheidenden Generaldirektor Adolf von Harnack zum 31. März 1921 überreicht von den wissenschaftlichen Beamten der Preussischen Staatsbibliothek. Berlin, 1921.

Bern. Schweizerische Landesbibliothek. Fünfzig Jahre Schweizerische Landesbibliothek. Bern, 1945.

Berthold, Arthur B. "Survey of Recent Russian Library Literature," LQ XVII (1947), 138-147.

Bertoni, Giulio. La Biblioteca Estense e la coltura ferrarese ai tempi del duca Ercole I (1471-1505). Turin, 1903.

Besterman, Theodore. The Beginnings of Systematic Bibliography. 2nd ed. London, 1936.

Beyerle, Konrad, ed. Die Kultur der Abtei Reichenau. Erinnerungsshrift zur zwölfhundertsten Widerkehr des Gründungsjahres des Inselklosters, 724-1924. Munich, 1925.

Bezold, Carl. "Bibliotheks- und Schriftwesen im alten Ninive," ZfB XXI (1904), 257-277.

Biagi, Guido. "Le biblioteche nel passato e nell'avvenire," Rivista delle biblioteche e degli archivi XVI (1905), 1-11.

"Bibliotheca," in Thesaurus linguae latinae, Vol. II.

"Bibliotheken," in Pauly-Wissowa, Realencyclopedie der classischen Altertumswissenschaften, Vol. III.

"Les Bibliothèques," L'Architecture d'aujourd'hui IX, no. 3 (March, 1938)

"Bibliothèques," Bulletin du livre français, no. 49 (July/August, 1938)

Binz, Gustav. "Literarische Kriegsbeute aus Mainz in schwedischen Bibliotheken," Mainzer Zeitschrift XII/XIII (1918), 157-165.

Birt, Theodor. Alexander der Grosse und das Weltgriechtum bis zum Erscheinen Jesu. 2nd ed. Leipzig, 1925.

------Das antike Buchwesen. Berlin, 1882.

------Die Buchrolle in der Kunst. Leipzig, 1907.

Bloch, Hermann. "Ein karolingischer Bibliothekskatalog aus Kloster Murbach," in Strassburger Festschrift zur XLVI Versammlung deutscher Philologen und Schulmänner (Strassburg, 1901), p. 257-285.

Bodley, Thomas. Letters...to the University of Oxford. Oxford, 1927.

------Letters...to Thomas James, First Keeper of the Bodleian Library. Oxford, 1926.

------The Life of Sir Thomas Bodley, Written by himself, Together with the First Draft of the Statutes of the Public Library at Oxon. Chicago, 1906. (Literature of Libraries in the Seventeenth and Eighteenth Centuries, III)

*Bömer, Alois. "Das literarische Leben in Münster," in Aus dem geistigen Leben und Schaffen in Westfalen; Festschrift zur Eröffnung des Neubaus der Königl. Universitätsbibliothek in Münster (Westfalen) am 8. November 1906. Münster, 1906.

Böhme, Paul. Nachrichten über die Königl. Bibliothek der Landesschule Pforta. Naumburg, 1880-1883.

Börsenverein der deutschen Buchhändler. Historische Kommission. Geschichte des deutschen Buchhandels. Leipzig, 1886-1923.

Bogeng, Gustav A.E. "Über Zacharias Conrad von Uffenbachs Erfahrungen und Erlebnisse bei der Benutzung deutscher, englischer, holländischer öffentlicher Büchersammlungen in den Jahren 1709-11," in Beiträge... Schwenke gewidmet. p. 30-46.

Bohn, Richard. Das Heiligtum der Athena Polias Nikephoros. Berlin, 1885. (Altertümer von Pergamon, II)

Bollert, Martin. "Johann Joachimm Winckelmann als Bibliothekar," ZfB LIII (1936), 482-489.

Bonfort, Helene. Das Bibliothekswesen in den Vereinigten Staaten. Hamburg, 1896.

Borden, Arnold K. "Seventeenth-Century American Libraries," LQ II (1932), 138-147.

Bosca, Pietro P. De origine et statu Bibliothecae Ambrosianae. Milan, 1672.

Bostwick, Arthur E. The American Public Library. 4th ed. New York, 1929.

------ed. Popular Libraries of the World. Chicago, 1933.

Boulting, William. Aeneas Silvius (Enea Silvio de Piccolomini--Pius II), Orator, Man of Letters, Statesman, and Pope. London, 1918.

Boyd, Clarence E. Public Libraries and Literary Culture in Ancient Rome. Chicago, 1916.

Boysen, Karl. "Systematischer oder Schlagwortkatalog," in Aufsätze Fritz Milkau gewidmet, p. 19-36.

Brandes, Ernst. Über die gegenwärtige Zustand der Universität Göttingen. Göttingen, 1802.

Braunsberger, Otto. "Ein Freund der Bibliotheken und ihrer Handschriften," in Miscellanea Francesco Ehrle, Vol. V, p. 455-472.

Bresslau, Harry. "Bamberger Studien," Neues Archiv der Gesellschaft für ältere deutsche Geschichtskunde XXI (1896), 141-234.

------Handbuch der Urkundenlehre für Deutschland und Italien. 2nd ed. Leipzig, 1912-1931.

Breycha-Vauthier, Arthur C. de. "The Federation of Library Associations," in William Warner Bishop, a Tribute, 1941, p. 34-49.

British Museum. Dept. of Egyptian and Assyrian Antiquities. Catalogue of the Cuneiform Tablets in the Kouyunjik Collection of the British Museum. London, 1889-1899.

------Dept. of Printed Books. The British Museum Catalogue of Printed Books, 1881-1900. Published under the auspices of a committee of the Association of Research Libraries. Ann Arbor, 1946.

------Catalogue of Printed Books. London, 1881-1900.

------General Catalogue of Printed Books. London, 1931-

------Subject Index of Books Published up to and including 1880. Series 1-3. London, 1933-1939.

------Subject Index of the Modern Works Added to the Library, 1881- London, 1902-

Brodrick, James. Saint Peter Canisius, S. J., 1521-1597. London, 1935.

Brooks, Constance. Antonio Panizzi: Scholar and Patriot. Manchester, 1931. (University of Manchester Publications, no. 208, Italian Series, no. 1)

Brown, James D. Library Classification and Cataloguing. London, 1912.

------Manual of Library Economy. 5th ed. London, 1907.

Brown, Karl, comp. A Guide to the Reference Collections of the New York Public Library. New York, 1941.

Bruch, Bernhard. "Die Entwicklung der deutschen Stadtbibliotheken vom Beginn des 19. Jahrhunderts bis zur Gegenwart," ZfB LIV (1937), 591-610.

Buchholtz, Arend. Die Volksbibliotheken und Lesehallen der Stadt Berlin, 1850-1900. Berlin, 1900.

Bürger, Richard. Friedrich Adolf Ebert; ein biographischer Versuch. Leipzig, 1910. (Sammlung bibliothekswissenschaftlicher Arbeiten, XXXXI)

Burckhardt, Jakob C. The Civilization of the Renaissance in Italy. Oxford, 1937.

Burdach, Konrad. "Die pfälzischen Wittelsbacher und die Handschriften der Palatina," ZfB V (1888), 111-133.

------"Zur Kenntnis altdeutscher Handschriften und zur Geschichte altdeutscher Literatur und Kunst," ZfB VIII (1891), 1-21, 145-176, 324-344, 433-488.

Burton, Margaret and Vosburgh, Marian E. A Bibliography of Librarianship. London, 1934.

Cagnat, M.R. "Les bibliothèques municipales dans l'empire romain," Mémoires de l'Academie des Inscriptions et Belles-Lettres XXXVIII (1909/1911), I, 1-26.

Cahier, Charles. Bibliothèques. Paris, 1877. (His Nouveaux mélanges d'archeologie, d'histoire et de littérature sur le moyen âge, IV)

Carini, Isidoro. La Biblioteca Vaticana. 2nd ed. Rome, 1893.

Carnegie Corporation of New York. Carnegie Grants for Library Buildings, 1890-1917. Philadelphia, 1943.

Castellani, Carlo. Le biblioteche nell'antichità. Bologna, 1884.

I Cataloghi delle biblioteche italiane. Rome, 1934.

Centenary of the Birth of Andrew Carnegie. The British Trusts and their Work, with a Chapter on the American Foundations. Edinburgh, 1935.

Champion, Pierre. La librairie de Charles d'Orléans. Paris, 1910. (Bibliothèque du XVe siècle, X1)

Chapman, John. St. Benedict and the Sixth Century. London, 1929.

Chiera, Edward. They Wrote on Clay. Chicago, 1938.

Christ, Karl. Die Bibliothek des Klosters Fulda im 16. Jahrhundert: die Handschriften-Verzeichnisse. Leipzig, 1933. (ZfB. Beiheft 64)

------Die Bibliothek Reuchlins in Pforzheim. Leipzig, 1924. (ZfB. Beiheft 52)

------"Kardinal Franz Ehrle," ZfB LII (1935), 1-47.

Christ, Wilhelm von. Geschichte der griechischen Literatur. 6th ed. Munich, 1912-1924. (Handbuch der classischen Altertumswissenschaft, VII)

Clark, James M. The Abbey of St. Gall as a Center of Literature and Art. Cambridge, 1926.

Clark, John W. The Care of Books. 2nd ed. Cambridge, 1909.

------Richard Bentley. Cambridge, 1908.

Clarke, Archibald L. "Leibnitz as a Librarian," The Library, ser. 3, V (1914), 140-154.

Clauss, Hermann. Die Schwabacher Kirchenbibliothek. Munich, 1921.

Clément, Claude. Musei sive bibliothecae, tam privatae quam publicae, extructio, instructio, cura, usus. Lyon, 1635.

Coggiola, Giulio. "Il prestito della Marciana dal 1474 al 1527," ZfB XXV (1908), 47-70.

Columbia University. School of Library Service. School of Library Economy of Columbia College, 1887-1889; Documents for a History. New York, 1937.

Comparetti, Domenico P.A. and Petra, Giulio de. La villa ercolanese dei Pisoni; i suoi monumenti e la sua biblioteca. Turin, 1883.

Conze, Alexander. "Die pergamenische Bibliothek," Sitzungsberichte der K. Preussischen Akademie der Wissenschaften, 1884, II, 1259-1270.

Cotton des Houssayes, Jean Baptiste. The Duties and Qualifications of a Librarian; a Discourse pronounced in the General Assembly of the Sorbonne, December 23, 1780. Chicago, 1906. (Literature of Libraries in the Seventeenth and Eighteenth Centuries, I)

Crouzel, Robert. Le dépôt légal. Toulouse, 1936.

Crüwell, G.A. "Der Bücherfluch," Mitteilungen des Österreichischen Vereins für Bibliothekswesen VIII (1904), 178-184; IX (1905), 27-31, 96-101, 129-135.

Dahl, Svend. Geschichte des Buches. Leipzig, 1928.

------ed. Haandbog i Bibliotekskundskab, 3rd ed. Copenhagen, 1924-1930.

------"Über die neueste Entwicklung des wissenschaftlichen Bibliothekswesens in Danemark," ZfB LVI (1939), 395-409.

D'Angelo, Maria. Il cardinale Girolamo Casanate (1620-1700). Luzzatti, 1923.

Danton, J. Periam. Education for Librarianship; Criticisms, Dilemmas, and Proposals. New York, 1946.

Dawe, Grosvenor. Melvil Dewey. Lake Placid, 1932.

*Decker, A. "Die Hildeboldsche Manuskriptensammlung des Kölner Doms," in Festschrift der 43. Versammlung deutscher Philologen und Schulmänner, dargeboten von den höheren lehranstalten Kölns (Bonn, 1895), p. 215-251.

Degener, Hermann. "Die Bibliothek des British Museum," Zeitschrift für Bücherfreunde VI (1902/03), I, 1-39.

------"Die Bodleian Library in Oxford, "Zeitschrift für Bücherfreunde VIII (1904/05), I, 89-119.

Degering, Hermann. "Französischer Kunstraub in Deutschland, 1794-1807," Internationale Monatsschrift für Wissenschaft, Kunst und Technik XI (1916/17), 1-47.

Delisle, Léopold V. Le cabinet des manuscrits de la Bibliothèque Impériale. Paris, 1868-1887.

------Inventaire des manuscrits de la Bibliothèque Nationale. Fonds de Cluni. Paris, 1884.

------"Notice sur un livre annoté par Pétrarque (Ms. Latin 2201 de la Bibliothèque Nationale," Notices et extraits des manuscrits de la Bibliothèque Nationale et autres bibliothèques XXXV (1896/97), II, 393-408.

------Recherches sur la librairie de Charles V. Paris, 1907.

Delitsch, Friedrich. Assurbanipal und die assyrische Kultur seiner Zeit. Leipzig, 1907. (Der alte Orient, XI, 1)

Delougaz, Nathalie. "Some Problems of Soviet Librarianship as Reflected in Russian Library Periodicals," LQ XV (1945), 213-223.

Denifle, Heinrich. "Die Constitutionen des Predigerordens vom Jahre 1228," Archiv für Litteratur und Kirchengeschichte des Mittelalters I (1885), 164-227.

Denk, Victor M.O. Geschichte des Gallo-fränkischen Unterrichts- und Bildungswesen von den ältesten Zeiten bis auf Karl den Grossen. Mainz, 1892.

De Roover, Florence E. "The Scriptorium," in J.W. Thompson, The Medieval Library, p. 594-612.

Des Coudres, Hans P. "Das verbotene Schrifttum und die wissenschaftlichen Bibliotheken," ZfB LII (1935), 459-471.

Ditzion, Sidney H. "The Anglo-American Library Scene: a Contribution to the Social History of the Library Movement," LQ XVI (1946), 281-301.

------Arsenals of a Democratic Culture; a Social History of the American Public Library Movement in New England and the Middle States from 1850 to 1900. Chicago, 1947.

------"Mechanics' and Mercantile Libraries," LQ X (1940), 192-219.

Döbner, Richard, ed. Annalen und Akten der Brüder des gemeinsamen Lebens im Lüchtenhofe zu Hildesheim. Hannover, 1903. (Quellen und Darstellungen zur Geschichte Niedersachsens, IX)

Donker Duyvis, F. "The International Federation for Documentation," Journal of Documentary Reproduction III (1940), 176-191.

Douais, C. "Assignations des livres aux religieux du convent des Frères Prêcheurs de Barcelone," Revue des bibliothèques III (1893), 49-83.

Doutrepont, Georges. La littérature française à la cour de Bourgogne: Philippe le Hardi - Jean sans Peur - Philippe le Bon - Charles le Téméraire. Paris, 1909. (Bibliothèque du 15e siecle, VIII)

Downs, Robert B. Resources of New York City Libraries; a Survey of Facilities for Advanced Study and Research. Chicago, 1942.

------Resources of Southern Libraries; a Survey of Facilities for Research. Chicago, 1938.

------ed. Union Catalogs in the United States. Chicago, 1942.

Düntzer, Heinrich. "Goethe und die Bibliotheken zu Weimar und Jena," ZfB I (1884), 89-105.

Duffus, Robert L. Our Starving Libraries; Studies in Ten American Communities during Depression Years. Boston, 1933.

Dummer, E. Heyse. "Cardinal Franz Ehrle: in Commemoration of a Double Anniversary," LQ XVI (1946), 335-340.

------"Johann Christian von Aretin: a Re-evaluation," LQ XVI (1946), 108-121.

Duncker, Albert. "Landgraf Wilhelm IV von Hessen, gennant der Weise, und die Begründung der Bibliothek zu Kassel im Jahre 1580. Kassel, 1881.

Dury, John. The Reformed Librarie Keeper. Chicago, 1906. (Literature of Libraries in the Seventeenth and Eighteenth Centuries, II)

Dvorák, Max. "Die Illuminatoren des Johann von Neumarkt," Jahrbuch der kunsthistorischen Sammlungen des allerhöchsten Kaiserhauses XXII (1901), 35-126.

Dziatzko, Karl. "Die Bibliothek und der Lesesaal des Britischen Museums," Preussische Jahrbucher XLVIII (1881), 346-376.

------"Die Bibliotheksanlage von Pergamon," in his Beiträge zum Kenntnis des Schrift-, Buch- und Bibliothekswesens, III. Leipzig, 1896. (Sammlung bibliothekswissenschaftlicher Arbeiten, X)

------"Eine Reise durch die grösseren Bibliotheken Italiens," in Sammlung bibliothekswissenschaftlicher Arbeiten VI (1894), 96-128.

------Entwicklung und gegenwärtiger Stand der wissenschaftlichen Bibliotheken Deutschlands mit besonderer Berücksichtigung Preussens. Leipzig, 1893. (Sammlung bibliothekswissenschaftlicher Arbeiten, V)

------"Die Göttinger Bibliothek in westfälischer Zeit," in Sammlung bibliothekswissenschaftlicher Arbeiten XVII (1904), 25-49.

Ebert, Friedrich A. "Bibliotheken," in Ersch and Gruber, Allgemeine Encyclopädie der Wissenschaften und Künste, X.

------A General Bibliographical Dictionary. Oxford, 1837.

------Geschichte und Beschreibung der königlichen öffentlichen Bibliothek zu Dresden. Leipzig, 1822.

------The Training of the Librarian. Woodstock, 1916. (The Librarian's Series, V)

------Über öffentliche Bibliotheken, besonders deutsche Universitätsbibliotheken. Freiburg, 1811. Cf. also the review by M. Schrettinger in Jenaische allgemeine Literaturzeitung, 1814, Ergänzungsblätter, II, 337-344, 346-347.

Ebrard, Friedrich C. Die Stadtbibliothek in Frankfurt am Main. Frankfurt, 1896.

Edwards, Edward. Lives of the Founders of the British Museum, with Notice of its Chief Augmentors and Other Benefactors. London, 1870.

------Memoirs of Libraries, of Museums, and of Archives. 2nd ed. London, 1901.

Ehl, Heinrich. Die Ottonische Kölner Buchmalerei. Bonn, 1922.

Ehrhardt, Albert. "Die griechische Patriarchal-Bibliothek zu Jerusalem. Ein Beitrag zur griechischen Palaeographie," Römische Quartalschrift für christliche Altertumskunde und für Kunstgeschichte V (1891), 217-265, 329-331.

Ehrle, Franz. "Bibliothektechnisches aus der Vaticana," ZfB XXXIII (1916), 197-227.

------"Die Frangipani und der Untergang des Archivs und der Bibliothek der Päpste am Anfang des 13. Jahrhunderts," in Mélanges offerts a M. Emile Chatelaine (Paris, 1910), p. 448-485.

------Historia bibliotheca Romanorum pontificum tum Bonifatianae tum Avenionensis, I. Rome, 1890.

Ehwald, Rudolf. "Geschichte der Gothaer Bibliothek," ZfB XVIII (1901), 434-463.

Eliot, Charles W. "The Division of a Library into Books in Use and Books not in Use, with Different Storage Methods for the two Classes of Books," LJ XXVII (1902), II, 51-56, Cf. also ibid. I, 256-260.

Eneström, Gustaf. "Schwedische Bibliotheken," ZfB IV (1887), 329-335.

Erfurt. Stadtbücherei. Beschreibendes Verzeichnis der Amplonianischen Handschriften zu Erfurt. Berlin, 1887. Introduction by Wilhelm Schum

Erman, Adolf. Aegypten und aegyptisches Leben im Altertum. Tübingen, 1923.

------Life in Ancient Egypt. London, 1894.

Erman, Wilhelm. Geschichte der Bonner Universitätsbibliothek (1818-1901). Halle a.S., 1919. (Sammlung bibliothekswissenschaftlicher Arbeiten, XXXVII/XXXVIII)

Ernesti, Johann A. Narratio de Ionne Matthia Gesnero et I.N. Niclasii de eodem Gesnero epistola familiaris... Accedit memoria Gesneri ab I.D. Michaeli. Leipzig, 1826. (Eloquentium virorum narrationes de vitis hominum doctrina et virtute excellentium... ed. C.H. Frotsche II)

Escher, Hermann. Aus dem amerikanischen Bibliothekswesen. Tübingen, 1923.

------"Vom schweizerischen Bibliothekswesen," ZfB XXVIII (1911), 537-544.

Esdaile, Arundell. "Between two Wars at the British Museum," LQ XII (1942), 794-804.

------The British Museum Library. London, 1946.

------and Burton, Margaret. The World's Great Libraries. London, 1934-1937.

Essays offered to Herbert Putnam by his Colleagues and Friends on his Thirtieth Anniversary as Librarian of Congress, 5 April 1929; ed. by William Warner Bishop and Andrew Keogh. New Haven, 1929.

Estienne, Henri. The Frankfort Book Fair, ed. and tr. by J.W. Thompson, Chicago, 1911.

Evans, Joan. Monastic Life at Cluny, 910-1157. London, 1931.

Fabre, Paul. "La Vaticane de Sixte IV." Mélanges d'archéologie et d'histoire XV (1895), 455-483.

Fagan, Louis A. The Life of Sir Anthony Panizzi. 2nd ed. London, 1880.

Faider, Paul. "Le Catalogue général des manuscrits des bibliothèques de Belgique," LQ VIII (1938), 523-527.

Falk, Franz. Beiträge zur Rekonstruktion der alten Bibliotheca Fuldensis und Laureshamensis. Leipzig, 1902. (Beihefte zum ZfB, 26)

------Die ehemalige Dombibliothek zu Mainz. Leipzig, 1897. (Beihefte zum ZfB, 18)

Farrar, Clarissa P. and Evans Austin P. Bibliography of English Translations from Medieval Sources. New York, 1946.

Faucon, Maurice. La librairie des papes d'Avignon. Paris, 1886-1887. (Bibliothèque des Ecoles françaises d'Athènes et de Rome, 43,50)

Fava, Domenico. La Biblioteca Nazionale Centrale di Firenze et le sue insigni raccolte. Milan, 1939.

Felder, Hilarin. Geschichte der wissenschaftlichen Studien im Franziskanerorden bis um die Mitte des 13. Jahrhunderts. Freiburg i.Br., 1904.

Festschrift für Georg Leidinger zum 60. Geburtstag am 30. Dezember 1930. Munich, 1930.

Festschrift Georg Leyh. Aufsätze zum Bibliothekswesen und zur Forschungsgeschichte dargebracht zum 60. Geburtstag am 6. Juni 1937 von Freunden und Fachgenossen. Leipzig, 1937.

Festschrift Martin Bollert zum 60. Geburtstag. Dresden, 1936.

Festschrift zur Feier des hundertfünfzigjahrigen Bestehens der Königlichen Gesellschaft der Wissenschaften zu Göttingen. Berlin, 1901.

Fick, Richard. Ein Bericht Heynes aus der westfälischen Zeit und seine programmatische Bedeutung. Göttingen, 1924. (Vorarbeiten zur Geschichte der Göttinger Universität und Bibliothek, I)

Fifty Years of Education for Librarianship. Papers Presented for the Celebration of the Fiftieth Anniversary of the University of Illinois Library School, March 2, 1943. Urbana, 1943.

Fischer, Hans. "Die Kgl. Bibliothek in Bamberg und ihre Handschriften," ZfB XXIV (1907), 364-394.

Fischer, Ludwig. König Matthias Corvinus und seine Bibliothek. Vienna, 1878.

Fliegel, M. "Die Dombibliothek zu Breslau im ausgehenden Mittelalter," Zeitschrift des Vereins für Geschichte Schlesiens LIII (1919), 84-133.

Florence. Biblioteca Mediceo-Laurenziana. Biblioteca Mediceo-Laurenziana di Firenze. Florence, 1872.

Focke, Rudolf. "Das Volksbibliothekswesen in der Provinz Posen," Blätter für Volksbibliotheken und Lesehallen X (1909), 73-76, 109-119.

Folz, Karl. Geschichte der Salzburger Bibliotheken. Vienna, 1877.

Franke, Johannes. Die Abgabe der Pflichtexemplare von Druckerzeugnissen, mit besonderer Berücksichtigung Deutschlands und des Deutschen Reiches. Berlin, 1889. (Sammlung bibliothekswissenschaftlicher Arbeiten, III)

Franklin, Alfred. Guide des savants, des littérateurs et des artistes dans les bibliothèques de Paris. Paris, 1908.

------Histoire de la Bibliothèque Mazarine et du palais de l'Institut. 2nd ed. Paris, 1901.

Franz, Adolph. M. Aurelius Cassiodorus Senator; ein Beitrag zur Geschichte der theologischen Literatur. Breslau, 1872.

Friedensburg, Walter. "Petruc Lambecuis an Lucas Holsteinus über die Errichtung der Hamburgischen Stadtbibliothek und den Stand der Gelehrsamkeit in Hamburg (1651)," ZfB XIX (1902), 321-328.

Fritz, Gottlieb. Das moderne Volksbildusgswesen. Leipzig, 1909. (Aus Natur- und Geisteswelt, 266)

------and Plate, Otto. Volksbüchereien (Bücher- und Lesehallen), ihre Einrichtung und Verwaltung. Berlin, 1924. (Sammlung Göschen, 332)

Fuchs, Hermann. "Der Deutsche Gesamtkatalog als Organisation und Leistung," ZfB LV (1938), 443-457.

------"The Gesamtkatalog of the Prussian Libraries," LQ IV (1934), 36-49.

Fussler, Herman H. Photographic Reproduction for Libraries. Chicago, 1942.

Gardner, Alice. Theodore of Studium, his Life and Times. London, 1905.

Gardthausen, Victor. "Die alexandrinische Bibliothek, ihr Vorbild, Katalog und Betrieb," Zeitschrift des deutschen Vereins für Buchwesen und Schrifttum V (1922), 73-104. Cf. the review by Carl Wendel in ZfB XL (1923), 258-259.

------Handbuch der wissenschaftlichen Bibliothekskunde. Leipzig, 1920.

Garnett, Richard. "Librarianship in the Seventeenth Century," in his Essays in Librarianship and Bibliography (London, 1899), p. 174-190.

------"The Printing of the British Museum Catalogue," ibid., p. 67-86.

------"Sir Anthony Panizzi, K.C.B.," ibid., p. 288-303.

Gasquet, Francis A. Monastic Life in the Middle Ages, with a Note on Great Britain and the Holy See, 1792-1806. London, 1922.

Gautier, Jean. Nos bibliothèques publiques, leur situation légale; avec appendice contenant les décrets, arrêtés et circulaires relatifs aux bibliothèques parus dans les vingt dernières années. 2nd ed. Paris, 1902.

Gebhardt, Oscar von. "Ein Bücherfund in Bobbio," ZfB V (1888), 383-431, 538.

Gedike, Friedrich. Der Universitäts-Bereiser Friedrich Gedike und sein Bericht an Friedrich Wilhelm II. Mitgeteilt von Dr. Richard Fester. Berlin, 1905. (Ergänzungshefte des Archivs für Kulturgeschichte, I)

Geiger, Karl. "Jeremias David Reuss und seine Bibliothek," ZfB XXII (1905), 465-490.

------"Robert von Mohl als Vorstand der Tübinger Universitäts-Bibliothek," ZfB XVII (1900), 161-191.

Germany. Statistisches Reichsamt. Die deutschen Volksbüchereien nach Ländern, Provinzen und Gemeinden. 1933/34. Berlin, 1935. (Statistik des Deutschen Reiches. Bd. 471)

Gesellschaft der Freunde der Deutschen Bücherei. Deutsche Bücherei (German Library). Objects and Functions. Leipzig, 1925.

Gesellschaft der Wissenschaften, Göttingen. Festschrift zur Feier des hundertfünfzigjährigen Bestehens der Königlichen Gesellschaft der Wissenschaften zu Göttingen. Berlin, 1901.

Gesner, Johann M. "Ein Gutachten Gesners über die Anforderungen des bibliothekarischen Berufes," in Sammlung bibliothekswissenschaftlicher Arbeiten, VIII, p. 98-104.

Gessert, Dr. "Theiner über die Schenkung der Heidelberger Bibliothek durch Kurfürst Maximilian I von Bayern an Papst Gregor XV," Serapeum VI (1815), 1-11.

Gibson, Strickland. Some Oxford Libraries. London, 1914.

Gillett, Charles R. Burned Books: Neglected Chapters in British History and Literature. New York, 1932.

Giordani, Igino. "The Vatican Library during Recent Years," LQ VII (1937), 1-25.

------"The Work of Italian Libraries," LQ IX (1939), 145-155.

Giubileo di cultura, MCMXI, per la nuova Biblioteca Nazionale Centrale. Florence, 1911.

Glauning, Otto. "Ein Jahrhundert bibliothekarischer Vergangenheit," ZfB XL (1923), 1-18.

Götze, Bernt. "Antike Bibliotheken," Jahrbuch des deutschen archäologischen Instituts LII (1937), 225-247.

Gomoll, Heinz. "Zu Cassiodors Bibliothek und ihrem Verhältnis zu Bobbio," ZfB LIII (1936), 185-189.

Gosnell, Charles F. and Schütz, Geza. "Goethe the Librarian," LQ II (1932), 367,374.

Gottlieb, Theodor. Büchersammlung Kaiser Maximilians I. Leipzig, 1900.

------Über mittelalterliche Bibliotheken. Leipzig, 1890.

------Die Weissenburger Handschriften in Wolfenbüttel. Vienna, 1909. (Sitzungsberichte der Philosophisch-historischen Klasse der K. Adademie der Wissenschaften in Wien, CLXIII, 6)

Gourley, James E. and Lester, Robert M. The Diffusion of Knowledge; a List of Books Made Possible Wholly or in Part by Grants from the Carnegie Corporation of New York and Published...during the Years 1911-1935. Philadelphia, 1935.

Graesel, Arnim. Handbuch der Bibliothekslehre. 2nd ed. Leipzig, 1902.

------"Otto Hartwig," ZfB XXI (1904), 97-103.

Grässe, Johann G.T. "Zur Geschichte der Bibliotheken in Frankreich," Serapeum IV (1843), 332-336; 344-348.

Graham, Hugh. The Early Irish Monastic Schools. Dublin, 1923.

Gray, Austin K. Benjamin Franklin's Library. New York, 1937.

Great Britain. Board of Education. Public Libraries Committee. Report on Public Libraries in England and Wales. London, 1927. (Parliamentary Papers by Command, no. 2868)

Great Britain. Royal Commission on National Museums and Galleries. Final Report. London, 1929-1930.

Green, Samuel S. The Public Library Movement in the United States, 1853-1893. Boston, 1913. (Useful Reference Series, 8)

Greenwood, Thomas. Edward Edwards, the Chief Pioneer of Municipal Public Libraries. London, 1902.

Grimm, Werner von. "Studien zur älteren Geschichte der Kaiserlichen Öffentlichen Bibliothek in St. Petersburg (Leningrad), 1794-1861," ZfB L (1933), 301-315, 353-377.

Grisar, H. "Le biblioteche nell'antichità classica e nei primi tempi cristiani," La civiltà cattolica, ser. 18, vol. VII (1902), 715-729; VIII (1902), 463-477.

Guasti, C. "Inventario della Libreria Urbinate, compilato nel secolo XV da Federigo Veterano, bibliotecario di Federigo I da Montefeltro, duca d'Urbino," Giornale storico degli archivi toscani VI (1862), 127-147; VII (1863), 46-55, 130-154.

Guide to Catholic Literature, 1888-1940. Detroit, 1940.

Haeberlin, Carl. "Beiträge zur Kentniss des antiken Bibliotheks- und Buchwesens," ZfB VII (1890), 271-302.

Haebler, Konrad. Deutsche Bibliophilen des 16. Jahrhunderts; die Fürsten von Anhalt, ihre Bücher und Bucheinbände. Leipzig, 1923.

Hamburg. Staats- und Universitätsbibliothek. Mitteilungen aus der Stadtbibliothek zu Hamburg. Vol. XI. Hamburg, 1894.

Hamdorff, G. "Die dänischen Volksbüchereien im Johre 1912," Monatshefte der Comenius-Gesellschaft für Volkserziehung, n.s. V (1913), 7-12.

Hamel, Frank. "The Librarians of the Royal Library at Fontainebleau," The Library III, ser. 1 (1910), 190-199.

Handbuch der deutschen Volksbüchereien, hrsg. vom Verband deutscher Volksbibliothekare. Leipzig, 1935. (Jahrbuch der deutschen Volksbüchereien, V)

Handwerker, Otto. Geschichte der Würzburger Universitäts-bibliothek bis zur Säkularisation. Wurzburg, 1904.

Hanslik, Josef A. Geschichte und Beschreibung der Prager Universitätsbibliothek. Prague, 1851.

Hanson, James C.M. A Comparative Study of Cataloging Rules Based on the Anglo-American Code of 1908. Chicago, 1939.

Hardy, Thomas D. Descriptive Catalogue of Materials Relating to the History of Great Britain and Ireland, to the End of the Reign of Henry VII. London, 1862-1871. Cf. especially the Introduction to Vol. III.

Harnack, Adolf von. "Die älteste Inschrift über eine öffentlichen Kirchen-Bibliothek," in Beiträge...Schwenke gewidmet, p. 111-114.

------"Die Benutzung der Königlichen Bibliothek und die deutsche Nationalbibliothek," in his Reden und Aufsätze, N.F. III (Giessen, 1916), p. 227-261.

------"Die Geschichte der Königl. Bibliothek," ibid., III, p. 263-276.

------"Die Königliche Bibliothek zu Berlin," ibid., I (Giessen, 1911), p. 126-162.

------"Tertullians Bibliothek christlicher Schriften," Sitzungsberichte der K. Preussischen Akademie von Wissenschaften, 1914, I, 303-334.

Hartig, Otto. Die Gründung der Münchener Hofbibliothek durch Albrecht V und Johann Jakob Fugger. Munich, 1917. (Abhandlungen der K. Bayerische Akademie der Wissenschaften, Philosophisch-philologische und historische Klasse, XXVIII, 3)

Hartmann, Karl J. and Füchsel, Hans, eds. Geschichte der Göttinger Universitäts-Bibliothek. Verfasst von Göttinger Bibliothekaren. Göttingen, 1937.

Hartwig, Otto. "Karl August Barack," ZfB XVII (1900), 542-544.

------Schema des Realkatalogs der Universitätsbibliothek zu Halle. Leipzig, 1888. (Beihefte zum ZfB, 3)

Hauck, Albert. Kirchengeschichte Deutschlands. 3rd & 4th ed. Leipzig, 1929. See especially Vol. I and VI.

Hausmann, Sebastian. Die Kaiserliche Universitäts- und Landesbibliothek in Strassburg. Strassburg, 1895.

Heberdey, Rudolf. "Vorläufiger Bericht über die Grabungen in Ephesus, 1904," Jahreshefte des österreichischen aechäologischen Instituts in Wien VIII (1905), Beiblatt, 61-80.

Heeren, Arnold H. L. Christian Gottlob Heyne. Gottingen, 1813.

Heiberg, Johan L. "Bobbio," Nordisk Tidskrift för Bok- och Biblioteksväsen V (1918), 112-138.

Heinemann, Otto von. Die Herzogliche Bibliothek zu Wolfenbüttel. 2nd ed. Wolfenbüttel, 1894.

The Hellenistic Age; Aspects of Hellenistic Civilization. Cambridge, 1923.

Herrmann, Max. Albrecht von Eyb und die Frühzeit des deutschen Humanismus. Berlin, 1893.

------Die Reception des Humanismus in Nürnberg. Berlin, 1898.

Hessel, Alfred. "Heyne als Bibliothekar," ZfB XLV (1928), 455-470.

------Leibniz und die Anfänge der Göttinger Bibliothek. Göttingen, 1924. (Vorarbeiten zur Geschichte der Göttinger Universität und Bibliothek, III)

Heuser, Emil. Beiträge zur Geschichte der Universitätsbibliothek Giessen. Leipzig, 1891. (Beihefte zum ZfB, 6)

Hevesy, André de. La bibliothèque du roi Matthias Corvin. Paris, 1923.

Hilgers, Joseph. "Zur Bibliothek Nikolaus' V," ZfB XIX (1902), 1-11.

Hill, Richard S. "The Former Prussian State Library," Music Library Association Notes III (1945/46), 327-350, 404-410.

Hilsenbeck, Adolf. "Eine Denkschrift Aretins," in Aufsätze Fritz Milkau gewidmet, p. 153-161.

------"Martin Schrettinger und die Aufstellung in der Kgl. Hof- und Staatsbibliothek München," ZfB XXXI (1914), 407-433.

Himmelbaur, J. "Eduard Reyer," Blätter für Volksbibliotheken und Lesehallen XVI (1915), 1-4.

Hirsch, Felix E. "The Scholar as Librarian; to the Memory of Adolf von Harnack," LQ IX (1939), 299-320.

Hirschfeld, Otto. Die kaiserlichen Verwaltungsbeamten bis auf Diocletian. 2nd ed. Berlin, 1905.

Hirsching, Friedrich K.G. Versuch einer Beschreibung sehenswürdiger Bibliotheken Teutschlands, nach alphabetischer Ordnung der Oerten. Erlangen, 1786-1791.

Hoecker, Rudolf. "Zum hundertjährigen Bestehen der Universitätsbibliothek zu Berlin," ZfB XLVIII (1931), 105-113.

Hörle, Georg H. Frühmittelalterliche Mönchs- und Klerikerbildung in Italien. Freiburg i.Br., 1914. (Freiburger theologische Studien, XIII)

Hoffmann, Friedrich L. "Christoff Hendreich," Serapeum XXIX (1868), 257-266.

Hoffmann von Fallersleben, August H. "Universitäts-Bibliotheken und ihre Verwaltung," Serapeum I (1840), 3-8.

Hofmann, Walter and Erdberg, Robert von. "Die Lausteiner Tagung," Hefte für Büchereiwesen IX (1924-25), 269-289.

Hortzschansky, Adalbert. Die Königliche Bibliothek zu Berlin, ihre Geschichte und ihre Organisation. Berlin, 1908.

Houlette, William D. "Parish Libraries and the Work of the Reverend Thomas Bray," LQ IV (1934), 588-609.

Hulth, Johan M. "Upsala Universitets Bibliotek," Nordisk Tidskrift för Bok- och Biblioteksväsen VIII (1921), 225-230.

Ihm, Max. "Die Bibliotheken im alten Rom," ZfB X (1893), 513-532.

Inter-American Bibliographical and Library Association. Proceedings. New York, 1938-1940.

International Federation of Library Associations. Répertoire des associations de bibliothécaires membres de la Fédération Internationale. La Haye, 1938.

------"Report of the Sub-Committee on Uniform Catalog Rules," Actes du Comité International des Bibliothèques X (1938), 55-69.

International Institute of Intellectual Cooperation. Mission sociale et intellectuelle des bibliothèques populaires; son organisation, ses moyens d'action. Paris, 1937.

------Le rôle et la formation du bibliothécaire. Paris, 1935.

Italy. Direzione Generale delle Accademie e Biblioteche. Le accademie e le biblioteche d'Italia nel sessennio 1926/27-1931/32. Rome, 1933.

Italy. Ministero dell'Educazione Nazionale. Le biblioteche governative italiane nel MDCCCXCVIII. Rome, 1900.

Jacobs, Emil. "Eine Instruktion Noccolò Niccolis für die Durchsuchung deutscher Klöster nach Handschriften," Wochenschrift für klassische Philologie XXX (1913), 701-702.

------"Neue Forschungen über antike Bibliotheksgebäude," ZfB XXIV (1907), 118-123. Cf. also ibid. XXVI (1909), 31-33.

Jaeger, Werner. Aristotle; Fundamentals of the History of his Development. Oxford, 1934.

James, Montague R. The Ancient Libraries of Canterbury and Dover. Cambridge, 1903.

Joachimsohn, Paul. "Aus der Bibliothek Sigismund Gossembrots," ZfB XI (1894), 249-268, 297-307.

Joeckel, Carleton B. The Government of the American Public Library. Chicago, 1935.

------Library Service. Washington, 1938. (Advisory Committee on Education. Staff Study no. 11)

------and Carnovsky, Leon. A Metropolitan Library in Action; a Survey of the Chicago Public Library. Chicago, 1940.

Johnson, Alvin. The Public Library - a People's University, New York, 1938.

Johnston, William D. History of the Library of Congress. Vol. I, 1800-1864. Washington, 1904.

Jourdain, Abbé. "La Bibliothèque du Roi au début du règne de Louis XV (1718-1736); journal de l'abbé Jourdain, secrétaire de la Bibliothèque, publié par Henri Omont," Mémoires de la Société de l'Histoire de Paris et de l'Isle de France XX (1893), 207-294.

Juchhoff, Rudolf. "[Englische Bibliotheken]," ZfB XLII (1925), 46-51.

Judeich, Walther. Topographie von Athen. Munich, 1905. (Handbuch der klassischen Altertumswissenschaft 3, II, 2)

Jürgens, Adolph. "Skandinavische Bibliotheken," ZfB XXXIX (1922), 208-213; XLII (1925), 183-189.

Juntke, Fritz. "Magazinierung der toten Literatur," ZfB XLVIII (1931), 391-421, 565.

Justi, Karl. Winckelmann und seine Zeitgenossen. 3rd ed. Vol. I. Leipzig, 1923.

Kaerst, Julius. Geschichte des Hellenismus. 2nd ed. Leipzig, 1926-1927.

Karlsruhe. Badische Landesbibliothek. Die Reichenauer Handschriften; beschrieben und erläutert von Alfred Holder. Leipzig, 1906-1918. (Handschriften der Grossherzoglich badischen Hof- und Landesbibliothek in Karlsruhe, V-VII)

Kelchner, Ernst. "Eine Bibliotheksordnung aus dem Jahre 1259," ZfB I (1884), 307-313.

Keller, Ferdinand. Bauriss des Klosters St. Gallen vom Jahre 820. Zurich, 1844. Cf. Alfons Dopsch, Wirtschaftsentwicklung der Karolinger, vornehmlich in Deutschland, 2nd ed. (Weimar, 1921-22), I, 100-101.

Kenyon, Frederick G. Books and Readers in Ancient Greece and Rome. London, 1935.

------Libraries and Museums. London, 1930.

Keogh, Andrew. "English and American Libraries; a Comparison," Public Libraries VI (1901), 388-395.

Ker, Neil R. Medeival Libraries of Great Britain, a List of Surviving Books. London, 1941. (Royal Historical Society Guides and Handbooks, no. 3)

Kibre, Pearl. The Library of Pico della Mirandola. New York, 1936.

Klette, Anton. Die Selbständigkeit des bibliothekarischen Berufes in Deutschland als Grundlage einer allgemeinen Bibliotheksreform. Jubiliäums-Ausgabe. Marburg, 1897.

Knod, Gustav C. Aus der Bibliothek des Beatus Rhenanus. Strassburg, 1889. (Sélestat, Alsace. Bibliothèque Municipale. Die Stadtbibliothek zu Schlettstadt. Festschrift zur Einweihung des neuen Bibliotheksgebäudes am 6. Juni 1889. 2. Buch)

Koch, Theodore W. "The Bibliothèque Nationale," LJ XXXIX (1914), I, 339-350, 419-430.

------"The Bodleian Library at Oxford," LJ XXXIX (1914), II, 739-746, 803-810.

------A Book of Carnegie Libraries. White Plains, 1917.

------"The British Museum Library," LJ XXXVIII (1913), II, 499-509, 547-556.

------"The Imperial Public Library, St. Petersburg," LJ XL (1915), I, 5-23, 93-108.

König, Erich. Peutingerstudien. Freiburg i.Br., 1914. (Studien und Darstellungen aus dem Gebiete der Geschichte, IX, 1/2)

Königsberg. Staats- und Universitätsbibliothek. Die Silberbibliothek Herzog Albrechts von Preussen und seiner Gemahlin Anna Maria. Festgabe der Königlichen und Universitätsbibliothek Königsberg i/Pr. zur 350-jahrigen Jubelfeier der Albertus-Universität. Bearb. von P. Schwenke...und K. Lange. Leipzig, 1894.

Kohlfeldt, Gustav. "Zur Geschichte der Büchersammlungen und des Bücherbesitzes in Deutschland," Zeitschrift für Kulturgeschichte, ser. 4, vol. VII (1900), 325-388.

Kohl, Johann G. "Etwas über die Geschichte der Stadtbibliothek der freien Stadt Bremen," Serapeum XXVI (1865) , 113-121.

Kortum, Albert. "Anlage und Einrichtung von Bibliotheken," Allgemeine Bauzeitung XLIX (1884), 49-52, 57-64.

------"Bibliotheken," in Handbuch der Architektur, 2nd ed., Teil 4, Bd. VI, Heft 4, p. 53-218.

Kramm, Heinrich. Deutsche Bibliotheken unter dem Einfluss von Humanismus und Reformation. Leipzig, 1938. (Beihefte zum ZfB, 70)

Krassovsky, Dimitry M. "Bibliographical Work in Russia," LQ IV (1934), 449-466.

Kreis, Friedrich. "Wilhelm von Humboldt und die Bibliotheken," ZfB LIII (1936), 196-209.

Kraus, Franz X. "Zur Geschichte des Bücherwesens im 15. Jahrhundert,"
Publikationen des Börsenvereins der deutschen Buchhändler, N.F.
VII (1882), 250-252.

Kremer, Alfred von. Culturgeschichte des Orients unter den Chalifen.
Vol. II. Vienna, 1877.

Kretschmayr, Heinrich. Geschichte von Venedig. Vol. II. Gotha, 1920.

Krieger, Bogdan. Frederick the Great and his Books. New York, 1913.

Krüss, Hugo A. Die Stadtbibliothek zu Berlin als Zentralbibliothek.
Berlin, 1928.

Krumbacher, Karl. Geschichte der byzantinischen Literatur von Justinian
bis zum Ende des Oströmischen Reiches (527-1453). 2nd ed. Munich,
1897. (Handbuch der klassischen Altertumswissenschaft, IX, 1)

Künstle, Karl. Reichenau, seine berühmteste Äbte, Lehrer und Theologen.
Freiburg i.Br., 1924.

Kuhnert, Ernst. "Die Nova Bibliotheca des Herzog Albrecht," in Aufsätze
Fritz Milkau gewidmet, p. 209-219.

Kummer, Rudolf. "Das wissenschaftliche Bibliothekswesen im nazional-
sozialistischen Deutschland," ZfB LV (1938), 399-413.

Kurpiun, Robert. "Der Stand der Volksbüchereien in Oberschlesien,"
Blätter für Volksbibliotheken und Lesehallen VI (1905), 113-116.

Ladewig, Paul. Politik der Bücherei. 3rd ed. Leipzig, 1934.

Lambeck, Peter. Commentarii de augustissima Bibliotheca Caesarea
Vindobonensi liber I-VIII. Vienna, 1665-1679.

Lampros, Spyridon P. Die Bibliotheken der Klöster des Athos. Bonn, 1881

------Catalogue of the Greek Manuscripts on Mount Athos. Cambridge,
1895-1900.

Lanciani, Rodolfo A. The Ruins and Excavations of Ancient Rome.
Boston, 1897.

Lange, Hans O. "Über einen Katalog der Erfurter Universitätsbibliothek
aus dem 15. Jahrhundert," ZfB II (1885), 277-287.

Langfeldt, J. "Die Entwicklung der Volksbüchereien in Dänemark,"
Bücherei und Bildungspflege IV (1924), 87-91.

Learned, William S. The American Public Library and the Diffusion of
Knowledge. New York, 1924.

Ledos, Eugène G. Histoire des catalogues des livres imprimés de la
Bibliothèque Nationale. Paris, 1936.

Lehmann, Paul. Corveyer Studien. Munich, 1919. (Abhandlungen der
Bayerischen Akademie der Wissenschaften, Philosophisch-philologische
und historische Klasse, XXX, 5)

------Iohannes Sichardus und die von ihm benutzten Bibliotheken und
Handschriften. Munich, 1911. (Quellen und Untersuchungen für
lateinische Philologie des Mittelalters, IV, 1)

------"Nachrichten von der Sponheimer Bibliothek des Abtes Johannes
Tritheimus," in Hermann Grauert zur Vollendung des 60. Lebens-
jahres gewidmet von seinen Schülern (Freiburg i.Br., 1910), p. 205-
220.

Lehmann-Haupt, Hellmut, et. al. The Book in America; a History of the
Making, the Selling, and the Collecting of Books in the United States,
New York, 1939.

Leidinger, Georg. "Aus der Geschichte der K. Hof- und Staatsbibliothek
zu München," ZfB XXIX (1912), 339-349.

Leipzig. Deutsche Bücherei. Denkschrift zur Einweihungsfeier der
Deutschen Bücherei. Leipzig, 1916.

------Deutsche Bücherei des Börsenvereins der deutschen Buchhändler
zu Leipzig: Urkunden und Beiträge zu ihrer Begründung und Entwicklung. Leipzig, 1915.

------Die Deutsche Bücherei nach dem ersten Jahrzehnt ihres Bestehens,
Rückblicke und Ausblicke. Leipzig, 1925.

Leistle, David. "Über Klosterbibliotheken des Mittelalters," Studien und
Mittheilungen zur Geschichte des Benediktiner-Ordens und seiner
Zweige XXXVI (1915), 197-228.

Lemaître, Henri. Histoire du dépôt légal. 1re partie (France). Paris,
1910.

------Léopold Delisle," Zeitschrift des österreichischen Vereins für
Bibliothekswesen I (1910), 113-121.

------"Les richesses des bibliothèques municipales de France," ZfB L
(1933), 94-106.

Leo, Friedrich. "Heyne," in Festschrift zur Feier des hundertfünfzigjährigen Bestehens der Königlichen Gesellschaft der Wissenschaften
zu Göttingen, p. 153-234.

Le Prince, Nicolas T. Essai historique sur la Bibliothèque du Roi.
Paris, 1782.

Lerche, Otto. "Das älteste Ausleihverzeichnis einer deutschen Bibliothek,"
ZfB XXVII (1910), 441-450.

------Goethe und die Weimarer Bibliothek. Leipzig, 1929.

Leroy, Emile. Guide pratique des bibliothèques de Paris. Paris, 1937.

Lesne, Emile. Les livres, "scriptoria," et bibliothèques du commencement du VIIIe à la fin du XIe siècle. Lille, 1938. (Histoire de la
propriété ecclésiastique en France, IV)

Lester, Robert M. Forty Years of Carnegie Giving. New York, 1941.

Leyh, Georg. "Aus der älteren Bibliothekspraxis," in Beiträge...Schwenke
gewidmet, p. 159-174.

------"Chr. F. Heynes Eintritt in die Göttinger Bibliothek," in Aufsätze Fritz Milkau gewidmet, p. 220-228.

------Die deutschen wissenschaftlichen Bibliotheken nach dem Krieg. Tübingen, 1947.

------"Das Dogma von der systematischen Aufstellung," ZfB XXIX (1912), 241-259; XXX (1913), 97-136.

------"Friedrich Adolf Ebert zum 100-jährigen Todestag," ZfB LI (1934), 599-606.

------"Die Gesetze der Universitätsbibliothek zu Göttingen vom 28. Oktober 1761," ZfB XXXVII (1920), 1-30.

------"Das Haus und seine Einrichtung," in F. Milkau, ed., Handbuch der Bibliothekswissenschaft, II, 1-115.

------Die wissenschaftliche Stadtbibliothek. Tübingen, 1929.

"Libraries," Encyclopedia Britannica. 11th ed. Vol. XVI.

Lindsay, Wallace M. "The Bobbio Scriptorium: its Early Minuscule Abbreviations" ZfB XXVI (1909), 293-306.

------"The (Early) Lorsch Scriptorium," Palaeographia latina III (1924), 5-48.

Linneborn, Johannes. "Die Reformation der westfälischen Benedictinerklöster im 15. Jahrhundert durch die Bursfelder Congregation," Studien und Mitteilungen aus den Benedictiner- und Cistercienser-Order XX (1899), 266-314, 531-570; XXI (1900), 53-68, 315-332, 554-578; XXII (1901), 48-71, 396-418.

Lipsius, Justus. A Brief Outline of the History of Libraries. Chicago, 1907. (Literature of Libraries in the Seventeenth and Eighteenth Centuries, V)

Löffler, Karl. Geschichte der Württembergischen Landesbibliothek. Leipzig, 1923. (Beihefte zum ZfB, 50)

Löffler, Klemens. "Die Bibliothek von Korvei," Zeitschrift für Bücherfreunde, N.F. X (1918/19), 136-143.

------Deutsche Klosterbibliotheken. 2nd ed. Bonn, 1922. (Bücherei der Kultur und Geschichte, 27)

------"Die Fuldaer Klosterbibliothek," Zeitschrift für Bucherfreunde, N.F. X (1918/19), 194-202.

------Kölnische Bibliotheksgeschichte in Umriss. Cologne, 1923.

------"Papst Nikolaus V. als Bücherfreund," Zeitschrift für Bücherfreunde, N.F. I (1909), I, 174-179.

------"Das Schrift- und Buchwesen der Brüder vom gemeinsamen Leben," Zeitschrift für Bücherfreunde XI (1907/08), II, 286-293.

Loserth, Johann. "Der älteste Katalog der Prager Universitäts-Bibliothek Mitteilungen des Instituts für österreichischen Geschichtsforschung XI (1890), 301-318.

Loubier, Hans. Der Bucheinband von seinen Anfängen bis zum Ende des 18. Jahrhunderts. 2nd ed. Leipzig, 1926. (Monographien des Kunstgewerbes, XXI/XXII)

Lowe, Elias A. The Beneventan Script; a History of the South Italian Minuscule. Oxford, 1914.

Lydenberg, Harry M. History of the New York Public Library. New York, 1923.

------John Shaw Billings. Chicago, 1924.

Lyle, G.R. "A Royal Book-Collector," LQ III (1933), 180-191.

Lynd, Robert S. and Helen M. Middletown. New York, 1929.

------Middletown in Transition. New York, 1937.

Maass, Ernest. "Leibnitz' Contribution to Librarianship," College and Research Libraries IV (1942/43), 245-249.

McColvin, Lionel R. The Public Library System of Great Britain. London, 1942.

Mackensen, Ruth S. "Arabic Books and Libraries in the Umaiyad Period," American Journal of Semitic Languages and Literatures LII (1935/36), 245-253; LIII (1936/37), 239-250; LIV (1937), 41-61.

------"Background of the History of Moslem Libraries," American Journal of Semitic Languages and Literatures LI (1934/35), 114-125; LII (1935/36), 22-33, 104-110.

------"Four Great Libraries of Medieval Baghdad," LQ II (1932), 279-299.

MacLeish, Archibald. "The Reorganization of the Library of Congress, 1939-44," LQ XIV (1944), 277-315. Reprinted in the Annual Report of the Librarian of Congress...1945.

Macleod, Robert D. County Rural Libraries; their Policy and Organization. London, 1923.

McMurtrie, Douglas C. The Book; the Story of Printing and Bookmaking. New York, 1943.

Madan, Falconer. The Bodleian Library at Oxford. London, 1919.

------Books in Manuscript. 2nd ed. London, 1927.

Maderus, J.J. "De scriptis et bibliothecis antediluvianis," in his De bibliothecis atque archivis virorum clarissimorum libelli et commentationes. 2nd ed. Helmstedt, 1702.

Mancini, Girolamo. Giovanni Tortelli, cooperatore de Niccolò V nel fondare la Biblioteca Vaticana, con appendice di Giovanni Mercati. Florence, 1921.

Manitius, Maximilianus. Handschriften antiker Autoren in mittelalterlichen Bibliothekskatalogen. Leipzig, 1935. (Beihefte zum ZfB, 67)

------Geschichte der lateinischen Literature des Mittelalters. Munich, 1911-1923. (Handbuch der klassischen Altertumswissenschaft, IX, 2)

Marin, Eugène. Les moines de Constantinople depuis la fondation de la ville jusqu'à la mort de Photius (330-898). Paris, 1897.

Martin, Lowell. "The American Public Library as a Social Institution," LQ VII (1937), 546-563.

Marx, Jakob. Verzeichnis der Hss.-Sammlung des Hospitals zu Cues bei Bernkastel a. Mosel. Trier, 1905. Introduction.

Mazzinati, Giuseppe. La biblioteca dei rei d'Aragona in Napoli. Rocca S. Casciano, 1897.

Mearns, David C. The Story up to Now; the Library of Congress, 1800-1946. Washington, 1947.

Medical Library Association. A Handbook of Medical Library Practice. Chicago, 1943.

Meier, Gabriel. Heinrich von Ligerz. Bibliothekar von Einsiedeln im 14. Jahrhundert. Leipzig, 1896. (Beihefte zum ZfB, 17)

------"Die Schweizer Landesbibliothek (Bibliothèque Nationale Suisse)," ZfB XIX (1902), 165-172.

Meiners, Christoph. Göttingische akademische Annalen. Vol. I. Hannover, 1804.

Meinsma, Koenraad O. Middeleeuwsche Bibliotheken. Zutphen, 1903.

Meissner, Bruno. Babylon und Assyrien. Vol. II. Heidelberg, 1925. (Kulturgeschichtliche Bibliothek...1. Reihe: Ethnologische Bibliothek...4)

------"Wie hat Assurbanipal seine Bibliothek zusammengebracht?" in Aufsätze Fritz Milkau gewidmet, p. 244-248.

Mélanges offerts à M. Marcel Godet...à l'occasion de son soixantième anniversaire. Neuchâtel, 1937.

Menant, Joachim. La bibliothèque du palais de Ninève. Paris, 1880.

Mercati, Giovanni. "Il catalogo della biblioteca di Pomposa," Studi e documenti di storia e diritto XVII (1896), 143-177.

Merryweather, Frederick S. Bibliomania in the Middle Ages. New ed. London, 1933.

Metcalf, Keyes D. "The New England Deposit Library," LQ XII (1942), 622-628.

------"Some Trends in Research Libraries," in William Warner Bishop a Tribute, 1941, p. 145-166.

------"Spatial Growth in University Libraries," Harvard Library Bulletin I (1947), 133-154.

------and Williams, Edwin E. "Proposal for a Division of Responsibility among American Libraries in the Acquisition and Recording of Library Materials," College and Research Libraries VI (1944), 105-109.

------et. al. The Program of Instruction in Library Schools. Report of a Study Financed by the Carnegie Corporation and Made for the University of Illinois Library School on the Occasion of its Fiftieth Anniversary. Urbana, 1943.

Meyer, Adolf B. Amerikanische Bibliotheken und ihre Bestrebungen. Berlin, 1906.

Meyer, Conrad Ferdinand. "Plautus in the Convent," in German Classics of the Nineteenth Century, ed. Kuno Francke, Vol. XIV.

Meyer, Ernst. "Einige Mitteilungen über die Volksbibliotheken Schwedens," Blätter für Volksbibliotheken und Lesehallen VIII (1907), 109-113.

Meyer, Hermann. "Mittelalterliche Bibliotheksordnungen fur Paris und Erfurt," Archiv für Kulturgeschichte XI (1914), 152-165.

Meyer, José. "The Bibliothèque Nationale During the Last Decade: Fundamental Changes and Constructive Achievement," LQ XII (1942), 805-826.

Meyer, Kuno. Learning in Ireland in the Fifth Century and the Transmission of Letters. Dublin, 1913.

Mez, Adam. The Renaissance of Islam. London, 1937.

Michaelis, Johann D. Raisonnement über die protestantischen Universitäten. Teil 4. Frankfurt, 1776.

Middeldorpf, Heinrich. Commentatio de institutis literariis in Hispania quae autores habuerunt. Göttingen, 1810.

Milan. Biblioteca Ambrosiana. La Bibliothèque Ambrosienne. Paris, 1923. (A translation of Guida sommaria... della Biblioteca Ambrosiana... Milan, 1907)

Milkau, Fritz. "Die Bibliotheken," in Die Kultur der Gegenwart, 2nd ed., I, 1.

------Geschichte der Bibliotheken im alten Orient. Leipzig, 1935.

------ed. Handbuch der Bibliothekswissenschaft. Leipzig, 1931-1941.

------Die internationale Bibliographie der Naturwissenschaften nach dem Plane der Royal Society. Berlin, 1899.

------Die Königliche Universitäts-Bibliothek zu Breslau. Breslau, 1911.

------"Léopold Delisle," ZfB XXVII (1910), 385-401.

------Centralkataloge und Titeldrucke. Leipzig, 1898. (Beihefte zum ZfB, 20)

Minto, John. A History of the Public Library Movement in Great Britain and Ireland. London, 1932.

Molhuysen, Philip C. Geschiedenis der Universiteits-Bibliothek te Leiden. Leyden, 1905.

Mone, Franz J. "Bibliothek zu Alzey," Zeitschrift für die Geschichte des Oberrheins XIV (1862), 143-147.

------"Bibliotheken (Bibliothek zu Alzey)," Anzeiger für Kunde der teutschen Vorzeit VI (1837), 255.

Monnier, Philippe. Le Quattrocento; essai sur l'histoire du XVe siècle italien. Paris, 1901.

Mortet, Charles. "The Public Libraries of France, National, Communal, and University," Library Association Record, n.s. III (1925), 145-159.

Mortreuil, Théodore. La Bibliothèque Nationale: son origine et ses accroissements jusqu'à nos jours. Paris, 1878.

Mosel, Ignaz F. von. Geschichte der Kaiserl. Königl. Hofbibliothek zu Wien. Vienna, 1835.

Müller, K.K. "Neue Mitteilungen über Janos Laskaris und die Mediceische Bibliothek," ZfB I (1884), 333-412.

Müntz, Eugène and Fabre, Paul. La bibliothèque du Vatican au XVe siècle d'après des documents inédits. Paris, 1887. (Bibliothèque des Ecoles françaises d'Athènes et de Rome, XLVIII)

Müntz, Eugène. La bibliothèque du Vatican au XVIe siècle. Paris, 1886.

Munich. Bayerische Staatsbibliothek. Catalogus codicum manu scriptorum Bibliothecae Regiae Monacensis. Munich, 1866-1915.

Munn, Ralph. Conditions and Trends in Education for Librarianship. New York, 1936.

Munthe, Wilhelm. "Die bibliothekarische Ausbildung in Norwegen," ZfB L (1933), 177-181.

------American Librarianship from a European angle. Chicago, 1939.

------"The Library History of Norway," LJ XLV (1921), 19-24, 57-62.

------"Die neuesten amerikanischen Bibliotheksbauten," ZfB XLVIII (1931), 447-478.

Naudé, Gabriel. Instructions Concerning Erecting of a Library Presented to My Lord the President De Mesme...interpreted by Jo. Evelyn. Cambridge, 1903. (Reprint of the 1661 edition)

------News from France; or a Description of the Library of Cardinal Mazarin, preceded by The Surrender of the Library. Chicago, 1907. (Literature of Libraries in the Seventeenth and Eighteenth Centuries, VI)

Neuburger, Otto. Official Publications of Present-Day Germany, Washington, 1942.

Neveux, Pol L. and Dacier, Emile. Les richesses des bibliothèques provinciales de France. Paris, 1932.

Nicholson, Reynold A. A Literary History of the Arabs. 2nd ed. Cambridge, 1930.

Niederländisches Bibliothekswesen; eine Übersicht in acht Aufsätzen. Utrecht, 1914.

Niepce, Léopold. Les bibliothèques anciennes et modernes de Lyon. Lyon, 1876.

Nörrenberg, Constantin. Die Bücherhallenbewegung im Jahre 1897. Berlin, 1898. (Vorträge und Aufsätze aus der Comenius-Gesellschaft, VI, 2)

Nolhac, Pierre. Pétrarque et l'humanisme. New ed. Paris, 1907. (Bibliothèque de la renaissance. Nouv. sér. I-II)

Norris, Dorothy M. A History of Cataloguing and Cataloguing Methods, 1100-1850. London, 1939.

Ogilvy, J.D.A. Books Known to Anglo-Latin Writers from Adelhelm to Alcuin (670-804). Cambridge, 1936. (Medieval Academy of America. Studies and Documents, 2)

Ogle, John J. The Free Library. London, 1897. (The Library Series, I)

Omont, Henri. "La bibliothèque de Ferdinand Ier d'Aragon, Roi de Naples (1481)," Bibliothèque de l'École de Chartes LXX (1909), 456-470.

------La Collection Moreau. Paris, 1891.

Oppenheim, Gustav. Christoff Hendreich, churfürstlich brandenburgischer Rat and Bibliothekar. Berlin, 1904.

Ornstein, Martha. The Role of Scientific Societies in the 17th Century. Chicago, 1928.

Osborn, Andrew D. "Books for the Deposit Library," Harvard University Library Notes IV (1942), 80-83.

------"The Crisis in Cataloging," LQ XI (1941), 393-411.

Otten, Bennata. Die deutschen Volksbibliotheken und Lesehallen in Städten über 10,000 Einwohner. Leipzig, 1910. (Ergänzungsheft der Blätter für Volksbibliotheken, II)

Oxford University. Bodleian Library. Pietas Oxoniensis, in Memory of Sir Thomas Bodley, Knt., and the Foundation of the Bodleian Library. Oxford, 1902.

------Trecentale Bodleianum; a Memorial Volume for the Three Hundredth Anniversary of the Public Funeral of Sir Thomas Bodley. Oxford 1913.

Painter, Franklin V.N. Luther on Education. Philadelphia, 1890.

Paris. Bibliothèque Nationale. La Bibliothèque Nationale. Paris, 1907.

------Catalogue des livres imprimez de la Bibliothèque du Roy. Vol. I. Introduction. Paris, 1739.

------Catalogue général des livres imprimés. Vol. I. Introduction. Paris, 1897.

Partridge, Robert C.B. The History of the Legal Deposit of Books Throughout the British Empire. London, 1938.

Pastor, Ludwig. History of the Popes, from the Close of the Middle Ages. London, 1891-1941.

Perels, Ernst. Nikolaus I. und Anastasius Bibliothecarius; ein Beitrag zur Geschichte des Papstums im 9. Jahrhundert. Berlin, 1920.

Perlbach, Max. Versuch einer Geschichte der Universitätsbibliothek zu Greifswald. Greifswald, 1882.

Perrot, Georges. "Notice sur la vie et les travaux de Léopold-Victor Delisle," Bibliothèque de l'Ecole de Chartes LXXIII (1912), 1-72.

Peschek, Paul. "Die Entwicklung des neueren Bibliotheksbaues," in Aufsätze Fritz Milkau gewidmet, p. 264-280.

Petrarca, Francesco. Phisicke against Fortune, as well Prosperous as Adverse...Englished by Thomas Twyne. London, 1579.

Petzholdt, Julius. Adressbuch der Bibliotheken Deutschlands, mit Einschluss von Oesterreich-Ungarn und der Schweiz. Dresden, 1875.

------"Preusker, ein Veteran der Bibliothekswissenschaft," Neuer Anzeiger für Bibliographie und Bibliothekswissenschaft, 1870, p. 69-75.

Pfeiffer, H. F. "Roman Library at Timgad," Memoirs of the American Academy in Rome IX (1931), 157-165.

Pick, Hermann. "Der unvollendet gebliebene Bibliotheksbau des Grossen Kurfursten," in Beitrage...Schwenke gewidmet, p. 211-215.

Pietschmann, R. "Bibliotheken," in Handwörterbuch der Staatswissenschaften, 4th ed., Vol. II.

Pittoni, Laura. La libreria di S. Marco. Pistoia, 1903.

Poland, Franz. "Oeffentliche Bibliotheken in Griechenland und Kleinasien," in Historische Untersuchungen Ernst Förstemann zum fünfzigjährigen Doctorsjubiliäum gewidmet von der Historischen Gesellschaft zu Dresden (Leipzig, 1894), p. 7-14.

Potter, Alfred C. The Library of Harvard University; Descriptive and Historical Notes. 4th ed. Cambridge, 1934.

Pratt, R. A. "Chaucer and the Visconti Libraries," ELH; a Journal of English Literary History VI (1939), 191-200.

Predeek, Albert. A History of Libraries in Great Britain and North America, tr. by Lawrence S. Thompson. Chicago, 1947.

------Das moderne englische Bibliothekswesen. Leipzig, 1933. (Beihefte zum ZfB, 66)

The Prussian Instructions; Rules for the Alphabetical Catalogs of the Prussian Libraries, translated from the second edition...by Andrew D. Osborn. Ann Arbor, 1938.

Pütter, Johann S. Versuch einer academischen Gelehrten-Geschichte von der Georg-Augustus-Universität zu Göttingen. Göttingen, 1765-1838.

Putnam, George H. Books and Their Makers in the Middle Ages. New York, 1896-1897.

Quentin-Bauchart, Ernest. La bibliothèque de Fontainebleau et ses livres des dernier Valois à la Bibliothèque Nationale (1515-1589). Paris, 1891.

Rabbow, Paul. "Zur Geschichte des urkundlichen Sinns," Historische Zeitschrift CXXVI (1922), 58-79.

Rabe, Hugo. "Konstantin Laskaris," ZfB LXV (1928), 1-7.

Radlach, O. "Die Bibliotheken der evangelischen Kirche in ihrer rechtsgeschichtlichen Entwicklung," ZfB XII (1895), 153-173.

Rae, Walter S. C. Public Library Administration. London, 1913.

Rashdall, Hastings. The Universities of Europe in the Middle Ages. New ed. Oxford, 1936.

Rawlings, Gertrude B. The British Museum Library. London, 1916.

Reece, Ernest J. Programs for Library Schools. New York, 1943.

Reichmann, Felix. "The Book Trade at the Time of the Roman Empire," LQ VIII (1938), 40-76.

Ribbeck, Otto. Friedrich Wilhelm Ritschl; ein Beitrag zur Geschichte der Philologie. Leipzig, 1879-1881.

Ribera y Tarragó, Julian. Bibliófilos y bibliotecas en la España Musulmana. Saragossa, 1896.

Rice, James V. Gabriel Naudé, 1600-1653. Baltimore, 1939. (The Johns Hopkins Studies in Romance Literatures and Languages, XXXV)

Richard de Bury. Philobiblon. London, 1925.

Richardson, Ernest C. The Beginnings of Libraries. Princeton, 1914.

------Biblical Libraries. Princeton, 1914.

Richou, Gabriel. Traité de l'administration des bibliothèques publiques. Paris, 1885.

Richter, Otto L. Topographie der Stadt Rom. Munich, 1901. (Handbuch der klassischen Altertumswissenschaft, 3, III, 2)

Rider Fremont. Melvil Dewey. Chicago, 1944.

------The Scholar and the Future of the Research Library. New York, 1944.

Robathan, Dorothy M. "The Catalogues of the Princely and Papal Libraries of the Italian Renaissance," Transactions and Proceedings of the American Philological Association LXIV (1933), 138-149.

Robert, Ulysse. Recueil des lois, décrets, ordonnances, arrêtés, circulaires, etc. concernant les bibliotheques publiques, communales, universitaires, scolaires et populaires. Paris, 1883.

Roberts, Ethel D. "Notes on Early Christian Libraries in Rome," Speculum IX (1934), 190-194.

Rocholl, Rudolf. Bessarion; Studie zur Geschichte der Renaissance. Leipzig, 1904.

Rockinger, Ludwig. "Zum baierischen Schriftwesen im Mittelalter," Abhandlungen der Historischen Klasse der K. Bayerischen Akademie der Wissenschaften XII (1872/73), I, 1-72; II, 167-230.

Roethe, Gustav. "Göttingische Zeitungen von gelehrten Sachen," in Festschrift... der K. Gesellschaft der Wissenschaften zu Göttingen, p. 567-688.

Roland-Marcel, Pierre. R. L'évolution des bibliothèques en France. Paris, 1929.

Romanis, Humbertus de. Liber de instructione officialum Ordonis Fratrum Praedicatorum," in L. Holstenius, Codex regularum monasticarum et canonicarum quas ss. patres monachis, canonicis et virginibus sanctimonialibus servandas praescripserunt, Vol. IV (Augsburg, 1759), p. 150-218.

Rome. Biblioteca Angelica. Bibliotheca Angelica litteratorum litterarumque amatorum commoditati dictata Romae in Aedibus Augustinianis. Rome, 1608.

Rosse, Giovanni B. "Introduction" to Enrico Stevenson, Codices Palatini latini Bibliothecae Vaticanae, Vol. I. Rome, 1886.

Roth, Friedrich. Willibald Pirkheimer, ein Lebensbild aus dem Zeitalter des Humanismus und der Reformation. Halle, 1887. (Schriften des Vereins fur Reformationsgeschichte, 5, IV, 21)

Rother, Karl. "Die Philologie in den Realkatalogsystmen seit 1600 mit besonderer Berücksichtigung der klassischen Altertumswissenschaft," in Aufsätze Fritz Milkau gewidmet, p. 300-320.

Rott, Hans. Ott Heinrich und die Kunst. Heidelberg, 1905. (Mitteilungen zur Geschichte des Heidelberger Schlosses, V, 1/2)

Rózycki, K. von. "Die kaiserliche Bibliothek in St. Petersburg," ZfB (1900), 497-505.

Ruland, Anton. "Zur Geschichte der alten, nach Rom entführten Bibliothek zu Heidelberg," Serapeum XVII (1856), 185-191.

------"Die Vorschriften der Regular-Cleriker über das Anfertigen oder Abschreiben von Handschriften," Serapeum XXI (1860), 183-192.

Runge, Sigismund. "Some Recent Developments in Subject Cataloging in Germany," LQ XI (1941), 49-50.

Ryan, John. Irish Monasticism. London, 1931.

Sabbadini, Remigio. Le scoperte dei codici latini e greci ne' secoli XIV e XV. Florence, 1905-1914.

Sachse, Arnold. Friedrich Althoff und sein Werk. Berlin, 1928.

Sackur, Ernst. Die Cluniacenser in ihrer kirchlichen und allgemeingeschichtlichen Wirksamkeit, bis zur Mitte des elften Jahrhunderts, Vol. II. Halle a.S., 1894.

Sainte-Beuve, Charles A. Portraits littéraires (Naudé). 2nd ed. Paris, 1884. Vol. II, p. 467-512, 522-524.

Salamanca, Lucy. Fortress of Freedom; the Story of the Library of Congress. Philadelphia, 1942.

Savage, Ernest A. Old English Libraries; the Making, Collection and Use of Books in the Middle Ages. London, 1911.

------The Story of Libraries and Book-Collecting. London, 1909.

Sayle, C. "Annals of Cambridge University Library," The Library, ser. 3, vol. VI (1915), 38-76, 145-182, 197-227, 308-345.

Schachner, Nathan. The Mediaeval Universities. New York, 1938.

Scheffen, W. "Zwanzig Jahre 'Grenzbüchereidienst'," Die Bücherei VII (1940), 254-263.

Schildt, A. "Die Hamburger Bücherhalle, 1895-1905," Blätter fur Volksbibliotheken und Lesehallen VIII (1907), 5-11.

Schleimer, Hans. "Der bibliothekarische Schlagwortkatalog," ZfB XL (1923), 66-97.

Schmarsow, August. Melozzo da Forli; ein Beitrag zur Kunst- und Kulturgeschichte. Berlin, 1886.

Schmidt, Erich. Lessing; Geschichte seines Lebens und seiner Schriften. 4th ed. Vol. II. Berlin, 1923.

Schmidt, Friedrich. Die Pinakes des Kallimachos. Berlin, 1922. (Klassisch-philologische Studien, I)

Schmidt, Otto E. "Die Visconti und ihre Bibliothek zu Pavia," Zeitschrift für Geschichte und Politik V (1888), 444-474.

Schmidt, Philipp. "Die Bibliothek des Dominikanerklosters in Basel," Basler Zeitschrift für Geschichte und Altertumskunde XVIII (1919), 160-254.

Schmidt-Ott, Friedrich. "Althoff und die Bibliotheken," ZfB LVI (1939), 101-103.

Schneider, Georg. Handbuch der Bibliographie. 4th ed. Leipzig, 1930.

------Theory and History of Bibliography, tr. by Ralph R. Shaw. New York, 1934.

Schneider, Heinrich. Beiträge zur Geschichte der Universitätsbibliothek Helmstedt. Helmstedt, 1924. (Schriften des Helmstedter Universitätsbundes, I)

Schneider, Karl. "Die Bibliothek Petrarcas und ihre Schicksale," Zeitschrift für Bücherfreunde, N.F. I (1909/10), I, 157-160.

Schnürer, Gustav. Kirche und Kultur im Mittelalter, Paderborn, 1924-1929.

------Katholische Kirche und Kultur im 18. Jahrhundert. Paderborn, 1941.

------Katholische Kirche und Kultur in der Barockzeit. Paderborn, 1937.

Schottenloher, Karl. "Bamberger Privatbibliotheken aus alter und neuer Zeit," ZfB XXIV (1907), 417-460.

------"Schicksale von Büchern und Bibliotheken im Bauernkrieg," Zeitschrift für Bücherfreunde XII (1908/09), II, 391-408.

Schrettinger, Martin. Handbuch der Bibliothekswissenschaft. Vienna, 1834.

------Versuch eines vollständigen Lehrbuchs der Bibliothekswissenschaft. Munich, 1829.

Schriewer, Franz. Das ländliche Volksbüchereiwesen. Jena, 1937.

Schubart, Wilhelm. Das Buch bei den Griechen und Römern. Berlin, 1907. (Handbücher der Königlichen Museen zu Berlin, XII)

Schubert, Hans von. Geschichte der christlichen Kirche im Frühmittelalter Tubingen, 1921.

Schubert, Otto. Geschichte des Barock in Spanien. Erlangen, 1908. (Geschichte der neueren Baukunst, VIII)

Schubring, Paul. "Vespasiano da Bisticci," Mitteilungen des Kunsthistorischen Instituts in Florenz III (1919), 64-70.

Schürmeyer, Walter. Bibliotheksräume aus fünf Jahrhunderte. Frankfurt, 1929.

Schütz, Géza. "Bibliotheca Corvina," LQ IV (1934), 552-564.

Schultze, Ernst. Freie öffentliche Bibliotheken, Volksbibliotheken und Lesehallen. Dannenberg, 1900.

------Volksbildung und Volkswohlfahrt in England. Munich, 1912. (Die Kultur des modernen England in Einzeldarstellungen, II)

Schultze, Victor. Altchristliche Städte und Landschaften. I: Konstantinopel. Leipzig, 1913.

Schultze, Walther. "Die Bedeutung der iroschottischen Mönche für die Erhaltung und Fortpflanzung der mittelalterlichen Wissenschaft," ZfB VI (1889), 185-198, 223-241, 281-298.

Schulze, Werner. "Die Bibliothek Heinrich von Bünaus," ZfB LII (1935), 337-345.

Schuster, Wilhelm. "Neue Aufgaben der wissenschaftlichen Stadtbibliotheken," ZfB LIII (1936), 542-552.

------"Das neue deutsche Volksbüchereiwesen," ZfB LIII (1936), 144-154.

------"Die Zusammenarbeit der Stadtbibliothek mit den Volksbüchereien," ZfB LV (1938), 457-467.

Schwarber, Karl. Die Entwicklung der Universitätsbibliothek zu Basel. Basel, 1944.

Schwenke, Paul. "Eindrücke von einer amerikanischen Bibliotheksreise," ZfB XXIX (1912), 485-500; XXX (1913), 1-17, 49-58.

------"Friedrich Althoff," ZfB XXV (1908), 485-489.

------"Karl Dziatzko," ZfB XX (1903), 133-137.

Sélestat, Alsace. Bibliothèque Municipale. Die Stadtbibliothek zu Schlettstadt. Festschrift zur Einweihung des neuen Bibliothekgebäudes am 6. Juni 1889. Strassburg, 1889.

Serres de Mesplès, Christian de. Les bibliothèques publiques françaises, leur organisation--leur réforme. Thèse. Montpellier, 1933.

Sforza, Giovanni. La patria, la famiglia e la giovinezza di Papa Niccolo V. Lucca, 1884.

Shelley, Henry C. The British Museum: its History and Treasures. Boston, 1911.

Shera, Jesse H. Foundations of the Public Library; the Origins of the Public Library Movement in New England, 1629-1855. Chicago, 1949.

Sisson, M.A. "The Stoa of Hadrian at Athens," Papers of the British School at Rome XI (1929), 58-66.

Smith, George. "Gabriel Naudé: a Librarian of the 17th Century," Library Association Record I (1899), 423-431.

Sparn, Enrique. Las bibliotecas con 50,000 y mas volumenes y su distribucion geografica sobre la tierra. Cordova, 1924. (Academia Nacional de Ciencias, Miscellanea, VIII)

Special Libraries Association. Special Library Resources. New York, 1941-

Spencer, Gwladys. The Chicago Public Library: Origins and Backgrounds. Chicago, 1943.

Stauber, Richard and Hartig, Otto. Die Schedelsche Bibliothek. Ein Beitrag zur Geschichte der italienischer Renaissance, des deutschen Humanismus und der medizinischen Literatur. Freiburg i.Br., 1908. (Studien und Darstellungen aus dem Gebiete der Geschichte, VI, 2/3)

Steenberg, Andreas S. "Die Volksbibliotheken in Dänemark," Blätter für Volksbibliotheken und Lesehallen VII (1906), 117-120; XI (1910), 48-49.

Steiner, Bernard C., ed. Rev. Thomas Bray; his Life and Selected Works Relating to Maryland. Baltimore, 1901.

Stois, Max. "Die neuen Gesetze über die Freistücke im Dritten Reich," ZfB LIV (1937), 313-334.

Streck, Maximilian. Assurbanipal und die letzten assyrischen Könige bis zum Untergang Ninevahs. Leipzig, 1916. (Vorderasiatische Bibliothek, VII, 1)

Streeter, Burnett H. The Chained Library; a Survey of Four Centuries in t Evolution of the English Library. London, 1931.

Suchier, Wolfram. Kurze Geschichte der Universitätsbibliothek zu Halle, 1696 bis 1876. Halle, 1913.

Tatham, E.H.R. "The Library of Petrarch," Fornightly Review, n.s. LXXIX (1908), 1056-1067.

Taylor, Archer. Renaissance Guides to Books; an Inventory and Some Conclusions. Berkeley, 1945.

Tews, Johannes. Freiwillige Bildungsarbeit in Deutschland. Die Gesellschaft für Verbreitung von Volksbildung und ihre Wirksamkeit in den 25 Jahren ihres Bestehens. 1871-1896. Berlin, 1896.

Theele, Joseph. Die Handschriften des Benediktinerklosters S. Petri zu Erfurt. Leipzig, 1920. (Beihefte zum ZfB, 48)

Theiner, Augustin. Schenkung der Heidelberger Bibliothek durch Maximilian I, Herzog und Churfürsten von Bayern, an Papst Gregor XV und ihre Versendung nach Rom. Munich, 1844.

Thompson, Alexander H., ed. Bede: his Life, Times, and Writings; Essays in Commemoration of the Twelfth Centenary of his Death. Oxford, 1935.

Thompson, James W. Ancient Libraries. Berkeley, 1940.

------The Medieval Library. Chicago, 1939.

Thompson, Reginald C. and Hutchinson, Richard W. A Century of Exploration at Nineveh. London, 1929.

Thornton, John L. The Chronology of Librarianship. London, 1941.

Ticknor, George. Life, Letters and Journals. Boston, 1909.

Tiedemann, von. "Die Universitätsbibliothek in Halle a.S." Zeitschrift für Bauwesen XXXV (1885), 331-354.

Tisserant, Eugène. "Pius XI as Librarian," LQ IX (1939), 389-403.

------"The Preparation of a Main Index for the Vatican Library Manuscripts, in William Warner Bishop; a Tribute, 1941, p. 176-185.

------and Koch, Theodore W. The Vatican Library. Jersey City, 1929.

Traube, Ludwig. Textgeschichte der Regula S. Benedicti. 2nd ed. Munich, 1910. (Abhandlungen der K. Bayerischen Akademie der Wissenschaften Philosophisch-philologische und historische Klasse, XXV, 2)

------Vorlesungen und Abhandlungen. Vol. I-II. Munich, 1909-1911.

------and Ewald, Rudolf. Jean-Baptiste Maugérard. Ein Beitrag zur Kulturgeschichte. Munich, 1906. (Abhandlungen der K. Bayerischen Akademie der Wissenschaften, Historische Klasse, XXIII, Abt. II, 301-387.

Trebst, Hans. Die Kataloge der grösseren Bibliotheken des deutschen Sprachgebietes. Berlin, 1935.

Treitschke, Heinrich von. "Die Königliche Bibliothek in Berlin," Preussische Jahrbücher LIII (1884), 473-492.

Turin. Biblioteca Nazionale. Codici Bobbiesi nella Biblioteca Nazionale di Torino, ed. C. Cipolla. Vol. I. Turin, 1907.

Uffenbach, Zacharias K. von. Merkwürdige Reisen durch Niedersachsen, Holland und Engelland. Ulm, 1753.

Uhlendahl, Heinrich. "25 Jahre Deutsche Bücherei," ZfB LVI (1939), 1-17.

Uhlirz, Karl. "Beiträge zur Geschichte des Wiener Bücherwesens (1326-1445)," ZfB XIII (1896), 79-103.

Ullman, Berthold L. Ancient Writing and its Influence. New York, 1932.

United Nations Educational, Scientific and Cultural Organization. Survey of Losses and Needs of Libraries in Some European Countries. Paris, November 14, 1946. (UNESCO. Prep. Com/L&M/13. App.I)

U.S. Bureau of Education. Public Libraries in the United States... Pt. 1. Washington, 1876.

U. S. Library of Congress. The Hispanic Activities of the Library of Congress, with an Address by Archibald MacLeish. Washington, 1946.

------Advisory Committee on Descriptive Cataloging. Report... to the Librarian of Congress. Washington, 1946.

------Catalog Maintenance Division. Cumulative Catalog of Library of Congress Printed Cards. Washington, 1947-

------Descriptive Cataloging Division. Rules for Descriptive Cataloging in the Library of Congress. Washington, 1947.

------Processing Department. Studies of Descriptive Cataloging. Washington, 1946.

------Subject Cataloging Division. Subject Headings Used in the Dictionary Catalogs of the Library of Congress. 5th ed. Washington, 1948.

------Supplement. July 1947-   Washington, 1949-

Usener, Hermann. "Organization der wissenschaftlichen Arbeit," in his Vorträge und Aufsätze (Leipzig, 1907), p. 67-102.

------"Unser Platontext," in his Kleine Schriften, Vol. III (Leipzig, 1914), p. 104-162.

Valentinelli, Giuseppe. "Delle biblioteche della Spagna," Sitzungsberichte der K. Akademie der Wissenschaften in Wien, Philosophisch-historische Klasse, XXXIII (1860), I, 4-178.

Vatican, Biblioteca Vaticana. Codices Urbinates graeci Bibliothecae Vaticanae. Rome, 1895. Introduction.

------Rules for the Catalog of Printed Books, tr. from the 2d Italian ed., by Thomas J. Shanahan, Victor A. Schaefer and Constantin T. Vesselowsky, ed. by Wyllis E. Wright. Chicago, 1948.

Vienna. Nationalbibliothek. Festschrift der Nationalbibliothek in Wien. Hrsg. zur Feier des 200-jährigen Bestehens des Gebäudes. Vienna, 1926.

Vitruvius, Pollio. De architectura libri decem, ed. Friedrich Krohn. Leipzig, 1912.

Vogel, Ernest G. "Die Bibliothek der Benediktinerabtei Saint Benoit oder Fleury an der Loire," Serapeum V (1844), 16-29, 46-48.

------"Die Bibliothek der Benediktiner-Abtei zu Clugny," Serapeum V (1844), 123-128, 138-144.

------"Einiges über Amt und Stellung des Armarius in den abendländischen Klöstern des Mittelalters," Serapeum IV (1843), 17-29, 33-43, 49-55.

------"Einiges zur Geschichte der Escurialbibliothek unter Philipp II," Serapeum VIII (1847), 273-285.

------"Errinerungen an einige verdienstvolle Bibliophilen des vierzehnter und fünfzehnten Jahrhunderts. Vierter Artikel: Janus Laskaris. Quellen und Vorarbeiten," Serapeum X (1849), 65-74, 81-88.

------"Historisch-chronologische Übersicht des Ursprungs und Wachstums der literarischen Sammlunger im Britischen Museum zu London," Serapeum IV (1843), 219-223, 225-240, 241-252, 262-269.

------"Humphrey Herzog von Glocester," Serapeum VI (1845), 11-16.

Vogelsang, Friedrich. "Altägyptische Bibliothekare," ZfB XXX (1913), 17-22.

Voigt, Georg. Die Wiederbelebung des classischen Altertums, oder das erste Jahrhundert des Humanismus. 3rd ed. Berlin, 1893.

Vorstius, Joris. Grundzüge der Bibliotheksgeschichte. 3rd ed. Leipzig, 1941.

Vouilliéme, Ernst H. Die Inkunabeln der Königlichen Bibliothek und der anderen Berliner Sammlungen. Leipzig, 1906.

W.S. "Eine Katholische Zentralbibliothek für Deutschland," Historisch-politische Blätter für das katholische Deutschland CXXXIV (1904), 677-684.

Waas, Adolf. "Gegenwart und Zukunft der deutschen Volksbüchereien," Hefte für Büchereiwesen IX (1924/25), 325-332.

Wackernagel, Rudolf. Geschichte der Stadt Basel. Vol. III. Basel, 1924.

Wadlin, Horace G. The Public Library of the City of Boston, a History. Boston, 1911.

Walde, Otto W. C. Storhestidens litterära Krigsbyten, en kulturhistorisk-bibliografisk Studie. Vol. I. Uppsala, 1916.

Walser, Ernst. Poggius Florentinus. Leben und Werke. Leipzig, 1914. (Beiträge zur Kulturgeschichte des Mittelalters und der Renaissance, XIV)

Waples, Douglas. "The Public Library in the Depression," LQ II (1932), 321-343.

Wattenbach, Wilhelm. Das Schriftwesen im Mittelalter. 3rd ed. Leipzig, 1896.

Weinberger, Wilhelm. Beiträge zur Handschriftenkunde. I. (Die Bibliotheca Corvina). Vienna, 1908. (Sitzungsberichte der K. Akademie der Wissenschaften in Wien, Philosophisch-historische Klasse, CLIX, 6)

West, Andrew F. Alcuin and the Rise of Christian Schools. New York, 1892.

Westfälische Studien. Beiträge zur Geschichte der Wissenschaft, Kunst und Literatur in Westfalen Alois Börner zum 60. Geburtstag gewidmet. Leipzig, 1928.

Wheeler, Joseph L. Progress and Problems in Education for Librarianship. New York, 1946.

------and Githens, Alfred M. The American Public Library Building, New York, 1941.

Wickhoff, Franz. "Die Bibliothek Julius' II," Jahrbücher der kgl. preussischen Kunstsammlungen XIV (1893), 49-64.

Wiedemann, Alfred. Das alte Ägypten. Heidelberg, 1920. (Kulturgeschichtliche Bibliothek, ser. 1, vol. II)

Wieser, Max and Ackerknecht, Erwin. Der Volksbuchereibau. Stettin, 1930.

Wilamowitz-Moellendorff, Ulrich von. Antigonos von Karystos. Berlin, 1881. (Philologische Untersuchungen, IV)

------Hellenistische Dichtung. Berlin, 1924.

Wilberg, Wilhelm. "Die Fassade der Bibliothek in Ephesus," Jahreshefte des österreichichen archäologischen Instituts in Wien, XI (1908), 118-135

Wild, Helen. Aus englischen und schottischen Public and County Libraries. Zurich, 1924. (Publikationen der Vereinigung schweizerischer Bibliothekare, V)

Wilken, Friedrich. Geschichte der Bildung, Beraubung und Vernichtung der alten Heidelbergischen Büchersammlungen. Heidelberg, 1817.

------Geschichte der Königlichen Bibliothek zu Berlin. Berlin, 1828.

Wilkens, Nicolaus. Leben des Gelehrten Petri Lambeck. Hamburg, 1724.

Wille, Jakob. "Aus alter und neuer Zeit der Heidelberger Bibliothek," Neue Heidelberger Jahrbücher XIV (1906), 215-240.

William Warner Bishop; a Tribute, 1941. New Haven, 1941.

Williams, Edwin E. "Research Library Acquisitions from Eight Countries," LQ XV (1945), 313-323.

------ed. Conference on International Cultural, Educational and Scientific Exchanges, Princeton University, November 25-26, 1946. Chicago, 1947.

Williamson, Charles C. Training for Library Service. New York, 1923.

Wilson, Louis R. The Geography of Reading; a Study of the Distribution and Status of Libraries in the United States. Chicago, 1938.

------ed. The Role of the Library in Adult Education; Papers Presented before the Library Institute at the University of Chicago, August 2-13, 1937. Chicago, 1937.

------and Tauber, Maurice F. The University Library; its Organization, Administration, and Functions. Chicago, 1945.

World's Libraries and Librarians. London, 1939- (British Universities Encyclopedia, II)

Wustmann, Gustav. Geschichte der Leipziger Stadtbibliothek. Leipzig, 1906. (Neujahrsblätter der Bibliothek der Stadt Leipzig, II)

Wyss, Wilhelm, von. Die Bibliotheken des Altertums und ihre Aufgabe. Zürich, 1923. (Neujahrsblatt des Waisenhauses in Zürich, 86)

Zahn-Harnack, Agnes von. Adolf von Harnack. Berlin, 1936.

Zarncke, Eduard. Leipziger Bibliothekenführer. Leipzig, 1909.

Zimmermann, Friedrich. Die ägyptische Religion nach der Darstellung der Kirchenschriftsteller und die ägyptischen Denkmäler. Paderborn, 1912. (Studien zur Geschichte und Kultur des Altertums. V, 5/6)

Zimmermann, Heinrich, et al. Die beiden Hofmuseen und die Hofbibliothek Der Werdegang der Sammlungen, ihre Eigenart und Bedeutung. Vienna 1920.

Zimmermann, Paul. "Ein neuer Beitrag zu Lessings Wolfenbüttler Bibliothekariat," ZfB XL (1923), 181-184.

------"Herzog August der Jüngere zu Braunschweig und Lüneberg als Bibliothekar," ZfB XLV (1928), 665-679.

ILLUSTRATIONS

The illustrations in the original text were all reproduced from other sources and are therefore not reduplicated. References to the plates have been retained in the text of the translation for the convenience of readers who wish to consult the German edition of Hessel.

INDEX

Numbers refer to pages except when preceded by "n".
Numbers preceded by "n" refer to the numbered footnotes at the end of the text.

Academy (Platonic), 3.
Academy of Sciences (U.S.S.R.), 114.
Access, public, 64, 77, 79, 93, 104, 110, 118; see also Open Stack.
Accessions lists, 88.
Acquisition, cooperative, 122-123, n. 156.
Acta Sanctorum, 62.
Beatus Rhenanus, 49.
Actes du Comité Internationale des Bibliothèques, iv, 127.
Adelhard, 19.
Adelung, J. C., 73.
Administration, public, 125.
Aemelius Paulus, see Paulus, Aemelius.
Africa, 10, 31.
Agricola, Rudolf, 48.
Agricultural extension, 106.
Albareda, Anselmo, 97.
Albert V, Duke of Bavaria, 54.
Albert, Duke of Prussia, 53.
Albrecht von Eyb, 47.
Alcuin, 16, 17, 36, n. 22.
Aldine imprints, 49.
Aldus Manutius, 48.
Alexander the Great, 3.
Alexandria, 1, 2, 4, 5, 6, 10, 14, 31, 86.
Althoff, Friedrich, 87-89, 94, 122, 124, n. 98.
Alzey, 34.
Amboise, Cardinal, 46, 55.
Ambrosian Library, 57, 58, 97.
American Book Center, 128.
American Catalogue, 104.

American Library Association, 104, 106, 125, 127-128; Board of Education for Librarianship, 125; Cataloguing rules, 119.
American Revolution, 100.
Americana, 91.
Ammianus Marcellinus, 10, n. 15.
Amorbach, 68.
Amplonius of Erfurt, 37.
Anastasius, 12.
Anglican Church--U.S., 101.
Anglo-American catalogue code, 119.
Anna Marie, Duchess of Prussia, n. 61.
Apollo, temple of, 6.
Arabic civilization and literature, 30-31.
Aragon (family), 43, 46.
Architecture, library, 116, n. 140.
Aretin, C. von, 78.
Ariosto, n. 55.
Aristophanes, 3, n. 4.
Aristophanes of Byzantium, 4.
Aristotle, 3, 4, 31, n. 54.
Armarius, 25.
Arno, Bishop of Salzburg, 22.
Arrangement of books and manuscripts, see Classification; Shelving.
Arsenal Library, 77, 95.
Asinius Pollio, 6.
Association for Scientific Lectures, 111.
Association of German Librarians, 117.
Association of German Popular Librarians, 112.

- 181 -

Association of German Publishers and Bookdealers, 94.
Associazione Italiana per le Biblioteche, 114.
Assurbanipal, 2, n. 2.
Assyro-Babylonian civilization and literature, 2.
Astor, J. J., 103.
Athena Polias, Temple of, 5.
Athenaeus, n. 4.
Athens, 1, 7.
Athos, Mt., 12.
Atrium Libertatis, 6.
Atticus, 6.
Attali, 5.
Aubert, David, 33.
Audifreddi, G.B., 67.
Augsburg, 47, 49, 52.
August of Saxony, 53.
Augustine, St., 11, 31.
Augustinian Friars, 29.
Augustus, 6.
Augustus, Duke of Brunswick, 60.
Auskunftsbüro Deutscher Bibliotheken, 88.
Australasia, iv.
Austria, 29, 77, 93, 112.
Avignon, Papacy, 43; Library, 33.
Bacon, Francis, 57, 64, n. 75, n. 142.
Baden, 78.
Bagdad, 30, n. 37.
Balbulus, Notker, see Notker Balbulus.
Baltic provinces (Germany), 59.
Baluze, Etienne, 63, 67, 71.
Bamberg, 22, 59, 78.
Bandini, A.M., 67.
Barack, K. A., 86.
Barberini (family), 97.
Baronius, C., 59.
Basel, 48; Council of, 47.
Basel Group, 48.
Basra, 30.
Bavaria, 29, 78.

Bavarian State Library, 80, 84, 93, 120.
Bayle, Pierre, 62.
Bede, 16, 17, 18, n. 20.
Bedford, Duke of, n. 40.
Belgium, 121.
Benedict, St., 13, n.17.
Benedictines, 29, 62, n. 35; see also Maurists.
Bentley, Richard, 65, 72.
Berlin, 68, 79, 93, 111, 113, 124; Municipal Library, 111; Prussian State Library, 61, 69, 79, 80, 88, 93, 94, 120, n. 86, n. 111; Royal Library, see Prussian State Library; University, 79; Library, n. 86.
Berlin Accessions, 120, n. 102.
Berlin Information Bureau, 88.
Berliner Titeldrucke, 120, n. 102, n. 154.
Bern. Schweizerische Landesbibliothek, 98, n. 120.
Bernward of Hildesheim, 22.
Bessarion, Cardinal, 43.
Bible, 10, 14, 70, n. 54.
Bibliographie der Deutschen Bibliothek, Frankfurt A.M., n. 113.
Bibliographies, special, 121-122.
Bibliography, 71, 88, 92; Germany, 94-95; Italy, 96; Russia, n. 138; Scientific, 127; Switzerland, 98.
Bibliophily -- France, 31-32, 46, 63; Germany, 52-54; Reformation, 52; Renaissance, 42, 46; Rome, 6, 7; Spain, 31.
Biblioteca Casanatense, 67.
Biblioteca Nazionale Centrale di Firenze, 96.

Biblioteca Nazionale Centrale Vittorio Emmanuele II (Rome), 96.
Bibliotheca Augusta, 60.
Bibliotheca Ulpia, 6.
Bibliothecarius, 12, n. 19.
Bibliothèque Nationale, 31, 77, 78, 79, 82, 84, 85, 86, 95, 117, 118, n. 105; Catalogue général des livres imprimés, 85, 119-120, n. 96; Collection Moreau, n. 76; Dept. of Manuscripts, 85; Dept. of Printed Books, 77, 85.
Bignon, Jean Paul, 63.
Bignon (family), 63.
Billings, J.S., 103, n. 125.
Binding, see Bookbinding.
Biondo, 41.
Biscop, Benedict, 15.
Bishop, W. W., 97.
Bisticci, Vespasiano da, 42, 43, 45.
Black Forest, 51, 68.
Blätter fur Volksbibliotheken und Lesehallen, 112.
Blind, books for, 105.
Blois, 46.
Blotius, Hugo, 54.
Board of Education for Librarianship, 125.
Bobbio, 15, 41, 58, n. 19.
Boccaccio, 40.
Bodley, Sir Thomas, 57, n. 67.
Börsenblatt, n. 48.
Börsenverein der Deutschen Buchhändler, 94.
Bohemia, 60.
Boineburg, J.C. von, 71.
Bojardo, 82.
Bollettino delle opere moderne straniere acquisitate delle biblioteche pubbliche governative del Regno d'Italia, 96.
Bollettino delle pubblicazioni Italiane, 96.

Bologna, University, 28, 31, 37.
Boniface VIII, Pope, 33.
Boniface, St., 16, 17.
Bonn, 79, 86.
Bookbinding, 53.
Book-collections--France, 77, 95-96; Germany, 47, 93; Göttingen, 75; Italy, 47; Leibniz's theory of, 72; medieval, 23-24, 30; Renaissance, 45, 47.
Book-curse, 25.
Book-fairs, 34.
Book-trade--Alexandria, 4, 6; Basel, 48; Europe, 48; Florence, 42; Germany, 34; Netherlands, 34; Paris, 35, 64; Rome, 6, 13, n. 7; Venice, 41.
Borghese (family), 97.
Borromeo, Carlo, 58.
Borromeo, Federigo, 58.
Boston, 102-103, 108, 116, 117; Atheneum, 101; Public Library, 103, 117.
Bostwick, A.E., iii, iv.
Brant, Sebastian, 49.
Braunsberg, Academy, 120.
Bray, Thomas, 101, 107, n. 123.
Brera Library, 67.
Breslau, 59, 79, 81, 86.
British Museum, 65-66, 79, 82-84, 107, 117, n. 87, n. 94, n. 105; Catalogue of Printed Books, 83, 119-120; New Library, 84.
Brockhaus, Eduard, 94.
Broeders van de penne, 35.
Brothers of the Common Life, 34-35.
Brucheum, 1.
Brühl, Count, 73, 75.
Bruni, L., 41.
Buda, 42.
Budé, G., 46.
Bünau, Count, 73.
Bugenhagen, John, 51.

Buildings, library, 5, 7, 10, 25, 118, n. 5, n. 140
Burchard, 22.
Burgundy, Dukes of, 31-32.
Bursfeld, Congregation of, 29.
Burton, Margaret, iii, iv.
Byzantine culture, 11.
Byzantine Empire, 41.
Byzantium, 11-12, 30; see also Constantinople.
Cabinet des Chartes, 64.
Caesar, 6, 59.
Caesarea, 11.
Caesarius, Bishop of Arles, 13.
Caetani Archives, 97.
Cain, Julien, n. 96, n. 114.
Cairo, 31.
California, 93, 105, 115; University, Library School, 125.
Call numbers, 120.
Callimachus of Cyrene, 4.
Cambridge (England), University Library, 37.
Cambridge (Mass.), 116; see also Harvard University.
Canada, iv, 93, 122.
Canisius, St. Peter, 52, n. 60.
Canterbury, Christ Church, 23.
Carnegie, Andrew, 103, 105, 108.
Carnegie Corporation, 125, 126.
Carnegie Endowment for International Peace, 97.
Carnegie United Kingdom Trust, 108.
Carolingian Renaissance, 17, 18.
Carthusians, 29.
Casanate, Cardinal, 67.
Cassel, 53, 70.
Cassiodorus, 13, 14, 17, 36, 50.
Casus S. Galli, 20.

Catalogue cards, 91, 95, 115; Lenin Public Library, 97; Library of Congress, 98, 118-119; Vatican Library, 98.
Catalogue général des manuscrits des bibliothèques de Belgique, 121.
Catalogue général des manuscrits des bibliothèques publiques de France, 96.
Catalogue raisonné, 63, 69.
Catalogues, alphabetical, 72, 79, 83, 85; author, 75, 126; classed, 63, 69, 83, 84, 87, 118, 123, n. 147; dictionary, 98, 110, 118-119; monastic, 15, 19, 26; printed, 119-122; subject, 75, 118, 126; union, 29, 63, 66, 76, 92, 98, 109, 120-121.
Cataloguing, 64, 69, 72, 75, 80, 83, 84, 91, 97-98, 115, 117-120, n. 32, n. 149, n. 150; central, 95, 115; cooperative, 92; cost of, 119; rules, 83, 98, 119, n. 102, n. 118, n. 148; subject, 92, 117, n. 146.
Catalogus Bibliothecae Bunavianae, 73.
Catherine II, 70.
Catholic Church, see Church.
Cavour, Count, 82.
Censorship, 47.
Central Book Chamber (Moscow), 115.
Central Library for Students, 108.
Certification of librarians, 124.
Cesena, 45, 46.
Chained books, 26, n. 43.
Charging systems, 110.
Charlemagne, 14, 16-18, 19, 21.

- 184 -

Charles IV, Emperor of Germany, 33, 37.
Charles V, Emperor of Germany, 31, 33.
Charles VI, Emperor of Germany, 69.
Charles VIII, King of France, 46, 47.
Charles the Bald, 17, 18.
Charles the Bold, 33.
Charles Eugene, Duke of Württemberg, 69-70.
Charleston (S.C.) Library Society, 101.
Chatauqua, 99.
Chaucer, Geoffrey, 46, n. 57.
Chicago. Exposition (1896), 112; Public Library, n. 126; University, Library School, 125.
Chigi Library, 97.
Children, library service for, 105.
China, 63.
Choir-books, 29.
Christianity, 9.
Christina, Queen of Sweden, 59.
Christine de Pisan, 31.
Church, 11, 28; Spain, 14.
Church Fathers, 11, 13, 14, 32, n. 54.
Church literature, 10.
Cicero, 20, 39.
Circulation, see Lending service.
Cities, emergence of, 34, 106.
Classed catalogue, see Catalogue, classed.
Classification, 36, 45, 55, 56, 60, 63, 64, 69, 72, 75, 80, 84, 85, 115, 117-119, n. 147.
Clay tablets, 2, n. 2.
Clément, Claude, 63, 64, 71, 84.
Cluny, 23, 40, n. 28; Order of, 23.

Cobbett, William, 83, n. 94.
Cobham, Thomas, Bishop of Worcester, 37.
Codex, 9.
Cogswell, J. G., 103.
Colbert, J. B., 63, 71, n. 73.
Colindale, 117.
Collection Moreau, n. 76.
College of the Bohemian Nation, 37.
Collegium Carolinum, 37.
Columban, St., 15.
Columbia University, Library School, 125, n. 157.
Comenius-Gesellschaft, 112.
Commissioners of Edward VI, 51.
Commune, 85.
Condé, Prince of, 51.
Confiscation, 51, 59, 76, 78, 114.
Conrad III, 20.
Consolidation of libraries, 113.
Constance, Council of, 29, 40, 47.
Constantine, 10, 11, 13.
Constantinople, 41; see also Byzantium.
Coolidge Foundation, 92.
Cooperation, library, 109, 122-123, 126-128.
Copenhagen, Royal Library, 122.
Copenhagen, University Library, 122.
Copyright, 47, 54, 66, 69, 77, 83, 93, 94, 95, 115, n. 84, n. 95; Registry of, 90.
Corbie, 15, 19, 70.
Cordova, 31.
Corvey, 19, 20.
Corvinus, Matthias, see Matthias Corvinus.
Cotton, Robert, 66.
Cotton, Sir Robert Bruce, 65.

Cotton des Houssayes, J.B., 64.
Cottonian Library, 65.
Counter-Reformation, 52.
Crystal Palace, 84.
Cuneiform tablets, 2, n. 2.
Custos, 25.
Dalberg, Johann von, 48.
Damasus, Pope, 12.
Dante, 29.
Delisle, Léopold, 85.
Demetrius of Phalerum, 4.
Democracy, 100.
Denmark, 110, 111, 122.
Dépôts littéraires, 76, 78.
Depression--Gt. Britain, 109; U.S., 105.
Descartes, René, 57, 62.
Desiderius, Abbot, 23.
Deutsche Bücherei, 87, 94-95, n. 113.
Deutsche Nationalbibliographie, 95, n. 113.
Deutsche Volksbüchereischule, 124.
Deutscher Gesamtkatalog, 96, 120-121, n. 103, n. 153, n. 154.
Deutscher Leihverkehr, 88, 120, 122.
Dewey, Melvil, 123.
Dewey Decimal Classification, 104, 106, 118; Brussels Expansion, 115, 125-126.
Diadochi, 1, 3, 5.
Diocletian, 10.
Dissertations--Germany, 88, 95, n. 100, n. 101.
Documentation, 118, 127.
Documents, state, 92.
Dominicans, 28, 30, 36.
Downs, R. B., 22.
Dresden, 68, 73, 79, 80; Court Library, 53, 73; Japanese Palace, 73.
Dubrovsky, 70.
Duke University, 122.
Dury, John, 65, 72.
Dziatzko, Karl, 86, 87, 94, 123.

Ebert, F. A., 80, 81, 86, n. 89, n. 90, n. 91.
Eckhart, 72.
Ecole des Chartes, 85, 123.
Eddy, Harriet, 115.
Education, 99 ff., 125; adult, 99; compulsory, 101; medieval, 16-18, 28, 36; Renaissance, 47; Russia, 114; technical, 107; U. S., 100-101; vocational, 106.
Education for librarianship, 86, 123-125, 127, n. 158, n. 159, n. 161.
Edward VI, 51.
Edwards, Edward, 107, 108.
Edwards, J. P., 108.
Egypt, ancient, 1.
Ehrle, Franz, 97.
Eichsfeld, 59.
Einhard, 18.
Einheitsbibliothek, 112, n. 135.
Ekkehard I, 20.
Ekkehard IV, 20.
Eliot, C. W., 116, 117.
Encyclopedists, Byzantine, 12; French, 64.
England, see Great Britain.
Enlightenment, 62, 64, 65, 67, 71, 76, 100, 117, 118.
Enlumineurs, see Manuscripts, Illumination.
Ente Nazionale per le Biblioteche Populari e Scholastiche, 114.
Ephesus, 7.
Epstein, F. T., v.
Erasmus, 48.
Eratosthenes, 4.
Erfurt, 59.
Ernest the Pious of Gotha, 60-61.
Escheat, right of, 33.
Escorial, Library, 55.
Esdaile, Arundell, iii, iv.
Esslingen, 48.
Este (family), 43, 66.
Eugene, Prince of Savoy, 69.

Eumenes II, 5.
Euripides, 3, n. 4.
Europe, iv, 62, 90, 99, 109 ff., 118, 123, 124.
Evans, Luther, 92.
Ewart, William, 107.
Exhibits, 55, 68, 100.
Explicit, 37.
Far East, 30.
Farmington Plan, n. 156.
Ferdinand I, 43.
Ferrara, 43.
Ferreolus, Tonantius, 14.
Fischer von Erlach, 69.
Flanders, 56.
Fleury-sur-Loire, 23, 51.
Florence, 40, 43; Biblioteca Nazionale Centrale, 67, 96; Laurentian Library, 41, 46, 67; St. Mark, Monastery, n. 54; Via degli Librai, 42.
Fontainebleau, 46, 55.
Fontana, Domenico, 59.
Forli, Melozzo da, see Melozzo da Forli
France, 23, 28, 31, 46, 47, 49, 51, 62-66, 76-77, 82, 85, 90, 96, 113-114, 121, 124, n. 83, n. 114, n. 116, n. 156; Huguenot Wars, 51; National Assembly, 64; Revolution, 63, 68, 70, 76, 77, 96, 113.
Francia, East, 20.
Francis I, 46, 47.
Franciscans, 28, 29, 30.
Francke, J. M., 73, 80.
Frankfurt, 68; Book Fair, 34, 53, 55, n. 41; Parliament, 94.
Frankfurt an der Oder, 79.
Franklin, Benjamin, 100, 101.
Franks, Kingdom of, 14, 18, 21.
Frederick II (Hohenstaufen), 31.
Frederick Barbarossa, 22.
Frederick the Great, 69.

Frederick of Montefeltro, Duke of Urbino, 42, 45, 59.
Frederick Ulrich, Duke of Brunswick, 60.
Frederick William, the Great Elector, 61, 69.
Free Library Company, 101.
French Revolution, 63, 68, 70, 76, 77, 96, 113.
Fronde, 57.
Frontier Library Service, 112.
Froumund, 22.
Fugger, J. J., 54.
Fugger, Ulrich, 53.
Fugger (family), 52.
Fulda, 16, 19, 21.
Gärtner, F. von, 84.
Galileo, 57.
Garnett, Richard, 82.
Gaul, 14.
Geoffrey of St. Barbe, n. 26.
Geoffroy de Beaulieu, n. 38.
George II, King of England, 65, 66.
George III, King of England, 83.
Gerbert, Abbot, 68.
German Loan Exchange, 120, 122.
German School for Popular Libraries, 124.
German Union Catalogue, 120-121.
Germanic Museum (Nuremberg), 94.
Germany, iii, iv, 11, 16, 22, 28, 29, 34, 37, 46, 47, 50, 51, 54, 55, 56, 59, 60, 67-74, 77, 78-81, 86-89, 93-95, 96, 111-113, 117, 120-121, 122, 123, 124, 126, n. 121; Empire, 87, 94, 95, 112, n. 85; Imperial Deputation, 78, n. 85; Minister of Folk Enlightenment and

- 187 -

Germany (continued)
Propaganda, 75; Ministry for Science, Education and Popular Enlightenment, 95; National Socialists, 95; Peasants' War, 51; Reaction, 82, 111; regionalism, 93; Revolution, 82, 111; Third Reich, 93, 95, 112, 120, 124; Wars of Liberation, 111.
Gesamtkatalog der preussischen Bibliotheken, 120, n. 103, n. 154.
Gesamtkatalog der Wiegendrucke, 121, n. 155.
Gesellschaft fur Ethische Kultur, 112.
Gesellschaft zur Verbreitung der Volksbildung, 112.
Gesner, Conrad, 55, n. 64.
Gesner, J.M., 74, 75, n. 82.
Giustiniani, 41.
Goethe, 75, 81, n. 92.
Göttingen, 70, 73-75, 78, 79, 86, 103, 123.
Göttinger Gelehrte Anzeigen, 74.
Gossembrot, 47.
Gotha, 61.
Gourley, J. E., iv.
Gozbert, 21.
Granada, 31.
Great Britain, 15, 16, 23, 28, 46, 47, 51, 56, 64-66, 82, 90, 106-109, 110, 112, 123, 124, 126, n. 127, n. 128, n. 129; Parliament, 65, 66, 83, 107; Royal Commission on National Museums and Galleries, 109; Select Committee on the British Museum, 107; Royal Library, 65-66.
Greece, ancient, 2, 3, n. 1.

Greek literature, 4, 30, 44, 45; Renaissance collection of, 41.
Gregory the Great, Pope, 10.
Grenville, Thomas, 83.
Grenzbüchereidienst, 112, n. 133.
Grimald, 20.
Groot, Gerhard, 35.
Grossenhain, 111.
Grotius, Hugo, 57.
Guelphic princes, 71, 72.
Gustavus Adolfus, King of Sweden, 59.
Gutenberg, 48, 52.
Hadrian, 7.
Hagenau, 34.
Hahn, publisher, 94.
Hakam II, Caliph, 31.
Halle, 74, 87.
Hamburg, 52, 68, 69; Commercial Library, 68.
Handbuch der Bibliothekswissenschaft, iii, iv.
Hanover, 71, 72, 94.
Hardmut, 20.
Harleian Library, 65.
Harley, Robert, 66.
Harnack, Adolf von, 88, 92, n. 99.
Hartwig, Otto, 87, 88, 94.
Harun-al-Raschid, 30.
Harvard University, 100; Library, v, 93, 116, 117.
Heidelberg, 37, 48, 53, 59; Palatine Library, 48, 53, 59; University Library, 48.
Hellenism, 3, 5, 6.
Helmstedt, 52, 60, 72.
Hendon, 117.
Hendreich, Christoph, 61.
Henry IV, King of England, 46.
Henry VII, King of England, 66.
Henry, Prince, 66.
Herculaneum, 7.
Herder, J. G., 75.

Herrera, J. de, 55.
Hessen-Darmstadt, 78.
Heyne, C. G., 74-75, 79.
Hildebald of Cologne, 22.
Hippo, 11.
Hirsching, F.K.G., 67, 68, 70, 74.
Hispanic Foundation, 91.
Hispanic literature and history, 91.
History, study of, 62, 66, 71, 74.
Hobbes, Thomas, 57.
Hoffmann von Fallersleben, Heinrich, 81.
Hofmann, Walter, 115, 124.
Homer, 4.
Horace, n. 6.
Hugo von Trimberg, 34.
Huguenot Wars, 51.
Humanism, 39, 41, 45, 47, 48, 49, n. 58.
Humbert de Romanis, 30.
Humboldt, Wilhelm von, 75, 79.
Humphrey, Duke of Gloucester, 46.
Hungary, 42.
Huntington Library, 93.
Iberian peninsula, 31.
Iconoclastic controversy, 12.
Iconoclastic riots, 66.
Illiteracy -- Italy, 113; Russia, 114.
Illuminators, see Manuscripts, Illumination.
Incipit, 37.
Incunabula, 78, 79, 89, 121, n. 104.
Index Translationum, 127.
India, 63.
Indiana, 105.
Industrial Revolution, 106.
Innsbruck, 49.
Inter-Allied Book Center, 128.
Inter-American Library Association, 128.
Interlibrary loan, 88, 127.

International Catalogue of Scientific Literature, 121.
International cooperation, 62, 126-128, n. 164.
International Federation for Documentation, 118, 126, n. 160.
International Federation of Library Associations, 127, n. 163.
International Institute of Bibliography, 126.
International Institute of Intellectual Cooperation, 127.
Inventaire général des manuscrits des bibliothèques publiques de France, 121.
Ireland, 15, 107, n. 128.
Isidore of Seville, 14, 16, 36, n. 18.
Islam, see Arabic civilization and literature.
Italian literature, translation, 48.
Italy, 6, 13, 15, 21, 23, 27, 28, 29, 40-44, 46, 47, 49, 56, 65-66, 77, 96-98, 113-114, n. 117.
Jahresverzeichnis der deutschen Hochschulschriften, 95.
James I, King of England, 66.
Japanese Palace (Dresden), 73.
Jarrow, 15, n. 20.
Jefferson, Thomas, 90, 100, n. 75.
Jena, 52, 81.
Jerome, St., 11.
Jerome Bonaparte, 78.
Jerome of Pomposa, 23.
Jesuits, 52, 59, 62, 63, 71, 77.
Joeckel, C. B., 102, 105-106, 125.
Johann von Kirchdorff, 34.

Johann von Neumarkt, 33.
John XXII, Pope, 33.
John, Duke of Berry, 31.
John Scotus, 17.
Julius II, Pope, 45.
Julius, Duke of Brunswick, 53.
Julius, Duke of Brunswick and Lüneberg, 60.
Jutland, 61.
Kaiser Wilhelm Library (Posen), 112.
Karlsruhe, 78.
Karlsschule, 69.
Kepler, Johannes, 57.
Kharkov State Library, 114.
Klette, Anton, 86.
Königsberg, 53, 79; Silver Library, 53; University, 52.
Krabbe, Wilhelm, 124.
Kufa, 30.
Labeo, Notker, see Notker Labeo.
Laboring classes, 107.
Lambeck, Peter, 69.
Lanfranc, 23.
Lascaris, Janus, 42, 46.
Lateran, 12.
Latin America, see South America.
Latin language, 28.
Latin literature, 44, 45; translation, 48.
Lauber, Diebolt, 34.
Laurentian Library, 41, 46, 67.
League of Nations, 127.
Learned societies, 62, 110, n. 71.
Lechfeld, Battle, 21.
Lectures, in libraries, 100.
Legal deposit, see Copyright.
Legislation, library, 102, 107-108, n. 83.
Leibniz, G. W., 62, 71-75, 89, 116, n. 81.

Leipzig, 68, 94, 115, 124; Deutsche Bücherei, 87, 94-95, n. 113; University, 52.
Lending, medieval, 25; modern, 105, 110; see also Interlibrary loan.
Lenin Memorial Library, 99, 114.
Leningrad, 70; Public Library, 98, 114, 115.
Lenox Foundation, 103.
Leo XIII, Pope, 97.
Lessing, G. E., 70, 71.
Lester, R. M., iv.
Lexicography, ancient, 4.
Librarianship as a profession, 57, 70-71, 81, 82, 86-87, 123-125.
Libraries, academy, 99; administration of, 81, 87, 96, 125; ancient, 1-8, n. 1, n. 5; Arabic, 30, n. 37; aristocratic, 7, 28, 32, 43; as prizes of war, 59-60; association, 114; baroque, 55; cathedral, 22; Catholic, 52, 94; Christian, 9; college, 28, 36-37, 101, 118; communal, 76; county, 105, 108; deposit, 116-117, 119, n. 145, n. 151; ecclesiastical, 30, 51, 52, 67, 76, 96; Hellenistic, 5; institutional, 99, 110, 114; mass, 115; mechanics, 101-102, 107; medieval, 29, 36, 44-45, n. 21, n. 29; mercantile, 101-102, 107; military 114; monastic, 14-16, 19ff., 28ff., 50, 67-68; municipal, 51-52, 68, 93, 96, 107, 111ff; national, 90ff, 96; pagan, 10; parish, 101, 107; popular, 99, 109-115, 124, n. 162; princely, 68; private, 34, 39, 52, 68, 96,

Libraries (continued)
101, 110, 113, n. 46;
Protestant, 152; provincial, 99; public, 6, 34, 39, 41, 52, 90ff., 99ff., 101-105, 118, 123, 127, n. 9, n. 83, n. 90, n. 122, n. 126-128; reference, 72, 76, 92, 110, 125, 126; regional, 99, 105, 114; Renaissance, 44ff.; research, 92, 105, 116-118, n. 140; rural, see regional; scholarly, 71-72, 76, 90ff., 105, 110-113, 115, 124; school, 114; school-district, 102; scientific, 110; special, 105; state, 93, 96, 113-114; subscription, 101, 107; travelling, 111-112; university, 28, 36, 52, 74, 76, 79, 81, 88, 93, 96, 99, 105, 110, 113-114, 120, 122, n. 140; village, 111; workingmens', 113.
Librarius, 25, 26, 35.
Library Association, 106, 108, 124.
Library associations, 114.
Library Bureau, 104.
Library committee, 81, n. 93.
Library Journal, 104.
Library of Congress, 90-92, 97, 99, 105, 119, 127-128, n. 75, n. 106-110; card depositories, 97-98; cataloguing rules, 119; classification, 115, 118; Coolidge Foundation, 92; Hispanic Foundation, 91; Photoduplication Service, 92; printed catalogue, 91-92, 120, 121, n. 109; Union Catalog, 92, 121; Whittall Foundation, 92.
Library schools, 104,

Library schools (continued)
124-125.
Library science, 86.
Library service, 79-82, 95-96, 104-105, 106, 109; national, 105-106, 108, 114; regional, 109, 112, 115.
Libri, B. de, 85.
Ligator, 35.
Ligerz, Heinrich von, 29, n. 34.
Livre Suisse, 98.
Livy, 40.
London, 29, 65, 86, 108; Crystal Palace, 84; London Library, 107; London University School for Librarianship, 124; National Central Library, 108-109; see also British Museum.
Lorsch, 20, 53.
Louis IX, King of France, 31, 32, 35, n. 38.
Louis XII, King of France, 46.
Louis XIV, King of France, 63.
Louis the Pious, 19.
Louis Eugene, Duke of Württemberg, n. 79.
Lucullus, 6.
Ludwig III, 34.
Lullus, Archbishop of Mainz, 22.
Lupus of Ferrieres, 17, 18.
Luther, Martin, 51.
Luxeuil, 15, 19.
Lyceum movement, 99.
Lyche, H. T. 110.
Lydenberg, H. M., v.
Lyons, 48.
Mabillon, Jean, 63, 66, 67, n. 72.
McColvin, L. R., iii, iv, 109, 125.
MacLeish, Archibald, 92.
Magliabechi, 66-67, n. 78.

- 191 -

Main (river), 51.
Mainfranken, 19.
Mainz, 59, 71.
Majolus, 23.
Malatesta Novello, 45.
Mallet, Gilles, 31.
Mamun, 30.
Manchester, 108.
Mannheim, 78.
Manuscripts, 16, 17, 53, 54, 63, 78, 80, 121, n. 14; arrangement and shelving, 36-37; cataloguing and classification, 37, 69, 80, 85, 98, n. 119; copying of, 24-25; exchange of, 24; illumination, 21, 31, 32, 34; spread of, 16.
Manzoni, A. 58.
Maps, 91.
Marburg, University, 52.
Marcellinus, Ammianus, see Ammianus Marcellinus.
Martin, bookseller, 64.
Marxist library classification, 115.
Maryland, 101.
Massachusetts, 102-103, 105.
Matthias Corvinus, King of Hungary, 42-43.
Maugérard, J. B., 77-78.
Maurists, 62, 63, 66, 71, 73, 85, n. 72.
Maurus, Rabanus, see Rabanus Maurus.
Maximilian I, Duke of Bavaria, 49, 54, 59, n. 69.
Mazarin, Cardinal, 55, 63.
Mazarine Library, 55-56, 77, 95, n. 66.
Mechthild, Princess Palatine, 48.
Medici, Catherine de, 55.
Medici, Cosimo de, 40, 41, 42, 44, n. 54.
Medici, Lorenzo de, 41, 42.
Medo-Persian Kings, 2.

Melancthon, Philipp, 51.
Melk, 29.
Melozzo da Forli, 45.
Mendoza, D. U. de, 55.
Mercati, Giovanni, 97.
Merv, 31.
Metcalf, K. D., v.
Mexico City, 128.
Michaelis, J. D., 70.
Michelsberg, scriptorium, 22.
Michigan, University, 97; Library school, iii, 125.
Microfilm, 123, 127.
Middle Ages, 9, 10, 12, 14, 28, 29, 45, 76.
Middle classes, 28, 34, 47.
Middle grade, in German libraries, 124.
Milan, Ambrosian Library, 57, 58, 59; Brera Library, 67.
Miniature decoration, British, 16.
Minorites, English, 29.
Minsk, 114.
Missionaries, Anglo-Saxon, 16; Irish, 13-15.
Mittlerer Dienst, 124.
Modena, 66.
Mohl, Robert von, 82, 86.
Mommsen, Theodor, 6.
Monasteries--Bavaria, 21; France, 70; Ireland, 15; see also names of cities, countries, etc.
Monastic rules, 12, 13, 35.
Montaigne, 58, 59, n. 68.
Montano, A., 55.
Monte Cassino, 13, 23, 40.
Montfaucon, Bernard de, 62, 69.
Moorish civilization, 31.
Moravia, 60.
Moscow, Central Book Chamber, 115; Lenin Memorial Library, 99, 114.
Münchhausen, Baron von, 73, 74, 75.

Münster, 79.
Münsterberg, Hugo, 100.
Munich, 59, 78, 79, 86, 93, 120; Bavarian State Library, 80, 84, 93, 120; Court Library, 53, 78.
Muratori, L. A., 66.
Murbach, 20.
Museum (Alexandria), 4.
Museums, 107.
Music, collections, 88, 91; programs in libraries, 100.
Naples, 7, 43, 46.
Napoleon, 59.
Nassau, 78.
National and University Library, Strasbourg, 95.
National Central Library, Florence, 96.
National Central Library, London, 108-109.
National Socialists, Germany, 95.
National University of Wales, 124.
Nationalism, 90, 99, 112, 126.
Naudé, Gabriel, 55-56, 60, 63, 71, 72, n. 65, n. 66.
Near East, 31, 63.
Neithart, 34.
Netherlands, 77.
New England Deposit Library, 117, n. 145.
New Hampshire, 102.
New York (City), 103; Public Library, 93, 103-104, 117, n. 126.
New York (State), 102, 105.
New York Society Library, 101.
Newspaper Library (Colindale), 117.
Newspapers, shelving, 117.
Newton, Sir Isaac, 65.
Niccoli, Niccolo, 40, 41.
Nicholas V, Pope, 43-44, 45, n. 54.
Nicholas of Cusa, 47.

Nineveh, 2, n. 2.
Nörrenberg, Constantin, 112.
North Carolina, 101; University, 122.
Norway, 110, n. 30.
Notker Balbulus, 20.
Notker Labeo, 20.
Novello, Malatesta, see Malatesta Novello.
Numerus currens, 85.
Nuremberg, 47, 49, 52, 68; Germanic Museum, 94.
Nyhuus, Haakon, 110.
Odenwald, 51.
Odo, 23.
Ohio, 105.
Oliva, Peace of, 61.
Open stack, 106.
Order of St. Victor of Paris, 23.
Orient, iv, 44, 63, n. 1.
Orientalia, 58, 63, 69, 91.
Origen, 11.
Osborn, A. D., v, n. 102, n. 154.
Otfried, 20.
Othlo, 21.
Ott Heinrich, 53, n. 62.
Otto the Great, Emperor, 21.
Outliers, 109.
Oxford, 29; University, Bodleian Library, 37, 46, 51, 57-58, 65, n. 67; Duke Humphrey's Library, 46.
Pachomius, 12.
Palatine (Rome), 6.
Palatine Library, 48, 53, 59.
Paleography, 123.
Palestine, 11.
Palimpsests, 15.
Pamphilus, 11.
Panizzi, Sir Anthony, 82-84, 85, 86, 126.
Pantheon (Rome), 84.
Paper, 30.
Papyrus rolls, 6, 7, 8, 9.

Parchment codex, see Codex.
Paris, 33, 36, 55, 62, 71, 76, 79, 85, 86, 95; American Library, 113; Arsenal Library, 77, 95; Cabinet des Chartes, 64; Ecole des Chartes, 85, 123; Mazarine Library, 55-56, 77, 95, n. 66; Royal Library, 55, 63-64, 71; Sainte Chapelle, 31; Sorbonne, 35-36; University, 23, 28, 35; see also Bibliothèque Nationale.
Paschasius Radbertus, see Radbertus, Paschasius
Paul, Abbot of St. Albans, 23.
Paul the Deacon, 13, 16, 17.
Paulinus of Nola, 10.
Paulus, Aemelius, 6.
Pavia, 43, 46.
Peasants' War, 51.
Pergamum, 5, 7, 61.
Pericles, 3.
Peripatetic school, 3.
Persia, 31.
Personnel, library, 123, 124.
Peter the Great, 70.
Peterborough, N. H., 102.
Petrarch, 39-40, 41, 46.
Peutinger, Konrad, 49.
Philadelphia, 101.
Philanthropy, 105.
Philip II, King of Spain, 55.
Philip, Count Palatine of the Rhine, 48.
Philip the Good, 33.
Philobiblon, 29, 38.
Philology, study of, 74.
Philosophes, French, 100.
Photius, 12.
Piccolomini, Aeneas Silvius, see Pius II, Pope.
Pico della Mirandola, n. 46.

Pinakes, 4, 5.
Pirkheimer, Willibald, 49.
Pisan, see Christine de Pisan
Pico della Mirandola, n. 46.
Pisistratus, 2.
Pius II, Pope, 47.
Pius XI, Pope, 97.
Platina, B., 44.
Plato, 3.
Pliny, n. 8.
Poggio, Francesco, 40-41.
Poliziano, Angelo, 41, 42.
Polycrates of Samos, 2.
Popularization of knowledge, 99.
Porticus Octaviae, 6.
Posen, 112.
Praet, see Van Praet.
Prague, 33, 34; College of the Bohemian Nation, 37; Collegium Carolinum, 37; University, 37.
Precentor, 25.
Preusker, Karl, 111.
Preussische Jahrbücher, 88, 94.
Printing, 48-49.
Printing privilege, 47.
Prints, 91.
Provenance, principle of, 80.
Prussia, 59, 78-79, 86, 103, 120; Ministry of Education, 87, 88, 94, 122.
Prussian Instructions, n. 102, n. 154.
Ptolemeum, 5.
Ptolemy Philadelphus, 1.
Ptolemy Soter, 1, 4, 44.
Public Libraries Act, 107.
Publicity, library, 104.
Publishing, 99; Russia, 115.
Putnam, Herbert, 91, n. 107.
Quattrocento, 47.
Rabanus Maurus, 19, 36, n. 27.
Radbertus, Paschasius, 19.

Radio, 100.
Rainaldi, 59.
Ramwold, 21, 22.
Ranke, Leopold von, 59, 111.
Raphael, 45.
Rationalism, German, 74.
Ratti, Achille, see Pius XI, Pope.
Raumer, Friedrich von, iii.
Readers' service, 104.
Reading rooms, 118.
Reference service, 104-105, 106, 110.
Reformation, 51, 76, n. 58.
Regensburg, 21.
Reginbert, 21, 26.
Registrum librorum Angliae, 29.
Registry of Copyright, 90.
Reichenau, 21, 26.
Renaissance, 34, 42, 45, 46, 58, 62, 76.
Renner, 34.
Research, 62; bibliographical, 88.
Resources, library, 121-123.
Reuchlin, Johannes, 49.
Reuss, J. D., 75.
Reyer, Eduard, 110, 112.
Rheingau, 59.
Richard de Bury, 29, 37-38, 39.
Ritschl, Friedrich, 86, 87.
Robert de Sorbonne, 35.
Rockefeller Foundation, 126.
Roman Empire, 6, 7, 11, 30.
Romanis, Humbert de, see Humbert de Romanis.
Rome, 6, 15, 16, 44, n. 1, n. 7, n. 9; Biblioteca Angelica, 58; Biblioteca Casanatense, 67; Biblioteca Nazionale Centrale Vittorio Emmanuele II, 96; Bibliotheca Ulpia, 6;

Rome (continued)
  Leonine quarter, 44; Pantheon, 84.
Rottemberg, 48.
Royal Academy of Sciences, Sweden, 122.
Royal Society, 65, 66, 121.
Rubricator, 35.
Russia, 98-99, 114-115, n. 80, n. 137, n. 138
Russian culture, 70.
Sachs, Hans, 52.
Sächsische Ökonomische Gesellschaft, 111.
St. Albans, scriptorium, 23.
St. Blasien, 68.
St. Emmeram, 21, 22.
St. Gall, 15, 20, 25, 40.
St. Germain-des-Prés, 62, 77.
St. Maur, Congregation of, see Maurists.
St. Petersburg, see Leningrad.
St. Riquier, n. 24.
Sainte Chapelle, 31.
Sainte Geneviève Library, 77, 95.
Salomon, Bishop of Constance, 20.
Salutati, C., 40, 41.
San Lorenzo, Basilica, 12.
Sansovino, J. 43.
Saracens, 31, n. 38.
Sargonids, 2.
Saxon Economic Society, 111.
Saxony, 19, 73, 94, 111.
Scaliger, J. J., 57.
Scandinavia, 44, 98, 110, 114-115, 124.
Schedel, Hartmann, 49, 54.
Schedel, Hermann, 49.
Schlettstadt, 49.
Schmeller, J. A., 80, 85.
Scholarly grade, in German libraries, 124.
Scholarship, among librarians, 124, 125.

Scholarship, ancient, 3.
Scholasticism, 27, 28, 36, 39, 47.
Schrader, Julius, 79.
Schrettinger, Martin, 80, 81, 85.
Schweizer Buch, 98.
Scientific progress, 62, 99.
Scotland, 107.
Scotus, John, see John Scotus.
Scribe, 15.
Script, British, 16; Renaissance, 40.
Scriptorium, 12, 14, 16, 17, 24, 25, n. 30; see also names of monasteries.
Scripturarius, 35.
Seleucids, 5.
Seneca, 7, n. 11, n. 12.
Serapeum (Alexandria), 1.
Serapeum (journal), 81.
Sforza (family), 43, 46.
Shelving, 26, 45-46, 55, 75, 80, 84-85, 87, 116-119, n. 143.
Shera, J. H., v.
Shiraz, 31.
Sichardus, Johannes, 48.
Silesia, 60.
Silver Library (Königsberg), 53.
Sixtus IV, Pope, 44.
Sixtus V, Pope, 59.
Slavica, 91.
Sloane, Sir Hans, 65.
Sloane Collection, 65.
Society for Ethical Culture, 112.
Society for the Spread of Popular Education, 112.
Sodalitas Basiliensis, 48.
Sollmitz, Walter, v.
Sorbonne, Library, 33, 35-36.
South America, iv, 128.
South Carolina, 101.
Soviet Union, see Russia.

Space problem in libraries, 116-119, n. 139, n. 140.
Spain, 14, 31.
Special Libraries Association, 122.
Sponheim, 49, 50.
Stacks, see Shelving.
Stagirite, see Aristotle.
Stanza della Segnatura, 45, n. 56.
State library commissions, 105.
Stationarii, 35, 37.
Stationers' Company, 58.
Steenberg, A. S., 110.
Storage, see Shelving.
Strasbourg, 86; Bibliothèque Nationale et Universitaire, 95.
Studia generalia, 28.
Sturm, Abbot of Fulda, 16.
Stuttgart, 78.
Subject headings, 92, 127.
Sulla, 6.
Swabia, 20, 21, 29.
Sweden, 60, 110, 122, n. 156.
Swedish Royal Library, 122.
Swiss National Library, 98, n. 120.
Switzerland, 51, 98, n. 21, n. 156.
Taxation, library, 102, 107, 108.
Technical processes, 123.
Tegernsee, 21, 22, 25.
Tennessee Valley, 106.
Tertullian, 11.
Thangmar, 22.
Theodore of Studium, 12.
Theodoric, 13.
Thirty Years' War, 55.
Thompson, L. S., iii.
Thou, J. A. de, 57.
Ticknor, George, 103.
Tilden, S. J., 103.
Tilly, 59.
Timgad, n. 10.

Tisserant, Eugene, 97.
Tocqueville, Alexis de, 99-100.
Toledo, 31.
Tomaso de Sarzana, see Nicholas V, Pope.
Tonantius Ferreolus, see Ferreolus, Tonantius.
Trajan, 44.
Treitschke, Heinrich von, 88-94.
Tritheim, Johannes, 49-50, n. 64.
Tübingen, 82.
Uffenbach, Z. K., 67, 68, 70.
Ulm, 34.
UNESCO, 128; Bulletin for Libraries, 128.
Union Catalogue of Incunabula, 121.
Union Catalogue of Prussian Libraries, 120.
Union catalogues, 29, 63, 66, 76, 92, 98, 109, 120-121.
Union List of Serials, 121.
Union of Upper Silesian Popular Libraries, 112.
United States, iii, iv, 92, 97, 99, 101-106, 108, 110, 111, 112, 115, 116, 117, 118, 121, 122, 123, 124, 126, n. 127; Bureau of Education, 104; Office of Education, 106; see also Library of Congress.
Universal Decimal Classification, 118.
Universities -- Germany, 52; Gt. Britain, 65; Italy, 37; medieval, 28, 36, n. 33; U. S., 100.
University publications -- Germany, 88, n. 100, n. 101.
Upsala University Library, 60.
Urbino, 42, 43, 44, 59, n. 54.

Valla, Lorenzo, 41.
Valois, House of, 31, 32.
Van Praet, Joseph, 77, 84.
Varro, 6.
Vatican Library, 12, 43-44, 45, 58-59, 97-99, 126.
Venice, 39, 41, 43, 48; St. Mark, Monastery and Library, 39, 41.
Verband Deutscher Volksbibliothekare, 112.
Verband Oberschlesischer Volksbibliotheken, 112.
Verein Deutscher Bibliothekare, 88.
Verein für Wissenschaftliche Vorträge, 111.
Verein Zentralbibliothek, 112.
Versailles, 117.
Verzeichnis der Handschriften im Deutschen Reich, 121.
Victor Emmanuel National Central Library, 96.
Victoria, Queen of England, 108.
Vienna, 68; Court Library, 49, 54, 69; National Library, 93, 120.
Vincent of Beauvais, 31.
Virginia, 101.
Visconti (family), 43.
Vita S. Martini, 14.
Vitrivius, 5, 7.
Vivarium, 13, 14, 15, 50.
Volksbibliothekar (journal), n. 134.
Voltaire, 70.
Wala, 19.
Wales, 107, 124.
Waltharius, 20.
Warsaw, 70.
Washington, 90.
Wearmouth, 15, n. 20.
Weimar, 81.
Weissenburg, 20, 67.
Western Hemisphere, 127.
Westphalia, 78.

White Russian State Library, 114.
Whittall Foundation, 92.
Wibald, 20.
Widmanstetter, J. A., 54.
Widukind, 20.
Wiener-Neustadt, 49.
William of Hesse, 53.
William and Mary College, 100.
Williamson, C. C., 127.
Wilmanns, August, 94.
Wilson, H. W., Co., 119.
Winckelmann, J. J., 73, 75.
Wissenschaftlicher Dienst, 124.
Wittenberg, 53.

Wolfenbüttel, 53, 60, 68, 70, 71, 78, 80.
Wolfgang, Bishop of Regensburg, 21.
World War I, iii, 88, 108, 112, 127.
World War II, iii, 127, 128, n. 105, n. 111, n. 112.
Württemberg, 78.
Würzburg, 59, 72, 78.
Wyle, Nikolas von, 48.
Yale University, 100; Library, 93.
Zaluski (family), 70.
Zenodotus of Ephesus, 4.
Zentralblatt für Bibliothekswesen, 88.
Zutphen, 46.